PRAISE FOR *EATERNITY*

"I'm drooling over every page. This book makes plant-based eating so fun and is the choose-your-own-adventure of ultimate health."

— VANI HARI, *New York Times* best-selling author of *The Food Babe Way*

"In *Eaternity*, Jason walks you through those overwhelming aisles in the health-food store as your chill friend who knows their shit. With gorgeous photos and enough info to put Google out of commission, this book is gonna shine even on the most well-stocked bookshelf."

—MICHELLE DAVIS AND MATT HOLLOWAY, #1 *New York Times* best-selling authors of *Thug Kitchen*

"If you're looking for a better way of living, try *Eaternity*. I'll be cooking from this wonderful book for years to come."

— KRIS CARR, *New York Times* best-selling author of *Crazy Sexy Kitchen*

"When I opened this book, I was thrilled to see not only Jason's energy filling its pages, but a new style of wellness book that is at once filled with fresh, meaningful information and written in such an engaging fashion, it will be hard for anyone to put it down long enough to cook the wonderful recipes."

— MATTHEW KENNEY, award-winning chef, author, and founder of Matthew Kenney Cuisine

"Jason has given us a wonderful lifestyle guide and cookbook all in one."

— NEAL BARNARD, M.D., president and founder of the Physicians Committee for Responsible Medicine

"*Eaternity* [...] better and [...] hurdles to [...]

— ASHLEY [...] expert and [...] Nutrition, Simplified Program

"This is a must-have for your kitchen to share with family and friends!"

— KRISTINA CARRILLO-BUCARAM, founder of FullyRaw and author of *The FullyRaw Diet*

"Jason is a star and his light needs to be shared. This book will heal and help so many people."

— JOEL KAHN, M.D., FACC, author of *The Whole Heart Solution*

"*Eaternity* is a perfect example of Jason's vast knowledge and passion around plant-based cooking, superfoods, and eating for health."

— CHAD SARNO, chef, educator, plant-pusher, and co-author of the *New York Times* bestseller *Crazy Sexy Kitchen*

"Supercharge your health for all eternity with Jason's incredible health tips and mind-blowing food. No matter what your goals are, these delectable recipes will rock your world and help you be the best version of you."

— TESS MASTERS, author of *The Blender Girl*

"With *Eaternity*, Jason brilliantly teaches us how to nourish our bodies while delighting our senses, allowing us to reap the many miraculous benefits of a plant-based diet."

— MARCO BORGES, author of *The 22-Day Revolution*

Carrot Almond
Ice Cream Float (see
recipe page 300)

EATERNITY

HAY HOUSE TITLES OF RELATED INTEREST

EATERNITY

MORE THAN
150
deliciously
EASY -VEGAN- RECIPES

FOR A LONG, HEALTHY, SATISFIED, JOYFUL LIFE

JASON WROBEL

HAY HOUSE, INC.
Carlsbad, California · New York City
London · Sydney · Johannesburg
Vancouver · Hong Kong · New Delhi

Published and distributed in the United States by: Hay House, Inc.:
www.hayhouse.com® • *Published and distributed in Australia by:* Hay House Australia Pty.
Ltd.: www.hayhouse.com.au • *Published and distributed in the United Kingdom by:*
Hay House UK, Ltd.: www.hayhouse.co.uk • *Published and distributed in the Republic of
South Africa by:* Hay House SA (Pty), Ltd.: www.hayhouse.co.za • *Distributed in Canada
by:* Raincoast Books: www.raincoast.com • *Published in India by:* Hay House Publishers
India: www.hayhouse.co.in

Cover and interior lifestyle photography: Jeff Skeirik
Interior food photography: Jackie Sobon
Food styling: Jackie Sobon & Michelle Marquis
Recipe formatting: Michelle Marquis
Indexer: Jay Kreider

Library of Congress Cataloging-in-Publication Data
Name: Wrobel, Jason, author.
Title: Eaternity : more than 150 deliciously easy vegan recipes for
a long, healthy, satisfied, joyful life / Jason Wrobel.
Description: 1st edition. | Carlsbad, California : Hay House, Inc., 2016. | Includes index.
Identifiers: LCCN 2015038473 | ISBN 9781401947880 (tradepaper : alk. paper)
Subjects: LCSH: Veganism--Health aspects. | Nutrition. | Health. | Vegan   cooking.
Classification: LCC RM236 .W76 2016 | DDC 641.5/636--dc23 LC record available at http://
lccn.loc.gov/2015038473

Tradepaper ISBN: 978-1-4019-4788-0

10 9 8 7 6 5 4 3 2 1
1st edition, April 2016
Printed in the United States of America

SUSTAINABLE FORESTRY INITIATIVE

Certified Chain of Custody
Promoting Sustainable Forestry
www.sfiprogram.org
SFI-01268

SFI label applies to the text stock

THIS BOOK IS DEDICATED TO
ALL OF MY FELLOW EARTHLINGS.
MAY ALL BEINGS BE JOYFUL, FREE,
PEACEFUL, AND EMBRACED AS EQUALS.

CONTENTS

WHEN JASON AND I MET, IT WAS AN EXPLOSION OF ADMIRATION.

I knew his mother, Susan, and what solid stock Jason came from. Susan and I crossed paths at various vegan events in our mutual hometown of Detroit. To know Susan is to love her grace, beauty, and passion for health. Jason's "apple" doesn't fall far from Susan's "tree." His journey to find a plant-based community in the Motor City was similar to mine; I had pursued a vegan lifestyle for over 20 years while building a successful cardiology practice. The dramatic improvements I observed in patients who adhered to my diet motivated me to continue to teach and search out other leaders in the plant-based world. Jason is one such leader, and one of the brightest rising stars I have ever seen.

The organization of Jason's debut book, *Eaternity*—with chapters arranged by the specific benefits of eating certain foods—is absolutely brilliant. Want to know more about which foods support weight loss? Jump to Chapter 3. Or maybe you'd like to learn about the foods that will boost your immunity so you won't get sick so often? That's in Chapter 9. Whether you're looking to have more energy, stronger bones, better memory, less stress, or more, there's something for everyone. And the recipes are, to use a word I coined, one incredible *vegasm* after another. They will undoubtedly motivate any reader to incorporate them into his or her life.

Chapter 13, Eat for a Healthy Heart, will now be mandatory reading for my patients. It is a powerful, accurate, and tasty treatise on avoiding the number-one cause of death in the Western world: heart disease. Did you know that within 60 minutes of eating a meal, chemicals are circulating in the bloodstream that are either healing or hurting heart arteries? Choose fast food, and bacterial toxins are flooding the bloodstream through a damaged GI tract. The harmful effects of highly processed animal products can last for hours and progressively lead to clogged arteries that can choke off the heart and cause an early death. On the other hand, opting for one of Jason's heart-healthy, organic, meat-free meals can lead to a strong gut that provides a barrier and does not permit toxicity to enter the bloodstream.

I am so grateful to Jason and his team for taking the countless hours to create, research, photograph, package, and present *Eaternity* into the masterpiece that it is. More than a medical textbook sitting on a dusty shelf in a library, *Eaternity* is a gorgeous and delicious plan to live by. It will promote optimal health and well-being for the human body—and the planet—while sacrificing none of the aroma, texture, or eye candy that great cooking can provide. Jason's enormous talent as a chef, teacher, and writer in *Eaternity* offers both the beginner and advanced student of healthy eating an opportunity to enjoy meals that taste great, and just happen to heal the body, too.

JOEL KAHN, M.D., FACC, author of *The Whole Heart Solution*

Fancy Grilled Cheese with Golden
Fig Jam (see recipe page 359)

It all started in the late 1970s, when I was a curious and compassionate little boy growing up in Detroit. I had an inherent love of animals; the natural world; and fresh, healthy foods. Born lactose intolerant, I was unable to eat any dairy products without major digestive distress. Lucky for me, my mother was a super-dedicated health nut, giving me soy formula and driving two hours to Ann Arbor every Sunday afternoon to pick up organic produce and natural products from small specialty markets that carried farm-fresh foods. She would also frequently visit the biggest farmers market in Detroit, Eastern Market, to pick up locally grown produce and artisan products. As a result, I was a really healthy vegetarian for the first few years of my life.

Over time, though, through the strong urging of my pediatrician, combined with seeing my friends' Happy Meals and other fun, brightly packaged foods, I slowly fell off the veggie wagon and was swept into the Standard American Diet. For the next 15 years of my life, I consumed anything and everything that was put in front of my face, just as long as it looked cool and tasted good! Drive-through fast food runs for gooey seven-layer burritos, late-night eating with greasy double cheeseburgers, binging on fantastically fluorescent junk food candies—these were all commonplace activities that felt completely normal to me. Like most teenagers, I didn't think

this was weird, because everyone else was doing it. As a track sprinter and varsity cross-country runner in high school, I felt physically invincible and blissfully ignorant to what I was putting in my body.

Then, when I was 18 years old, my grandfather was diagnosed with a metastasized tumor—a remnant from his first bout with prostate cancer 30 years earlier. I didn't know it at the time, but his diagnosis would have a profound and lasting impact on the rest of my life. Watching my grandfather—the strong, reliable patriarch of our family—slowly wither away and die was mentally unsettling and emotionally painful for me to witness. After he lost his second battle with cancer in 1995, I wanted to learn more about the origins of disease and find out why people were getting sick for seemingly no reason. At the time, there was a lot of information coming out in the media about mad cow disease and its human variant, Creutzfeldt-Jakob disease. The more I learned about factory farming, the less I wanted to eat and live the way I did. It was heartbreaking and horrifying. The thought hit me: not only could the overconsumption of processed meat, cheese, milk, and eggs lead to life-threatening diseases, but this way of eating might also be massively contributing to global warming and environmental pollution.

After more than a year of detailed and exhaustive research, I began experimenting with my diet, gradually eliminating one animal product at a time. Over the course of three years, I transitioned to become fully vegan at the age of 20. I remember feeling like I was the only vegan in Detroit. Honestly, I was probably one of a dozen! It was a scary decision, but it resonated deeply with me. When I told my mom I had decided to be vegan, bracing myself for the inevitable backlash, surprisingly, she just said, "Okay, but just make sure you're doing it in a healthy way." In fact, several months later, she actually decided to become vegan herself! Fast-forward a few years, and more friends and family members are eating primarily plant-based, organic foods. It's been a true gift to watch them open their minds and hearts and take greater responsibility for their health and longevity. Little did I know that the decision to be vegan would not only affect my personal health and the health of my loved ones but also provide a passionate career direction for the future.

In my early 20s, after I completed my college education in marketing and theatre, I bounced around from job to job. In my heart, I really wanted to be an actor, comedian, and singer, but I settled for the cold comfort of a steady paycheck in the advertising world as a copywriter. After several years in advertising, I felt wealthy in my bank account but not in my soul. So after five years in the trenches, I quit my job, packed my bags, and did some much-needed soul-searching in Central America and Europe. It felt so liberating to give myself the space to explore and reimagine my life. By the end of that year, I made good on a childhood dream and moved to Los Angeles. I landed in Hollywood and started auditioning for acting roles and bands to play with. Nothing seemed to stick, and after a few months I found myself wondering how I was going to pay the rent. As fate would have it, I discovered a vegan culinary school in Northern California called the Living Light Culinary Arts Institute. When I saw their curriculum and chef's training program, I felt instantly compelled to drive up to the Bay Area and see what it was all about. I packed up my electric-blue Honda Prelude with a few outfits, some chef's knives, a book of CDs (full of '80s heavy metal and Motown classics), and drove up to Fort Bragg.

After graduating from Living Light, I began a journey into the culinary arts that led me back to Los Angeles, to a start-up café in my native Detroit, to an assistant chef position at the Jivamuktea Café in New York City with one of my future culinary mentors, Matthew Kenney, then to a vegan café in Silicon Valley, and finally back to Los Angeles. During my first few years as a professional chef, I definitely got a crash course in the tumult of the restaurant world. I started a few small businesses, including a raw food catering company, a boutique copywriting firm, and a private chef agency for celebrity clients. None of those ventures, though, truly fulfilled my deep desire to be on stage or in front of a camera, teaching others how to make healthy, vibrant, delicious food.

A few years after grinding it out with the catering business and private consulting, I was asked to cater an online launch for David Wolfe's new event, The Longevity

Now Conference, in the summer of 2009. That day, I was given a golden opportunity to start my speaking career and lecture to thousands of people in the global online audience. That experience jump-started my media career, which now includes a successful YouTube channel, *The J-Wro Show*; books; DVDs; teaching programs; and speaking tours. I was finally able to combine all of my talents in acting, marketing, presenting, and the culinary arts to create a potent amalgam that inspires change and transformation in others.

After a truly wild ride, it seems I've come full circle. I feel like I'm back in touch with that compassionate little boy who knew the truth in his heart all along and wasn't afraid to express it with reckless abandon. I'm doing my best to keep his spirit alive in me. I'm also constantly reminded that joyfulness, a playful attitude, and unquenchable curiosity are just as important as a healthy diet if you want to live a long, satisfied life. Longevity isn't just about what's on the end of your fork. It's about the whole, ecstatic enchilada: your diet, daily thoughts, belief systems, exercise regimen, loving relationships, and connection to the world.

At this point, I'm still searching for answers. My natural curiosity has taken me far beyond experimenting with healthy, plant-based foods. I'm deeply involved in cultivating a more expansive meditation practice, exploring the benefits of yoga, and engaging in constant self-inquiry. One of my favorite Bruce Lee quotes says, "For it is easy to criticize and break down the spirit of others, but to know yourself takes a lifetime." I am sure that the more self-knowledge we can cultivate—and awareness of our true needs and passions—the longer we will live. And who doesn't want that?

Beyond the fear of change, there lies unbounded excitement and the promise of a life even greater and more joyful than you've ever imagined. I wrote this book to help spark the natural curiosity, excitement, and passion for living within you—to encourage you to take a chance on a brand-new lifestyle, try some deliciously easy recipes, and to inspire you to feel amazing every day. In the words of Ralph Waldo Emerson, "All life is an experiment. The more experiments you make the better." *Eaternity* is an opportunity for you to experiment with a new way of eating, a more balanced, mindful way of living, and to adopt a fresh perspective on true health and the promise of longevity. So get ready to take the leap. I'll be right here alongside you on this journey!

People have been searching for the proverbial fountain of youth for centuries. From the legend of Ponce de León to the latest trendy superfoods from Dr. Oz, it seems that we have a deep cultural fascination with the idea of being able to drink a secret elixir, take a magic pill, or bathe in some blessed waters to achieve eternal life. Luckily, this isn't entirely out of reach. There is a magic pill that can give you all of this and more . . . only . . . well . . . it's not *actually* a pill. You want to know what it is? Real food.

So, what IS real food? Well, first of all, it's food whose name you can pronounce. It's also food that was actually grown by a human being with their bare hands. Food that has been nurtured, grown, cared for, and harvested without the use of synthetic pesticides, herbicides, insecticides, Harley rides, or paraglides. It's food that doesn't require a laboratory to manufacture or synthesize. In short, these are the types of foods that your grandparents and great-grandparents used to eat all the time. And those were hearty folk, let me tell you. They rarely got sick, lived a long time, and worked harder than snarling wildebeests. Part of me strongly believes that's because they were eating real, unprocessed, natural, organic foods that were grown in their local area. Your recent ancestors likely had their own gardens and grew most, if not all, of their food themselves. I mean, back in their day, there was no such thing as "organic" food labeling because ALL FOOD was intrinsically organic! Oh, how things have

changed in such a short time. So, I'm calling for a revolution to party in the kitchen like it's 1899, y'all! And this book is here to help!

In these pages, you'll get not only my best deliciously decadent and easy-to-prep plant-based recipes but also simple tips and strategies to live a long, healthy, happy, and

JASON'S CORE LONGEVITY PRINCIPLES

- Embrace an organic, unprocessed, whole-food vegan lifestyle
- Incorporate superfood ingredients and supplements in your daily recipes
- Move your body through daily exercises to energize and lift your mood
- Reduce your stress and anxiety through breathing, meditation, and daily mindfulness practices
- Consciously select the right ingredients to use in recipes that help you accomplish a specific health goal or remedy a present malady ("picking the right tool for the job")
- Be adventurous in the kitchen and willing to experiment with new foods and ways of living to find out what's right for your body
- Understand and accept that food is fuel for your body, not simply an emotional crutch or a means of escape
- Remember to indulge, and have fun in the kitchen with your loved ones!

satisfied life. So sit down, buckle up, and let's dive right in. I hope you brought your goggles and floaties, 'cause we're going in the deep end. We're going to learn how to eat well to live well—and to live long.

EAT TO LIVE

Do you eat to live, or live to eat? Take a moment to consider this; it's an important question. With our stressed-out, crazy fast, and technology-driven modern lifestyles, it's really easy to rely on food as an emotional crutch, a best friend, or an outlet for our fears and hostilities. If you're living to eat, it may be time to reconsider your relationship to food.

Biologically speaking, food is fuel for your body. It's as simple as that. You have been given this glorious, fleshy, fantastically powerful machine to carry you through life. It's as amazing, powerful, and sexy as a Ferrari, Lamborghini, Porsche, or Tesla. You would be certifiably insane to use 87-octane fuel in your $300,000 supercar, so why the hell would you put crappy fuel in YOUR priceless body? It's pure, unadulterated madness. Most of the time we treat our freakin' cars better than we treat ourselves!

Now, don't get me wrong, I'm not advocating that we become cold or dispassionate about our food or not fully enjoy it with every fiber of our being. I just don't want you to get confused about the real reason that we need to eat. We need food for energy, stamina, and vital life force. This biological principle is simple, true, and unambiguous. So eat like you're going to be traveling in this machine for the rest of your life—because, guess what, you are!

THE LANGUAGE OF FOOD

People often find the language of healthy nutrition to be confusing at best. Counting calories, multiplying fat grams, and memorizing words like "indole 3-carbinol" can have your head spinning like Linda Blair's in *The Exorcist*. Not a good look if you're trying to score a date at the food co-op. So, let me break it down for you.

Nutrients have their own language. Whether it's vitamins, minerals, proteins, or fats—the chemical structure of these food components is encoded in a specific molecular makeup. This chemical encoding is the "language" of nutrients, allowing them to communicate perfectly with the blood, cells, organs, and tissues of the human body in order to create health. When we eat natural, whole, unprocessed foods that are packed with high nutrient density, it's easy to have a perfectly flowing, engaged, and happy conversation. It's like when you meet a new person at a party and you instantly know you're going to be great friends. The conversation flows easily and gracefully, and, at its end, you both feel amazing, uplifted, and energized.

Conversely, when you eat foodlike substances that often contain a plethora of unpronounceable and artificial ingredients and their names come with a lot of "oxyl," "methyl," and "propyl" things in them plus combinations of strange numbers, the conversation doesn't exactly feel good. Again, it's like being at a party and meeting a stranger, only the conversation drains you and sucks out your life force. All you can think about is chewing off your own arm and bashing the person you're talking to over the head with it to escape their bloodsucking, lecherous energy. A pretty vivid picture, am I right? The question now becomes: if your body can't speak the same language as these artificial, toxic, unnatural, often petroleum-based ingredients, what does it DO after you consume them?

In all of its infinite wisdom, when your body realizes that it can't speak "toxicese" fluently and can't process these "foods" via normal digestive and excretory processes, it files them away in your organs or fatty tissues to deal with later. The problem is—unless you make a point to regularly detoxify and cleanse—your body doesn't deal with them. EVER. If you aren't diligent about detoxing from these substances on a regular basis, you can accumulate a lifetime of buildup and create a seriously toxic environment in your body.

My advice: eat whole, minimally processed, organic, plant-based foods.

My intention with this book is to motivate and inspire you to eat more fresh fruits, vegetables, seeds, and occasionally seaweed. I know, I know . . . seaweed can be scary. Just take my hand, and let's bring it on down to veganville!

THE POWER OF PLANTS

My food philosophy isn't about being militant, judgmental, or self-righteous. It's just the facts based on the most current research, plain and simple.

Thanks to the emerging research into the Blue Zones—the places with the highest concentrations of people living to 100 and beyond—we have uncovered some key secrets to living a long, healthy life. Though

RECIPE CODES

The recipes in this book are coded to designate the following dietary guidelines:

TR—TRANSITIONAL FOODS: Great meals for people who are new to a plant-based lifestyle and want to enjoy familiar, hearty meals.

SF—SOY-FREE: Perfect for people with hormone issues or soy allergies/sensitivities.

GF—GLUTEN-FREE: If you have wheat/gluten sensitivities or have been diagnosed with celiac disease, these meals are for you.

RA—RAW FOOD: For those who like it raw, the majority of ingredients in these dishes are uncooked or have been processed below 118 degrees to preserve natural enzymes, vitamins, and minerals.

OF—OIL-FREE: For those looking to reduce their overall fat intake while still enjoying flavorful meals, these recipes are free from extracted, bottled vegetable oils.

NF—NUT-FREE: Ideal for people with mild sensitivities or full-blown tree-nut allergies. These recipes are tree-nut-free dishes without almonds, cashews, peanuts, pecans, walnuts, Brazil nuts, pistachios, or pine nuts. Some of these recipes do contain coconut, as it is not considered a botanical nut.

these Blue Zones are spread across the globe—from Italy, to Costa Rica, Greece, Japan, and even California—research has pointed out some distinct commonalities between the lifestyle and food choices of all Blue Zone residents. Naturally, as a professional chef and health educator, I'm most intrigued by the nutritional aspects of longevity. It turns out that the majority of Blue Zone diets are anchored in minimally processed, locally grown, supermineralized, nutrient-dense plant foods. Their primary food staples are fresh, local fruits, vegetables, nuts, seeds, grains, legumes, sea vegetables, and cold-pressed oils with portion-controlled, minimal intake of animal-based products like cheese, fish, or meat (if they even consume them at all!). This consistent focus on eating mostly plant foods helps to keep inflammation down and prevent the onset of chronic disease.

Check out some other key stats about the relationship between longevity and plant-based (or non-plant-based) eating:

- A 2009 study that followed 547,000 older Americans found that those who ate the most red meat had a 31 to 36 percent higher risk of dying in a ten-year period.

- In California, Seventh-Day Adventists who are vegetarians live about a year and a half longer than those who eat meat, and those who also eat nuts frequently gain an additional two years of life expectancy.

- Researchers at the University of Cambridge followed 20,000 men and women aged 45–79. They created a point structure to assess the effects of four behaviors: not smoking, physical activity, moderate alcohol consumption, and five servings of fruits and vegetables daily. There was a drop in mortality risk in participants having all four behaviors—equivalent to being 14 years younger.

- Researchers from Loma Linda University found that vegetarians had a lower risk of dying compared with nonvegetarians. The study included more than 70,000 men and women. Specifically, vegans had a 15 percent lower risk of death, ovo-lacto vegetarians (vegetarians who do not eat meat, fish, or poultry) had a 9 percent lower risk of death, and semivegetarians (sometimes called flexitarians) had only an 8 percent lower risk of death.

Here's the bottom line: if you want to have the best shot at a long life, you've got to look way outside your current culinary box. I want you to jump up right now and scream at the top of your lungs, "That's it! I'm moving to Costa Rica and living in the jungle! Honey, pack me a loincloth and a bamboo toothbrush!" Okay, but seriously, it's important to recognize that the world's longest-lived people choose a lifestyle that includes a healthy, balanced diet; daily exercise; and a low-stress life that incorporates family, strong ties to a community, a clear life purpose, healthy sex, and a strong foundation of spirituality or religion.

So if you're looking for this in your own life, let's start together. Embrace a gentle shift in how you eat, explore new ideas about maintaining your daily health, and allow this simple yet profound truism to sink in: the better your food choices, the longer you'll be able to enjoy the best things in life.

BAD	BETTER	BEST
Bacon	Tempeh bacon	Coconut or eggplant bacon
Beef/turkey burger	Veggie burger	Portobello mushroom cap
Butter	Extra-virgin olive oil (sparingly)	Organic virgin coconut oil, grapeseed oil, hemp seed oil, or flax oil (sparingly)
Cheese	Soy or tapioca cheese	Cultured nut cheeses
Cold cuts	Veggie deli meat	Mandolin sliced veggies
Corn syrup	Agave nectar	Coconut nectar, maple syrup, yacon syrup, or stevia
Cream	Soy creamer	Coconut or almond creamer
Dairy milk	Soy milk	Almond, hemp, flax, rice, or coconut milk
Eggs	Egg-replacer powder	Ground flax or chia seed
Iodized salt	Sea salt	Himalayan crystal salt
Mayonnaise	Vegenaise	Cashew mayonnaise
Meat	Seitan, tofu, TVP	Tempeh, hemp tofu
White bread	Whole-wheat bread	Gluten-free or sprouted grain bread
White sugar	Turbinado sugar	Stevia, Lakanto, coconut sugar, maple sugar

HOW TO USE THIS BOOK

This book is a little different from the cookbooks you're probably used to. *Eaternity* will not only teach you how to prep delicious recipes, it will also empower you to select recipes based on the specific functional benefits that you want. For example, if you want to ramp up your love life, turn to the "Eat for Better Sex" chapter and you'll find recipes to get things moving in the right direction. Or if you're restless at night, check out the "Eat for Good Sleep" chapter and see what ingredients you can use to get your snooze on like a boss. My goal is to introduce you to my recipes and inspire a sense of adventure in your cooking so you can whip up healthy foods on your own.

I get that it's less than ideal to be thrown into the deep end of the pool without an inner tube or snorkel. That's why I'm here—to serve as your lifeguard and help you along the way. I'll motivate, support, and encourage you to keep an open mind and a curious attitude as you explore new ingredients and recipes. You can start by just dipping one toe in the water . . . then another, then another. Making small, incremental changes and mindful substitutions helps take the pressure off. That's how I did it.

You just have to be willing to experiment with better options. You may not want to use ingredients that are too strange or out of the ordinary. We all feel more comfortable with familiar tastes, textures, colors, and smells. For me, that's food reminiscent of my Puerto Rican and Polish heritage. I won't give up my mom's classic grilled plantains—but I will put a healthier spin on the recipe. Fortunately, we have a plethora of delicious ingredients at our disposal to use as healthy substitutes. Check out my sensational swaps list in the sidebar for some awesome ideas!

There are healthy substitutions for pretty much every bad ingredient, fattening food, cholesterol-laden treat, or diet-busting dessert on the market. Another thing that will help you put a healthy spin on recipes is becoming familiar with some new tastes and textures, like chia seeds and coconut kefir. Being familiar with new foods will give you even more options when you're looking to make some dietary shifts. Simple adjustments to your recipes and a little bit of extra effort to obtain these ingredients can result in incremental changes that eventually add up to a healthier and more balanced lifestyle.

Before I send you off on your merry way to start cooking, I wanted to address two other things: superfoods and your body's pH.

JASON'S TOP TEN LONGEVITY SUPERFOODS

- acai berries
- cacao
- chia seeds
- goji berries
- hemp seeds
- maca powder
- pumpkin seeds
- quinoa
- sea vegetables
- watercress

SUPERFOODS: NOT JUST FOR SUPERHEROES

Superfoods are a special category of foods found in natural, pristine growing environments and often cultivated by indigenous cultures that have enjoyed their benefits for hundreds or even thousands of years. They tend to be calorie sparse and nutrient dense, meaning they pack a lot of energetic and nutritional punch for their weight. They are superior sources of antioxidants, trace minerals, essential fatty acids, and vitamins—all nutrients the human body needs but cannot make on its own. Superfoods are considered highly beneficial to your health and may even help alleviate some medical conditions.

Many people are eating more fresh fruits and vegetables, but with concerns over the quality of the foods we grow—including the effects of mineral-stripped soil, contaminated water, and heavy pesticide usage—superfoods are now a more intelligent choice than ever. Basically, they're nutritious rocket fuel for your recipes. They're just really damn good for you. And we like that. We like that a lot.

LET'S ALKALIZE, GUYS!

Homeostasis—a state of perfect balance and harmony in all of the body's systems and processes—is one of the primary keys to longevity. And when it comes to your body's pH levels, homeostasis is crucial for vibrant health. pH is a measure of how acidic or alkaline something is, and your blood pH needs to stay at a slightly alkaline level to keep you healthy. So, what affects the pH of your blood? What you eat. Some foods make your blood more alkaline, and some make it more acidic.

Most fruits, vegetables, herbs, nuts, seeds, and herbal teas add alkalinity. Glutinous grains, beans, meats, dairy products, fish, fast foods, and processed foods add acidity. When you eat acid-forming foods, your body brings your blood pH back into balance by releasing alkaline-rich minerals into your bloodstream, the most abundant of which are calcium, phosphorus, and magnesium. And where do these come from? Your body leeches them from your bones, teeth, and organs, which compromises your immune system, causes fatigue, and decreases bone density. This makes you more vulnerable to diseases like diabetes, heart disease, and cancer and conditions like osteoporosis, among many others. Major diseases can only thrive in one type of environment: an acidic one.

Ideally, you want to aim for a diet of 80 percent alkaline-forming foods and 20 percent acid-forming foods. For the acid-forming foods, skip the fast food

JASON'S TOP ALKALIZING FOODS

Foods with a pH range of 7.0 to 9.0

artichoke	kelp
asparagus	leek
avocado	lemon
beet	lime
cauliflower	spinach
fennel	tomato
grapefruit	watercress
kale	watermelon

meals, artificial sweets, processed foods, and animal products—which come with other health problems—and choose options like beans, legumes, and whole grains. When it comes to alkaline-forming foods, it's important to choose organic fruits and vegetables whenever possible, as herbicides and pesticides are highly acidic and challenging for the body to detoxify.

WHAT IT'S ALL ABOUT

How we eat is a direct reflection of the amount of self-love we have cultivated. When we truly love and accept ourselves, we naturally gravitate toward more conscious, mindful food choices and a lifestyle that supports the desire to feel *alive*. That's why I talk about changing your lifestyle in this book. For many people, the way they eat might be better described as a *death*style.

At the end of the day, caring for yourself isn't just about the food. It's also about giving yourself more love. By doing this, you can be healthy, vibrant, and able to experience the joy of life—plus, you can continue to give your unique and awesome gifts to this world! The world needs you! So make a point to take care of yourself—if not for your own sake, then for the rest of us, okay?

I think we can all agree that when you choose to live a life full of joy, energy, positivity, purpose, and health, you're naturally going to want to live as long as possible! I mean, really, who would want to get off the roller coaster when the ride is *that* much fun? The nourishment that you choose to allow into your body—from the foods you eat, the impressions you take in, and the thoughts you think—has a tremendous impact on your longevity and overall well-being.

Everything is beautiful when you make it with love. When you are in the kitchen, it's important to remember to infuse all of your food with a conscious intention for the meal to nourish everyone who tastes it.

Now that you see it's about creating a healthy, supportive lifestyle on ALL levels of your being, let's jump right into the meat and potatoes—wait . . . just the potatoes—of this book and how it can help you in your quest for a long, healthy, and vibrant life. That said . . . let's start by talking about sex, shall we? Oh, do I have your attention NOW? Good!

1

EAT

FOR BETTER

SEX

WHAT IF I TOLD YOU that by adding a few really simple, delicious new foods to your current lifestyle, you could pump up your libido to levels unseen since the days of Greek Dionysian orgies? You'd better go stitch yourself a new pair of fig-leaf underwear, because I'm going to turn you into a superfood sex god or goddess before you know it!

But before I lay down the plan (so YOU can lay it down, Casanova), here are some key statistics about sex in the U.S.:

- 34 percent of all men between the ages of 40 and 70 suffer from some form of erectile dysfunction
- Roughly 20 million men use Viagra on a regular basis
- Between 30 and 50 percent of all women have been hit by prolonged periods of little or no sex drive

It's clear that millions of people are trying to improve their sex lives, or worse, are not having good sex at all. Having a consistently low sex drive can be incredibly frustrating, especially when you can't figure out why. For some, it can be a physical issue related to key nutrient deficiencies, lack of strong blood flow, or just low energy and fatigue. Others may have a psychological issue rooted in low self-esteem,

depression, or chronic anxiety. I've had some direct experience with this. I suffered from an extremely low libido for more than three years due to high stress levels mixed with consistent depressive emotional states that were left unaddressed and untreated. Luckily, I found a great holistic medical doctor who was able to identify some critically low nutrients in my system that I was eventually able to balance through natural supplementation. Along with my supportive new psychotherapist, I was empowered with the physical, mental, and emotional tools to boost my libido and get my confidence back.

As I encountered firsthand, when you experience persistent stress, negative thinking, depression, and feelings of hopelessness, these states of being can rob your body of the essential vitamins, nutrients, and minerals that fuel your sex drive, energy, and mental focus. Running low on these critical nutrients, including vitamin B, vitamin D, and testosterone (to name a few), causes your appetite for lovemaking to go straight out the window—make that the *bedroom* window. That's why it's important to make time for effective daily stress management techniques, to monitor your moods, and to address any potential nutritional deficiencies.

Regular exercise, fresh air, and meditation are a few great ways to de-stress. Regarding your diet, it's essential to cut out heavy, cholesterol-laden foods and high-fat animal products to ensure that your arteries keep your blood pumping to the areas that need it most (like, ahem, those below the belt!). Once you start eating a more natural, healthy, plant-based, whole-foods diet, you can begin to incorporate specific functional ingredients into your recipes to help boost your libido and get your sex drive back on track.

Cultivating a healthy, consistent, and balanced sex life has a host of wonderful physical and mental benefits for your long-term health and happiness. What's more, when you have consistently good sex, you create an intimate bond with your partner. Your brain gets flooded with all kinds of feel-good chemicals, including dopamine, serotonin, oxytocin, and vasopressin. And then, you start producing those essential nutrients again, too. That's what I call a win-win.

PUTTING THE B BACK IN YOUR BOOM-BOOM

For both men and women, the amount of vitamin B in the body is directly correlated to the amount of sex hormones that are released. Vitamin B deficiencies can also lead to symptoms such as lethargy and fatigue, which usually means more sleep and rest are needed, not sex. We've all heard the line, "Not tonight, honey, I'm too tired." It might not be a lack of interest but rather the body's way of preserving its dwindling nutrient stores.

What's more, as we get older, vitamin B is not absorbed as well as when we were young. You really need to keep an eye on your vitamin B levels if you want to keep the passion alive in the bedroom and be an elderly sex magnet. (I bet you never thought you'd see those three words together, did ya?)

Be sure to eat foods rich in B vitamins, such as dark green, leafy vegetables; lentils; nuts; legumes; and non-GMO soy products, to name but a few fantastic choices.

UNDERSTANDING TESTOSTERONE AND LOW LIBIDO

In the immortal words of Austin Powers, when you get "really randy, baby," it's generally because you have a healthy amount of testosterone in your body. Testosterone is the most important hormone in determining a healthy, consistent libido for both men and women. Low testosterone can reduce your ability to maintain your sexual stamina and have lasting, satisfying sex.

Researchers haven't totally unraveled the mystery of exactly how testosterone increases the libido. It's well known that a man's sex drive typically declines slowly from its peak in his teens and 20s; however, libido varies widely among men. What one man might consider a low sex drive, another might not. Also, sex drive changes within each man over time and is affected by stress, sleep, and the consistency of opportunities for sex. For these reasons, defining a "normal" sex drive is pretty close to impossible. It's kind of like defining a normal appetite—how much food is too much, or not enough? Usually, it's up to the individual or their partner to identify a lack of sex drive as a problem.

Low testosterone symptoms don't always include feeling like you have no sex drive. Some men maintain sexual desire at relatively low testosterone levels. For other men, libido may lag even with normal testosterone levels. However, low testosterone is only one of the possible causes of low libido. As we've learned, high levels of stress and excess cortisol, consistent sleep deprivation, clinical depression, or chronic medical illnesses can also greatly sap a man's sex drive.

THE 411 ON ED

Erectile dysfunction (ED) is the inability to get or keep an erection long enough to have sexual intercourse. Surprisingly, low testosterone by itself rarely causes ED. It's usually caused by atherosclerosis, a hardening of the arteries. Diabetes, high blood pressure, and high cholesterol are the three main causes of atherosclerosis and ED, in which the blood vessels supplying the penis can no longer dilate to supply the flow needed for a firm erection.

ED can be treated and likely healed directly with a shift to a cholesterol-free, lower-fat, whole-foods, plant-based lifestyle. In fact, Dr. Dean Ornish was the first American medical doctor verified to have reversed atherosclerosis in his patients with a whole-foods, plant-based lifestyle. His groundbreaking research and subsequent work on diet and nutrition has been nothing short of paradigm shifting for the entire medical establishment.

LADIES LIVING WITH A LOCO LIBIDO

Consistent loss of sexual desire, technically referred to as hypoactive sexual desire disorder (HSDD), is by far the most common form of sexual dysfunction among women of all ages. A research study from *The Archives of Sexual Behavior* by renowned sex psychologist Sheryl A. Kingsberg, Ph.D., showed that nearly one-third of women aged 18 to 59 suffer from a diminished interest in sex.

Unlike most men's primary sexual complaint, erectile dysfunction, women's biggest sexual problem is caused by a combination of both mental and physical factors that aren't likely treatable with pharmaceutical drugs. The situation is often much more complicated and multifaceted than a simple chemical imbalance. "Although we would love to simplify it so we could have the one-two or even a one-punch treatment, it doesn't tend to work that way," says Kingsberg. For women, there can be a host of reasons for a loss of libido, including:

- Interpersonal relationship issues: partner performance problems, lack of emotional satisfaction with the relationship, the birth of a child, or becoming a caregiver for a loved one
- Sociocultural influences: job stress, peer pressure, and media images of sexuality

- **Medical problems:** mental illnesses such as depression, or medical conditions such as endometriosis, fibroids, or thyroid disorders
- **Medications:** certain antidepressants (including the new generation of SSRIs), blood pressure lowering drugs, and oral contraceptives
- **Age:** continuous decline of blood androgen levels with age that drop dramatically at menopause

The introduction of anti-impotence treatments in the last few years has spurred even more research into the causes of sexual dysfunction among both men and women. Luckily, effective therapies with balanced, healthy nutrition as a foundational component are available to help put the lust and passion back into people's lives.

Several therapies involving testosterone pills or skin patches specifically designed to treat female sexual problems are currently being studied in hopes of FDA approval in the near future. There are research studies using these testosterone skin patches to treat low sexual desire in women. Initial studies showed that the patch significantly improved both sexual desire and satisfaction compared with a placebo among postmenopausal women who had had their ovaries removed.

Again, however, because a loss of sexual desire in women is caused by a combination of physical and psychological factors, it usually requires more than one treatment approach to fix the problem.

COOKIN' UP AND HOOKIN' UP

From familiar, everyday ingredients such as walnuts, watermelon, and asparagus to high-potency Chinese herbs like cistanche and cordyceps fungus, there are a variety of powerful options for you to effectively boost your libido and have a tasty time doing it.

When it comes to incorporating these herbs and superfoods, I suggest adding them in gradually. It can be easy to unbalance your hormones or tax your endocrine system with too many new "stimulating" ingredients that your body needs time to get familiar with. Start with a small amount of one new ingredient and play with it, preferably under the guidance of a holistic medical doctor or nutritionist, before moving on to the next.

I like to keep a journal in my kitchen to document how new ingredients and recipes affect my body and my state of being. It's also important to be aware of any feeling that a particular supplement has lost its original potency. For example, with maca powder, I find it's best for my body if I take a staggered approach with my consumption. I've found that consuming it with a five-days-on, two-days-off approach is pretty effective and helps to prevent its potency from plateauing. With many superfoods and herbs, it's a good idea to be mindful and use them in moderation while carefully monitoring the effects on your body, mind, and spirit.

Preparing food with your partner and infusing love into your meal can be a very intimate and sensual experience. There's a beautiful connection that is fostered with your lover when you prepare a nourishing, delectable meal together. You can set the mood—and enhance the magic—by lighting candles and putting on music. It's truly a wonderful way to bond with your partner and enjoy the connection of culinary creativity.

It's time now to rev up your libido and take your love life to the next level with recipes designed to balance your hormones, increase your sex drive, and boost your overall energy. Get ready to become a food porn star!

MY TOP NUTRIENTS FOR GOOD SEX

Vitamin A: Helps regulate the synthesis of the sex hormone progesterone, which is important for that loving feeling.

Vitamin B1: Essential for optimal nerve transmission and energy production throughout the body, which is vital to increase libido.

Vitamin B3: Enhance the sexual flush, increase blood flow to the skin and mucous membranes, and intensify the orgasm!

Vitamin E: Known as the king of sex vitamins due to its ability to boost libido, increase sperm count, improve sperm motility and support healthy circulation throughout the body.

Magnesium: Important for the production of sex hormones and neurotransmitters that modulate the primal urges down yonder.

MY TOP LIBIDO-BOOSTING FOODS

- asparagus
- Brazil nuts
- cacao
- cinnamon
- cistanche herb
- cordyceps mushroom
- cranberries
- epimedium extract (horny goat weed)
- ginkgo biloba
- ginseng root
- kabocha squash
- kava kava
- maca powder
- pomegranate
- pumpkin seeds
- raspberries
- sea vegetables
- spinach
- walnuts
- watercress
- watermelon

RECIPES
FOR
BETTER SEX

· · · · · · · · · · · · · · · ·

MACA MALT
MILKSHAKE

I CREATED THIS MAGICAL SHAKE IN response to a lady friend's request for something to help her during that "special" time of the month. Maca powder is a powerful adaptogen that regulates hormone levels, including testosterone. The cistanche herb tonifies your kidneys and is also affectionately known as "cistanche in your pants," which gives you an idea of its libido-boosting powers. Combined with coconut, dates, raw almond butter, and a host of spices, this drink tastes like a 1950s classic, frothy milkshake meets modern-day Peruvian shamanic circle. Talk about a mellifluous mash-up!

4 cups coconut milk or 4 young Thai coconuts

1 cup dates, pitted

1 cup ice cubes

4 tablespoons raw almond butter

4 tablespoons maca powder

3 teaspoons ground vanilla bean

2 teaspoons cistanche extract powder

2 teaspoons mesquite powder

1 teaspoon ground cinnamon

½ teaspoon ground cloves

½ teaspoon sea salt

1 cinnamon stick, reserved for garnish

1 For this recipe, you can either buy organic coconut milk or make it fresh yourself. To make fresh, raw coconut milk, blend the water and meat from the 4 young Thai coconuts in a high-speed blender for 30 seconds. Add the dates, ice cubes, almond butter, maca powder, vanilla bean, cistanche, mesquite powder, cinnamon, cloves, and sea salt. Blend at high speed for another 30 seconds. Garnish with the cinnamon stick.

JASON'S TIP

Put a thick glass mug in the freezer and serve the milkshake in the frosted glass for a truly authentic experience. You can also top with hemp seeds, buckwheat, granola, or a sprinkling of cinnamon powder.

LUCUMA LIBIDO
LEMONADE

SERVES 4

DRINKING LEMON JUICE AND FILTERED WATER is one of the easiest ways to instantly alkalize your body. By adding superfoods like maca and cistanche extract, we have turned this seemingly mild-mannered lemonade into a creamy, luscious libido booster that helps to regulate your hormone levels. The pear adds dietary fiber, while the goji berries add antioxidants and help boost your levels of human growth hormone (HGH). This saucy lemonade stand is definitely for adults only!

6 cups filtered water

6 tablespoons coconut nectar

3 tablespoons organic virgin coconut oil or raw coconut butter

3 to 4 lemons, peeled, with the white pith intact

1 large pear, cored

1 tablespoon maca powder

1 tablespoon lucuma powder

4 capsules cistanche extract

¼ cup goji berries

1 teaspoon sea salt

1 handful ice cubes (optional)

1 Blend all ingredients in a high-speed blender until frothy, about 30 to 45 seconds. Add some ice if you want it chilled.

CHOCOLATE AVOCADO JUNGLE
PEANUT PUDDING

SERVES 4

THIS RECIPE IS ONE OF THOSE perfect dishes to serve to health food skeptics. This pudding is creamy, dense, complex, and oh-so-satisfying. People can't believe there's avocado in the mix because it's so well hidden with all of the other flavors. The magnesium in the raw cacao powder is awesome for blood flow, while the heart-healthy fats, vitamin B6, and potassium in avocado help boost hormone levels and provide more energy.

½ cup hemp milk

½ cup coconut nectar or maple syrup

1 tablespoon organic virgin coconut oil

½ teaspoon sea salt

½ tablespoon ground vanilla bean

½ cup raw cacao powder

2 large avocados, pitted

¼ cup raw jungle peanuts

¼ cup raw shredded coconut, reserved for topping

¾ cup gluten-free granola, reserved for topping

1 Blend all ingredients, except the shredded coconut and granola, in a high-speed blender for 50 seconds. Transfer the pudding to a mixing bowl and mix in the shredded coconut and granola by hand.

SEXY SUPERFOOD
SUSHI ROLLS

WHEN I STARTED WORKING WITH QUINOA, I had a blast thinking of all the ways I could substitute this "supergrain" for brown rice in my recipes. Sushi is one of my all-time favorite dishes, so it was only natural for me to pump up the protein with quinoa. These sushi rolls are sweet, light, crunchy, flavorful, and healthy. Plus, rolling sushi is a fun way to make dinner with your partner and get your hands dirty together. The nori seaweed in this dish is full of manganese, vitamin B2, and vitamin E, which increase libido, sex hormones, and healthy sperm production.

¼ cup chickpea miso

2 tablespoons toasted sesame oil

⅛ teaspoon smoked paprika

1 tablespoon wasabi powder

3 tablespoons water

½ tablespoon coconut aminos

4 to 6 large nori sheets

1 cup cooked quinoa, chilled

1 red bell pepper, julienned

1 carrot, julienned

1 cucumber, julienned

1 avocado, sliced thinly

1 tablespoon black sesame seeds, to taste

1 bunch microgreens or sprouts

1. In a small mixing bowl, combine the miso paste, sesame oil, and smoked paprika. Mix and set aside.

2. In a separate small mixing bowl, combine the wasabi powder, water, and coconut aminos. Mix and set aside.

3. Lay out a nori sheet with plenty of space to work. On the first ⅓ of the nori sheet closest to you, spread a bit of your miso paste mix. Evenly spread a couple of tablespoons of cooked quinoa, and then lay down a few strips of each of your fresh, julienned vegetables. Sprinkle generously with sesame seeds and add a pinch of microgreens on top.

4. To roll your sushi, roll away from you using four fingers or a sushi rolling mat. Apply light but firm pressure to keep the rolls neat. Your thumbs roll and push the roll forward as your other fingers keep the roll together. When you arrive at the last ⅛ at the end of the nori roll, use fingers dipped in water or half a lemon wedge to wet the nori roll so it stays together. Slice your nori roll with a sharp knife dipped in water after each cut. Repeat these steps for each nori roll.

5. Plate and top with black sesame seeds. Serve your dipping sauce alongside.

CHERRY CHOCOLATE
SMOOTHIE

SERVES 2

I'LL ADMIT IT . . . cherries and chocolate together make me weak in the knees. There's something earthshaking and baby making about their unique flavor combination of tart, bitter, and sweet. This smoothie is just killer—it's going to rock your world no matter what time of day you drink it. The raw cacao helps to create more PEA in your brain (that's phenylethylamine, the love/bliss chemical), along with goji berries and acai—this smoothie is overflowing with antioxidants to scavenge those pesky free radicals and keep your cells super healthy.

1½ cups coconut milk

2 teaspoons maca powder

1 tablespoon raw cacao powder

1 tablespoon superfood greens powder

1 scoop vanilla vegan protein

½ 3.5-ounce pack frozen acai berry

1 frozen banana

¾ cup frozen cherries

½ avocado, pitted

½ cup goji berries, reserved for garnish

1 Blend all ingredients together, then pour into glasses. Garnish with the goji berries. Enjoy!

CHESTNUT & KABOCHA
SQUASH DIP

SERVES 4

THIS RECIPE IS THE RESULT OF a really fun collaboration with Eco-Vegan Gal. We were experimenting with holiday recipes featuring two of our favorite ingredients (chestnuts and kabocha squash), and this divine dip was the outcome! The rich, nutty flavor and creamy texture is amazing with the crunchy pop of the pomegranate seeds and delicious, sweet taste of sweet potato tortilla chips. The ruby-red pomegranate seeds contain a compound called punicalagin that benefits the heart and blood vessels. The kabocha squash contains B vitamins and significant amounts of iron, which is important, as studies have shown that women with anemia (low iron levels) have lower sex drives.

1 kabocha squash

1 tablespoon organic virgin coconut oil

1 tablespoon fresh sage, minced

1 tablespoon fresh rosemary, minced

Dash white truffle salt or sea salt

Dash black pepper

One 16-ounce bag sweet potato chips

½ cup roasted chestnuts

1 pomegranate, seeded

1 Preheat the oven to 375 degrees Fahrenheit. Slice the kabocha squash into thin pieces, about ½ inch thick. Arrange the pieces in a single layer in one or two baking dishes. Do not stack them.

2 Melt the coconut oil in a small saucepan and then drizzle it over the squash. Add the sage, rosemary, salt, and pepper. Bake for 30 to 35 minutes. The squash is fully cooked when a knife inserted through the middle comes out clean.

3 Lay out sweet potato chips onto plates in one layer. When the squash is done, place the slices in a high-speed blender or food processor along with the chestnuts. Blend for about 30 seconds or until pureed. Spoon the puree onto chips and then top with pomegranate seeds. Serve warm.

PAD THAI
NOODLES

I AM OBSESSED WITH THAI FOOD. Other than Japanese food, it's the one ethnic cuisine that I crave incessantly. So, you can imagine how excited I was to finally nail a really delicious and flavorful pad thai noodle recipe. This dish kicks out the jams with al dente, raw kelp noodles and a mind-blowing spicy sauce full of antioxidants, protein, vitamin E, and vitamin C. Plus, kelp noodles contain iodine, which is essential for the health of your thyroid gland and the hormones it produces. Sweet, spicy, crunchy, and cool—the taste of these noodles will go straight to your noggin!

NOODLES:

Two 12-ounce bags kelp noodles, drained

¼ cup extra-virgin olive oil, divided

2 tablespoons fresh lemon juice

½ teaspoon sea salt

1 small red bell pepper, julienned

½ red onion, thinly sliced

2 scallions, thinly sliced on the diagonal

½ cup snap peas, halved lengthwise

½ cup torn fresh basil

½ cup torn cilantro

1 tablespoon fresh lime juice

SAUCE:

¼ cup dry-packed sun-dried tomatoes

2 tablespoons extra-virgin olive oil

1 tablespoon fresh lime juice

2 cloves garlic, peeled

2 teaspoons coconut sugar

2 teaspoons coconut aminos

¼ habanero pepper, seeded

1½ teaspoons finely chopped lemongrass

1½ teaspoons grated ginger root

¼ teaspoon cayenne pepper

¼ cup raw almond butter

5 large pitted dates, chopped

GARNISH:

1 tablespoon black sesame seeds

1 tablespoon hemp seeds

⅓ cup crushed cashews or almonds

⅓ cup torn cilantro

1 **To make the noodles:** soak the kelp noodles in hot water in a medium bowl for 20 minutes, then rinse and drain. Return to the bowl and stir in the olive oil, lemon juice, and salt. Massage vigorously and let marinate for 2 hours.

2 **To make the sauce:** cover the sun-dried tomatoes with hot water in a small bowl. Let soak for 30 to 45 minutes until softened, then drain. Combine all sauce ingredients, except the almond butter and dates, in a high-speed blender. Blend until almost smooth, but with some texture. Slowly blend in the almond butter and dates.

3 **To assemble:** drain any excess liquid from the marinated noodles. Toss the bell pepper, red onion, scallions, snap peas, basil, cilantro, and lime juice with the noodles. Mix in the sauce. Divide the noodles between two serving bowls and garnish with the sesame seeds, hemp seeds, crushed cashews, and torn cilantro.

COCONUT LEMONGRASS
RISOTTO

MAKING RISOTTO REQUIRES THE PATIENCE OF a saint and the tenacity of a honey badger. So, if you're going to put that much time and energy into the creation of a dish, why not funk it up like George Clinton? This radical risotto recipe takes classic Italian techniques and spices them up with some titillating Thai influence, including coconut milk, lemongrass, and basil. It's ultra creamy, tastes super decadent, and also happens to be cholesterol free. The coconut milk naturally balances your hormones and gives you more energy, while lemongrass contains good amounts of zinc, which is essential for male sexual health. The recipe is the culinary equivalent of DeNiro and Pacino tearing up the streets of Bangkok. Can you say *The Godfather: Part IV*?

7 to 8 cups low-sodium vegetable broth

1½ tablespoons organic virgin coconut oil

1½ tablespoons extra-virgin olive oil

⅔ cup yellow onion, diced

¼ cup plus 2 tablespoons fresh lemongrass, finely chopped

2 teaspoons ginger root, peeled and minced

1½ cups arborio rice

½ cup sweet rice wine

2 cups asparagus, chopped into ½-inch pieces

1 teaspoon dried basil

Dash white truffle salt, to taste

1 cup unsweetened coconut milk

1 In a large saucepan, bring the vegetable broth to a simmer on low heat. In a separate large stockpot, heat the coconut oil and olive oil over medium-high heat. Cook the yellow onion, lemongrass, and ginger until the onion softens and turns translucent, about 5 to 7 minutes. Reduce the heat to medium low. Stir in the arborio rice and cook for 1 to 2 minutes, thoroughly coating the rice with oil. Stir in the sweet rice wine and cook until the wine is completely absorbed. Add the vegetable broth ½ cup at a time, stirring very frequently.

2 Wait until each portion of broth is completely absorbed by the rice before adding more broth. When only about 1 cup of vegetable broth is left to put in, add the asparagus, dried basil, and white truffle salt to the stockpot. Continue to add the broth as before.

3 When all of the broth is completely absorbed, the rice should be tender and very creamy. The entire cooking process for the rice is about 35 to 40 minutes. If the rice is still a little firm at that point, add more vegetable broth ½ cup at a time and continue cooking until tender but still al dente. Stir in the coconut milk and cook until fully absorbed, another 1 to 2 minutes. Serve immediately.

Arborio rice can soak up
an incredible amount of
broth and therefore takes
a long time to cook and
become al dente. Do not
rush this recipe. Take your
time with the rice and
be methodical with the
steps, adding the broth
gradually. The results
are spectacular and well
worth the extra patience
and effort.

CREAM OF ASPARAGUS
SOUP

SERVES 4

CREAMED SOUPS ARE ONE OF MY favorite comforting meals during the wintertime. This recipe features a rich, dairy-free cashew cream to play off the woody, bright flavor of the asparagus. With the inclusion of yellow onion, bay leaves, and baby spinach, this dish offers a clean, savory flavor while achieving the thick, velvety texture you expect from a warm cream soup. Asparagus is rich in vitamin B6 and folate, both of which help to boost arousal. And it also boasts vitamin E, which helps stimulate sex hormones in both men and women.

SOUP:

2 tablespoons extra-virgin olive oil

2 pinches salt

1 yellow onion, chopped

1 stalk celery, diced

1 handful asparagus spears, chopped

1 quart low-sodium vegetable broth

2 to 3 bay leaves

Dash black pepper

1 cup baby spinach

CASHEW CREAM:

1 cup raw cashews

½ to ¾ cup filtered water

½ lemon, juiced

½ teaspoon sea salt

½ teaspoon apple cider vinegar

1 garlic clove, crushed

1 tablespoon extra-virgin olive oil

1 **To make the soup:** heat the olive oil and 1 pinch of salt in a saucepan over medium heat. Add the onion, celery, and asparagus and cook for about 10 minutes, until the onion is translucent and the asparagus and celery are golden brown. Add the vegetable broth and bay leaves and simmer uncovered for 30 minutes. Discard the bay leaves.

2 **To make the cashew cream:** blend all the ingredients in a high-speed blender for 30 to 40 seconds until very smooth.

3 Add ½ cup of cashew cream to the soup and simmer for another 10 minutes. Blend the soup with the remaining 1 pinch of salt, pepper, and baby spinach in a high-speed blender for 30 seconds.

 For style and additional nutrition, drizzle with pumpkin oil and top with microgreens.

WATERMELON POMEGRANATE
SALAD

SERVES 2 TO 4

SF GF RA OF NF

THIS CRAZY CRUNCHY SALAD FEATURES TWO of my favorite antioxidant-rich fruits, watermelon and pomegranate. The star of the recipe, watermelon, is high in libido-boosting phytonutrients. The lycopene, citrulline, and beta-carotene found in watermelon may help relax blood vessels and provide a natural enhancement for revving up your sex drive. This is one of my favorite quick lunch meals during the late summer/early fall when you can still find fresh watermelon, and pomegranate is just starting to come into season. The addition of lime juice and fresh mint gives this salad another layer of bright, refreshing flavor.

½ medium watermelon, seeded
   and cubed

1 large pomegranate, seeded

1 lime, juiced

Pinch sea salt

2 tablespoons minced fresh mint

1 Combine all ingredients in a large salad bowl and gently toss until well combined. Plate up a healthy portion in a bowl and enjoy!

CRANBERRY ORANGE
SMOOTHIE

YOU WOULDN'T NECESSARILY EXPECT CRANBERRIES TO taste good in a smoothie. However, the addition of sweet orange juice, frozen bananas, and creamy coconut yogurt helps to balance the tart cranberry flavor. Cranberries bring a potent libido trifecta of nutrients to the blender for this one: B vitamins for hormone balance, vitamin C for healthy sperm function, and vitamin A for good circulatory function and blood flow. And this smoothie is a great option for breakfast or dessert when you want something sweet, but not overpoweringly so.

¾ cup fresh orange juice

1 cup fresh or frozen cranberries

1 cup coconut yogurt

1 teaspoon ground vanilla bean

2 pinches sea salt

2 frozen bananas

2 cups ice cubes

1 Blend all ingredients in a high-speed blender for 40 seconds until smooth and creamy.

2

EAT FOR

GOOD
SLEEP

WE ALL KNOW THE FEELING of trying to wake up after a horrible night's sleep. You feel groggier than Frogger after running across a busy video game highway, and you're definitely not shakin' like a footloose Kevin Bacon (all right . . . two '80s pop culture references to start this chapter might be a wee bit too much).

Seriously, though, the last thing you feel like doing after a night of crappy sleep is leaping gleefully into your day with enthusiasm and focus. What often happens is, you reach for your morning coffee or some kind of energy drink to get you going and out the door.

According to a recent study from the Centers for Disease Control, insufficient sleep is now a major public health epidemic. They estimate that 50 to 70 million U.S. adults have sleep or wakefulness disorders. People are turning to all kinds of therapies to help them sleep, usually involving daily doses of pharmaceutical drugs and even more extreme modalities.

Before we explore some natural and delicious sleep solutions, let's take a look at how big our national sleep debt really is:

- 50 percent of Americans are clinically sleep deprived
- In a National Health Interview Survey, nearly 30 percent of adults reported an average of just six hours of sleep per night (medical doctors say seven to eight hours is optimal)
- More than 9 million Americans use pharmaceutical sleeping pills on a regular basis

The main problem is that people are looking for solutions at the bottom of an aluminum can. Artificial energy drinks, caffeinated sodas, and sugary coffees that claim to keep you going like the Energizer bunny are dominating the grocery and drugstore shelves these days. If it was available, I bet some people would set up intravenous coffee drips right into their veins. (Raise your hand if you just thought, *Hey, that's not a bad idea!*) Everyone wants to work harder, faster, longer, and stronger—which is super admirable—but there are major downsides to working those longer hours, inviting more stress into your life, and enduring the rigors of your daily responsibilities. Without proper time to rest and recharge, you'll enjoy far less sleep than you really need . . . and whatever sleep you *do* get won't be quality, rejuvenating sleep.

Getting enough sleep and taking time for radical self-care is now more important than ever. It does require courage, and some might say selfishness, to take good care of yourself amid a culture that pushes you to GO, GO, GO until you drop from exhaustion. But you deserve to feel good, and I'll show you why.

"I'LL SLEEP WHEN I'M DEAD!"

While we know our bodies need good sleep to function properly, scientists are not exactly sure of all the reasons *why* humans sleep. But there are a variety of fascinating theories. There's the energy conservation theory, which suggests that the primary function of sleep is to reduce your energy demand and expenditure during part of the day, especially at times when it is not efficient to search for food. Research has shown that energy metabolism, the process of generating energy from nutrients, is significantly reduced during sleep (as much as 10 percent in humans). For example, both your body temperature and caloric demand decrease while you sleep as compared to in your waking state. This evidence supports the theory that one of the primary functions of sleep is to help us conserve our precious stores of energy.

Another explanation for why you need sleep is based on the long-held belief that sleep in some way serves to "restore" what is lost in your body while you're awake. Sleep provides an opportunity for your body to repair and rejuvenate itself.

Research findings show that many of our major restorative functions, such as muscle growth, tissue repair, protein synthesis, and growth hormone release occur mostly, or in some cases only, during deep sleep. Other rejuvenating aspects of sleep are specific to the brain and cognitive function. For example, while you are awake, neurons in your brain produce adenosine, a by-product of your cells' activities. The buildup of adenosine in your brain is thought to be one factor that leads to your perception of being tired. Interestingly enough, this feeling is completely nullified by the use of caffeine, which blocks the actions of adenosine in the brain and keeps you awake, alert, and "cracked out." Scientists think that the buildup of adenosine during wakefulness may promote your body's drive to fall asleep. As long as we are awake, adenosine accumulates and remains at a high level. While you sleep, your body has a chance to clear adenosine from your system, and, as a result, you feel much more alert when you wake up.

One thing is for sure, and that's this: no matter what, you need sleep to live. Period.

THE HANGOVER PART IV

If you want a razor-sharp memory, sleep is a crucial activity for optimal information retention, especially after learning a new skill. Unfortunately, with many people choosing crazy, fast-paced lifestyles with myriad distractions, we are experiencing sleep deficiency at a much higher rate than ever. We end up compromising the production of key brain chemicals that are needed for relaxation and rejuvenation, to the massive detriment of our learning abilities.

So, how are sleep and learning related? And what happens to your brain the morning after an all-night bender laden with artificial energy drinks and triple-espresso macchiatos? Let me tell you, it's a hell of a lot worse than a hangover. And Bradley Cooper ain't around to help your ass.

Learning and memory are complex, interrelated phenomena that are not entirely understood by scientists and researchers. However, new studies indicate that the quantity and quality of sleep have a profound impact on our learning and memory in two distinct ways. First, a sleep-deprived person cannot focus attention optimally and therefore cannot learn efficiently while awake. Second, sleep plays a major role in the consolidation of memory, which is absolutely essential for learning and retaining new information. Without adequate sleep and rest, overworked neurons can no longer function to coordinate information properly, and you lose your ability to access previously learned information. Plus, your interpretation of events may be affected. You can lose your ability to make sound decisions because you can no longer accurately assess a situation to plan accordingly and choose the correct, most beneficial behavior for yourself.

Being chronically tired to the point of fatigue or exhaustion means that you are less likely to perform well. Major lapses in focus from sleep deprivation can even result in accidents or injury. Low-quality sleep and sleep deprivation also negatively impact mood, which has major consequences for learning and information retention. Although chronic sleep deprivation affects different people in a variety of ways, it's clear that a good night's rest has a huge impact on effective learning and long-term memory.

BRAIN BATTER

I can personally attest that sleep deprivation can have devastating effects on both psychological and physical condition. The most extreme example of how sleep loss created negative effects on me was during my early days working as a vegan chef. I volunteered to prepare food at the Raw Spirit Festival in Sedona, Arizona, and was put in charge of making raw brownies for more than 3,000 people. Well, the only way to mix enough brownie batter for that many servings was in a trough with my arms. After well over 36 work hours in the kitchen over three days, plus insane amounts of cacao (an adrenal stimulant if it's in too high a dosage) *literally at my fingertips*, I woke up the morning of the last day feeling like someone had stuck my finger into an electrical outlet. I was completely and totally fried. My brain was as goopy as that brownie batter!

The scary thing is that there are millions of people who experience a version of this on a consistent basis—though, probably not with a big-ass bucket full of raw brownie batter.

You might be able to pull off this kind of workload and push yourself beyond your natural boundaries for several days, but in the long run, you're going to compromise your energy, memory, well-being, and longevity.

NIFTY TRICKS FOR NAPTIME

So how can you naturally remediate insomnia or restlessness and experience deep, rejuvenating sleep every night? It's easier than you think. In fact, you've probably got more than a few of these insomnia-fighting ingredients in your kitchen right now. Peanut butter and jelly sandwich with fresh banana slices, anyone? Yep, it appears that some of your favorite go-to foods and celebrated snacks from childhood—including oatmeal, bananas, nut butters, and cherry juice—are actually some of nature's best "Ambiens"!

My absolute favorite sleep aid is liquid magnesium. I take one to two ounces before bedtime in a small glass of filtered water.

Magnesium plays a key role in the bodily function that regulates sleep. Insomnia is one of the symptoms of magnesium deficiency, and in fact, a 2006 analysis in the journal *Medical Hypothesis* suggests that a magnesium deficiency may be the cause of most major clinical depressions and mental health problems. Some health professionals actually refer to it as "the master mineral" because of all the important functions it facilitates in the body. You'll find healthy doses of natural magnesium in food sources such as dark leafy greens, pumpkin seeds, sesame seeds, Brazil nuts, beans, and all varieties of lentil.

Also, putting organic lavender oil on your pillow or sheets and doing restorative yoga poses, relaxing meditations, or gentle stretching before bedtime can be beneficial for a good night's sleep—not to mention an incredibly pleasurable, calming experience. You can even go the extra mile to boost nightly melatonin production by using blackout shades in your bedroom while unplugging your Wi-Fi and all EMF-emitting devices before you turn in for the night.

So, the good news is, you don't have to count sheep anymore or rely on pharmaceutical drugs to help you sleep. There are a variety of ways to prepare your body and mind for a seriously sound snoozin'.

MY TOP NUTRIENTS FOR GOOD SLEEP

Calcium: Has a sedative effect on the body. A calcium deficiency causes restlessness and wakefulness.

Magnesium: In addition to boosting your libido, this mineral is key to inducing slumber. Magnesium deficiency is partly responsible for nervousness that can prevent sleep.

Phosphatidylserine: An amino acid that helps the brain regulate the amount of cortisone produced by the adrenals. It is helpful for those who cannot sleep because of high cortisone levels, usually induced by stress. PPS is a hormone secreted naturally by the pineal gland.

Melatonin: The sleep hormone. It is said to induce sleep without any negative side effects and is secreted mainly at night. Melatonin is found naturally in plants and in algae.

Tryptophan: An amino acid that plays a key role in the repair of protein tissues and in creating new protein. In the brain, tryptophan is converted into serotonin, a natural sleep-inducing chemical. It also enhances the brain's ability to produce melatonin, the hormone that regulates your body's natural inner clock.

MY TOP FOODS FOR GOOD SLEEP

- 5-HTP
- almonds
- ashwagandha
- bananas
- chamomile tea
- cherries
- chickpeas
- GABA
- hops
- jasmine rice
- kale
- magnolia bark
- melatonin
- oatmeal
- passion flower
- poppy seeds
- Rescue Sleep
- rice
- St. John's wort
- valerian root
- walnuts
- white sapote
- whole grains

RECIPES
FOR
GOOD SLEEP

··················

ALMOND BUTTER BANANA
CHERRY SANDWICH

SERVES 1

THIS SANDWICH IS PERFECT FOR A late-night snack attack. Bananas and almonds are two of nature's top sleep aids due to their potassium and B vitamin content. The complex carbs of the bread also help you release more melatonin to support seriously sound sleep. When you slap on some fresh cherries or preserves, this is a delicious way to drift off to dreamland.

2 tablespoons raw almond butter

2 slices gluten-free bread, toasted

¼ apple, sliced

½ banana, peeled and sliced

⅓ cup fresh cherries, pitted and sliced (or sugar-free cherry preserves)

¼ teaspoon ground cinnamon

1 Spread the almond butter on the toasted slices of gluten-free bread. Layer with the apple slices, banana slices, and fresh cherries. Sprinkle with the ground cinnamon.

BLACK BEAN GARBANZO SALAD
WITH JICAMA CHIPS

THE BOMBTASTIC BEAN DUO OF BLACK beans and garbanzos highlights the fresh, crunchy, light flavor of this salad. Black beans are highly restorative for the adrenal glands, and garbanzos are loaded with high levels of B vitamins to help you relax. This recipe is awesome to eat as a lunch option or as an evening snack. The sweet, crunchy snap of the raw jicama chips makes this recipe extra magical and unique.

1¾ cups canned black beans, drained and rinsed

1 cup canned garbanzo beans, drained and rinsed

1½ cups fresh corn kernels

3 roma tomatoes, diced

1 large avocado, pitted and diced

4 scallions, sliced thin on the diagonal

1 red bell pepper, seeded and diced

1 small jalapeno, minced

1 lime, juiced

2 tablespoons black sesame seeds

Pinch sea salt, or to taste

Pinch black pepper, or to taste

Pinch ground cumin, or to taste

1 medium jicama root, peeled and sliced crosswise

1 Combine all ingredients, except the jicama root, in a medium mixing bowl and serve immediately. Serve with fresh jicama rounds as chips.

If you can't find fresh jicama root to serve as chips, substitute organic corn chips or your favorite healthy cracker for scooping this delicious and satisfying salad.

SOUTHWESTERN
WALNUT TACOS

SERVES 4 TO 6

TACOS ARE ONE OF MY ALL-TIME favorite comfort food dishes. I have multiple versions for awesome, meat-free taco recipes, and this one happens to be the easiest. The ground walnuts work fantastically well with the seasonings to create a "ground beef" type of consistency and flavor. Pair these tacos with fresh salsa, guacamole, and shredded romaine lettuce for the ultimate experience. Walnuts are a good source of tryptophan, a sleep-enhancing amino acid that helps make serotonin as well as melatonin, the "body clock" hormone that sets your sleep-wake cycles.

4 cups raw walnuts, soaked for 2 hours

1 tablespoon taco seasoning

½ teaspoon ground coriander

Pinch ground black pepper

¼ teaspoon sea salt

½ tablespoon coconut aminos

1 tablespoon organic virgin coconut oil

2 tablespoons extra-virgin olive oil

4 organic taco shells

3 cups shredded romaine lettuce, reserved for topping

½ cup salsa, reserved for topping

1 Pulse the walnuts for about 15 seconds in a high-speed food processor until a small, crumbly texture is achieved. Add all spices, coconut oil, and olive oil. Process again until the consistency resembles ground beef. Fill the taco shells with the walnut mixture and top with the shredded romaine lettuce and salsa.

BANANA NUT
PROTEIN BARS

SERVES 4

EVER GET BURNT OUT ON THE mind-numbing malaise of typical protein bars—none of which really taste all that good? Yep, me too! Hence the birth of these homemade banana nut protein bars, which are a mash-up of my Grandma Rose's famous banana bread and a nut-based, densely nutritious bar. These soft, cakey little beauties are both portable and packed with protein. Bananas contain the amino acid L-tryptophan, which turns to 5-HTP and releases relaxing serotonin in your brain. They're also full of calcium, potassium, and magnesium, which help promote muscle relaxation and better sleep.

3 large bananas, peeled and sliced

1 cup gluten-free oats

½ cup raw almonds

¼ cup raw Brazil nuts

4 tablespoons coconut flour

3 scoops vegan vanilla protein powder

Pinch ground clove, cardamom, cinnamon, or chicory root

⅛ teaspoon sea salt

1 cup coconut milk

1 tablespoon organic virgin coconut oil

½ cup toasted quinoa, reserved for garnish

1 Preheat the oven to 325 degrees Fahrenheit. Add 2 bananas, oats, almonds, Brazil nuts, coconut flour, vegan protein powder, ground clove, and sea salt to a food processor and blend until broken down but not yet binding together. Add the coconut milk and continue blending. The mixture is ready when the dough balls up.

2 Lightly grease an 8 x 8-inch glass or metal baking dish with coconut oil. Press the dough evenly into the pan. Bake for 30 to 35 minutes or until golden brown. Cut into square or rectangular bars. Top with the reserved fresh banana slices and toasted quinoa as desired and enjoy!

HAZELNUT
HORCHATA

HORCHATA IS A TRADITIONAL LATIN AMERICAN sweet beverage made from nuts or seeds. In this version, hazelnuts are the star with their woodsy, slightly bitter flavor. The vitamin B6 in hazelnuts enriches serotonin, melatonin, and epinephrine in the brain, which affect your mood and sleep cycle. The cooked white rice gives it a nice milky consistency, and the coconut nectar serves as a light and delicious low-glycemic sweetener.

½ cup cooked white rice

1 cup filtered water

1 cup hazelnuts, soaked 2 hours

2 tablespoons coconut nectar

1 teaspoon ground cinnamon

Pinch sea salt

1 handful of ice cubes

1 Cook the white rice according to the directions on the box. After the rice is done cooking, add it to a high-speed blender with all remaining ingredients, except for the ice cubes, and blend for 40 seconds. Add the ice cubes and blend for a few seconds more until creamy.

PUMPKIN ORANGE
GINGER SNAPS

MAKES 24 COOKIES

NEXT TO CHOCOLATE CHIP COOKIES, THESE snazzy snaps are tops in my cookie jar. I love their soft, chewy texture and spicy, gingery bite. The addition of orange extract perfectly complements the classic pumpkin flavor. Plus, they're gluten free and don't sacrifice any of the masterful moisture that you expect from these classic cookies. The best part? You can have one of these snaps before bedtime. Pumpkin seeds contain high levels of zinc, which can assist the brain in converting tryptophan into serotonin.

1 tablespoon golden flax meal

1 tablespoon ground pumpkin seeds

1 cup coconut sugar

2⅓ cups gluten-free baking mix

2 teaspoons baking soda

2 teaspoons ground cinnamon

1½ teaspoons minced ginger root

1 teaspoon ground cloves

½ teaspoon guar gum

½ teaspoon sea salt

½ cup organic virgin coconut oil, melted

½ cup unsweetened pumpkin puree

¼ cup blackstrap molasses

1 teaspoon orange extract

1 Combine the dry ingredients in a large mixing bowl and whisk until fully combined. In a separate mixing bowl, combine the wet ingredients, stirring well. Add the wet mixture to the dry mixture, combining until everything is fully mixed. This will develop a very sticky cookie dough consistency. Cover with plastic wrap and chill in the refrigerator for 1 hour.

2 Preheat the oven to 350 degrees Fahrenheit. Using a cookie scoop or large spoon, scoop out and drop your cookies onto an oiled or parchment-lined cookie sheet. Flatten each cookie with a fork, making a crisscross pattern. Bake for 12 minutes. Gently remove the cookies and place on a cooling rack for 10 minutes. Enjoy!

SWEET SAPOTE
SORBET

SERVES 2

SAPOTE FRUIT IS JUICY, CREAMY, AND has a sweet, mild flavor that hints at essences such as coconut, vanilla, and lemon. It's really the perfect base for an exotic sorbet. The addition of fresh lemon or lime juice and a dash of sweetener helps to amplify the natural flavor balance even more. This light, heavenly, refreshing dessert is best enjoyed in the summertime, especially on those lazy Sunday afternoons. If you're in need of a midday nap, you'll be happy to know that white sapote has a slight soporific effect and was used by the ancient Aztecs as a natural sleep aid.

2½ cups white sapote, peeled, seeded, and frozen

1 tablespoon fresh lemon juice

1 bunch fresh mint

Pinch sea salt

½ teaspoon liquid stevia

1 Blend all ingredients in a high-speed blender for 35 seconds until thick and creamy. Be careful not to overblend, as the sorbet will eventually warm up and melt.

VEGGIE
"FRIED" RICE

BOY, OH BOY, WHEN THE CRAVING for greasy Chinese take-out food strikes, there's nothing quite like a steaming-hot container of fried rice. Unfortunately, there's usually a lot of fat that comes along with it. This healthy, vegan version of fried rice is delicious and satisfying, with a kaleidoscope of fresh veggies and brown rice. Fun fact: brown rice is a natural source of melatonin, which enhances the quality of sleep by relaxing the nerves and increasing the sleep cycle. The sweet potatoes provide sleep-promoting complex carbohydrates and also contain the muscle relaxant potassium. For fun, fill a Chinese food take-out container with this healthier version and cozy up for a movie night chillaxin' on the couch.

3 cups cooked brown rice

1 cup chopped red bell pepper

1 cup sliced carrots

½ cup minced scallions

½ cup julienned beets

¼ cup shredded purple cabbage

½ cup cooked green peas

½ cup julienned sweet potato

1 cup water chestnuts, peeled and chopped

½ cup sprouted wheat berries (optional)

1 tablespoon minced ginger root

1 tablespoon minced garlic

1 teaspoon minced jalapeno pepper

¼ cup coconut aminos

¼ cup fresh lemon juice

½ cup extra-virgin olive oil

2 tablespoons orange zest, reserved for garnish

1 Cook the brown rice according to the directions on the package, as they may vary depending on the varietal. Combine the cooked rice and the remaining ingredients, except the orange zest, in a large mixing bowl. Stir gently to combine well, and serve garnished with the orange zest on top.

BLACK CHERRY
SODA

THIS SUPERFOOD SODA TASTES JUST LIKE Dr. Pepper, yo. Guzzle it by the gallon for all I care. It's a heck of a lot better for you than the commercial version with high-fructose corn syrup and a plethora of artificial ingredients. Plus, the cherry juice acts as a natural soporific to help you fall asleep easier. Instead of having you bounce off the walls from a sugar high, this soda will actually help you sleep like a baby.

1½ cups black cherry juice

1½ tablespoons coconut nectar

One 1-liter bottle sparkling mineral water

½ teaspoon liquid stevia

¼ teaspoon cinnamon extract

1 Using a small whisk, combine the cherry juice and coconut nectar in a small mixing bowl. Transfer the juice mix to a large mason jar or pitcher, add the remaining ingredients, and stir with a large wooden spoon. Be careful not to stir too vigorously, as this will diminish the carbonation in the soda more quickly. Serve immediately in your coolest glasses over a few ice cubes.

SPIRULINA
APPLESAUCE

SERVES 1 TO 2

THIS APPLESAUCE IS AS SWEET AND delicious as you would expect but is actually full of plant-based protein thanks to the addition of spirulina. I created this recipe with the idea of making a raw, vegan baby food product. If you do happen to serve this to your children, just tell them it's what the Incredible Hulk eats and that's why he's so strong. Apples are a good source of vitamin C and can supply you with vitamin B6 and potassium, both of which may promote proper sleep. So when it's getting to be naptime and someone's a little cranky, give 'em a little applesauce and see what happens.

2 large apples, cored and chopped

½ teaspoon ground vanilla bean

½ teaspoon ground cinnamon

2 teaspoons spirulina powder

Pinch sea salt

1 Blend all the ingredients in a high-speed blender or food processor for 15 to 20 seconds or until you achieve your desired applesauce consistency.

CREAMY COCONUT CHICKPEAS
WITH SWEET POTATOES

SERVES 4

ROASTED SWEET POTATOES ARE ONE OF life's simple pleasures. The natural sweetness of the root vegetable comes out with aplomb when you caramelize it. The creamy, spicy chickpeas and coconut milk in this dish perfectly complement the sweetness of the potato. The final result is an Indian-inspired main course that is as filling as it is flavorful. Plus, the sweet potato is loaded with potassium to relax your muscles, and the chickpeas boast vitamin B6, which is needed to make melatonin. As Steven Tyler once said, dream on!

1 large red bell pepper

2 cups canned chickpeas, drained and rinsed

2 medium sweet potatoes

1 tablespoon plus ½ teaspoon organic virgin coconut oil

1 large lime, juiced and zested

2 teaspoons ground cumin, divided

4 medium tomatoes, seeded and diced

½ cup yellow onion, finely diced

4 to 5 cloves garlic, minced

1½ teaspoons ground coriander

Dash red pepper flakes

13.5 ounces light unsweetened coconut milk

1 large bunch spinach, chopped

Dash sea salt, to taste

Dash ground black pepper, to taste

½ cup shredded unsweetened coconut

½ cup cilantro, chopped

¼ cup green onion, chopped

1 Preheat the oven to 400 degrees Fahrenheit. Slice the pepper lengthwise into 1½ to 2-inch strips and remove the seeds and stem. Place on a medium baking sheet, skin side up. Broil for approximately 10 to 15 minutes until the pepper strips are charred on the top. Remove from the oven and place the strips in a small paper bag for about 5 to 10 minutes to soften. Remove the charred skin by scraping or running under water.

2 Place the chickpeas in a small saucepan with enough water to cover. Bring to a boil and simmer for 15 minutes. Drain the water and set aside.

3 Slice the sweet potatoes lengthwise in half. Place them in a 13 x 9-inch baking pan, cut side facing up. Evenly drizzle the potatoes with ½ teaspoon of coconut oil. Sprinkle with the lime zest and ½ teaspoon ground cumin. Bake for 30 to 35 minutes until fork tender.

4 Pulse the tomatoes in a food processor until finely chopped. Puree the roasted red pepper in a blender until very smooth and creamy. Set aside.

JASON'S
TIP

You can easily substitute different greens in this recipe in place of the spinach. Feel free to add freshly steamed kale, steamed collard greens, or baby arugula, depending on the flavor and mouthfeel that you desire.

5 In a large skillet, add 1 tablespoon of coconut oil over medium-low heat. Add the onion and sauté for 5 minutes and then add the garlic and sauté for 1 minute more. Stir in the tomatoes and cook on low heat for 10 minutes. Add the coriander, 1½ teaspoons cumin, red pepper puree, and red pepper flakes, cooking for 1 minute more. Stir in the coconut milk and lime juice. Bring to a low boil and simmer gently for 5 minutes. Fold in the chopped spinach and the chickpeas and cook for an additional 3 minutes. Season the mixture with salt and pepper. Spoon this mixture over the prepared sweet potatoes and garnish with the shredded coconut, cilantro, and green onion. Serve immediately.

3

EAT FOR

WEIGHT LOSS

IF YOU'VE EVER BATTLED WEIGHT GAIN, body image issues, social pressure to stay slim, or even clinical obesity, you're not alone in your struggle—not by a long shot!

The current statistics regarding obesity and the fight to stay slim are nothing short of staggering:

- The weight loss industry generates more than $20 billion annually from diet books, drugs, foodlike products, and extreme weight loss surgeries
- More than 220,000 morbidly obese people had gastric bypass surgery in 2009
- More than 108 million Americans have indicated they have been (or are currently) on some kind of diet protocol

Chronic obesity profoundly affects the long-term health of Americans. According to the recent statistics from the Centers for Disease Control, more than one-third of American adults are now clinically obese, with no signs of abatement. Can you believe that stat? One out of every three people in the U.S. is now clinically obese. That is beyond shocking—it is completely unacceptable. In total, 65 million U.S. adults and 10 million U.S. children are obese. Now the truly frightening part about this epidemic is the laundry list of major obesity-related health conditions, including coronary heart disease, stroke, type 2 diabetes, and many different types of cancer—all of which are leading causes of preventable death in America.

Those statistics are totally mind-blowing to me. As a nation, we can't expect to have a good quality of life or a real shot at longevity if we continue down this path. Luckily, there are some real-world solutions that work. It all starts with modifying your daily choices, thoughts, habits, and ultimately, your entire lifestyle. So, the first step is to start visualizing yourself healthier, slimmer, and more energetic. Feel what it would be like to achieve your ideal weight. Your passion, drive, and enthusiasm will make you more likely to succeed in your weight loss goals.

The next step is to start incorporating specific foods that can help to boost your metabolism and burn fat while creating healthier substitutions for the unhealthy ingredients in your kitchen. From an overall lifestyle perspective, you will find tremendous benefits by switching to a minimally processed, organic, whole-food, plant-based diet. Last, you've got to move your body every single day and do some form of cardiovascular and weight-bearing exercise to boost your metabolic rate and activate the fat-burning capabilities of your body. There's muscle under the fat, and much like Michelangelo, you've got to chip away with persistence, determination, and unflappable vision to reveal the masterpiece that lies underneath!

HOW A PLANT-BASED DIET TIPS THE SCALES

Now, you may be curious how vegetarian and vegan diets rank compare to other diets when it comes to overall weight loss. Further, is there typically a difference in weight between vegetarians and nonvegetarians?

A review of the scientific literature on the subject found that 29 out of 40 clinical studies reported that vegetarians weighed significantly less than nonvegetarians. This was observed in both males and females across a wide range of ethnic groups. Although vegetarians tend to have healthier lifestyle habits that may influence weight (e.g., more exercise and less smoking), some studies were performed within a population with similar lifestyles, and the differences in weight were still seen.

Results from a study of more than 37,000 men and women participating in the Oxford cohort of the European Prospective Investigation into Cancer and Nutrition found that after adjusting for age, mean body mass index (BMI) was significantly highest among meat eaters and lowest in vegans. Vegetarians and fish eaters had a comparable mean BMI in between the other groups.

In addition, vegetarians have significantly lower rates of obesity. Data analyzed in more than 55,000 healthy women in the Swedish Mammography Cohort revealed a 40 percent prevalence of overweight among meat eaters versus a 25 percent prevalence among vegetarians.

A vegetarian diet also may impact the accumulation of excess weight. Participants in the EPIC-Oxford Study who cut back on animal-based foods showed the absolute lowest rate of weight gain.

Because vegetarian and vegan diets are associated with lower body weight, rate of overweight, and obesity, chances are good that plant-based eaters are at lower risk for certain related diseases such as heart disease and diabetes.

WHATCHU KNOW ABOUT CALORIES, VALERIE?

So, what the heck is a calorie, anyway? And what's the difference between a calorie and a nutrient? Let me break it down for you like M.C. Hammer. (If that was actually my rap name, you know it would totally stand for "Mighty Clean," yo.)

Calories are simply a way to measure the energy in food and the energy that's created and released in the body. Although the technically correct name is *kilocalorie*, everyone uses the abbreviated term *calorie*. One calorie is the amount of energy necessary to raise the temperature of one gram of water by one degree Centigrade. You expend about one calorie per minute when sitting in a relaxed position. That's about the same amount of heat released by an average candle or a 75-watt lightbulb.

Calories are rounded measurements on food labels, or, as the industry refers to them, "nutrition fact panels." So, when you multiply the grams of protein, carbohydrates, or fats, you may come out with a completely different value than what appears on the label. Foods that contain 50 calories or fewer are rounded to the nearest five-calorie increment, while foods with more than 50 calories are rounded to the nearest ten-calorie increment. For example, a 47-calorie food would be rounded to 45 calories, while a 96-calorie food would be rounded to 100. Foods that have fewer than five calories can actually be listed as having zero calories—isn't that crazy? A calorie is not a nutrient, but certain nutrients do provide calories. Protein, carbohydrates, and fats make up the calorie content of many foods. Although not considered a nutrient, alcohol also provides calories.

Here's a list of what one gram of each type of nutrient is calorically equivalent to:

- Protein: 4 calories per gram
- Carbohydrate: 4 calories per gram
- Fat: 9 calories per gram
- Alcohol: 7 calories per gram

As a point of note, water, minerals, and vitamins do not provide calories, neither do fiber or cholesterol.

Few foods are composed 100 percent of any single nutrient. Most foods and beverages are a combination of protein, fats, and carbohydrates, so the calorie count of a food is the sum of the calories provided by each individual nutrient. Here's how the breakdown works:

A bowl of vegetable soup contains 3 grams of protein, 7 grams of carbohydrate, and 2 grams of fat, for a grand total of 58 calories:

3 grams protein x 4 calories per gram = 12 calories

7 grams carbohydrate x 4 calories per gram = 28 calories

2 grams fat x 9 calories per gram = 18 calories

Total = 58 calories

Now, I'm not advocating that you become a strict calorie counter. I just want to make sure you understand how calories are calculated in the foods you eat so you can make more empowered choices at the grocery store. I'd much rather you focus on the quality of the foods you eat than micromanage your overall caloric intake like some kind of carb-hating dictator on a mission to wipe out fusilli from the face of the planet!

LOOKING FOR A FEW GOOD QUALITARIANS

From a nutritional perspective, it's clear that creating a consistent caloric deficit can be an effective approach to consistently lose excess weight. Also, in terms of overall longevity, the majority of centenarian diets include consistent caloric restriction. These older folks eat lower-calorie, more nutrient-dense foods most of the time.

But is there more to weight loss and health than just counting calories? Within the global, multibillion-dollar diet industry, I think there is a lot of misleading information and too many strategies from well-meaning doctors and experts who try to create "easy" solutions for people. The danger is that often, these diets are just faddish. What we want to do is focus on the *quality* of foods, not just the *quantity*. For example, there's a massive qualitative difference between 20 grams of saturated trans fats in lard and 20 grams of unprocessed fat in cold-pressed, extra-virgin olive oil. Sure, the numerical quantity of the fat grams is the same, but the quality, nutrient density, and level of assimilability for the body is vastly more beneficial with the latter.

Make no mistake here: I am not advocating a super-high-calorie, high-fat lifestyle for anyone, with the exception of maybe hardcore athletes who have everyday physical demands requiring that level of nutritional intake. However, I am advocating a shift in focus from the categorical demonization of calories and fat toward a higher awareness of the *quality* and *nutritional density* of foods that you're putting in your body. My friend Ashley Koff, celebrity nutritionist, author, and frequent Dr. Oz guest, advocates that people become "qualitarians." I love that term, as it summarizes the essence of the philosophy I'm espousing.

When we focus on the quality of our foods and the density of nutrients therein, we can shift our focus away from counting calories and the pressure to burn off those empty caloric units of energy from artificial, heavily processed foods. Just to provide another, more detailed example: 1,200 calories from a fast food take-out meal is qualitatively VERY different from a 1,200-calorie meal featuring a kale avocado salad, mushroom soup, curried tempeh, and a fresh-fruit smoothie. In fact, fresh, organic, ripe fruit is one of the most calorie-dense foods you can eat. And, coincidentally, it's an awesome source of carbohydrates that provide a sustainable source of energy that is easy to burn off during a workout. A huge serving of fresh, ripe, organic fruit can have the exact same calorie count as a fast food value meal, yet the quality of its nutrients and the energetic yield it creates result in a vastly different effect on the human body.

When it comes to my personal nutrition protocol, I approach my dietary choices with this basic underlying aim: to eat what produces the most energy for the longest sustained period AND is the easiest to digest, assimilate, and eliminate. By eating clean, organic, minimally processed, whole, plant-based foods, you are supplying your body with a clean-burning, highly assimilable, sustainable energy source that always has a net gain effect. To put it simply, the amount of energy that you gain from your food should always be higher than the amount of energy it takes to process. Much like the stock market, you always want to focus on good returns, minimal losses, and wise investments when it comes to your food choices. After all, YOU are your life's biggest asset!

MEET DAVE, THE RAW FOOD TRUCKER

Dave Conrardy is actually no longer a trucker today, but his journey to a healthier lifestyle took place while he was. It all began when he was teaching David and Judith Whiting how to drive a big rig. In exchange, they offered to teach him how to change to a diet that could save his life. At that time, Dave was weighing in around 430 pounds, taking 19 prescription drugs, 6 over-the-counter medications, and eating 4 packs of Rolaids a day. On top of that, he was diabetic and facing stage 2 colon cancer. He ate tons of red meat as part of his unhealthy diet and was staring death squarely in the face.

He agreed to try a raw, vegan diet with the help of his new friends in an effort to lose the excess weight and cure himself of his diseases. Dave took the ball and ran with it to the end zone—even doing some hardcore juice fasting to cleanse his body of harmful chemicals and rejuvenate it with healthy, plant-based nutrients. Over time, Dave was able to lose more than 230 pounds and reverse his cancer and diabetes. Talk about doing a 180 and turning a deathstyle into a lifestyle!

BUT IT'S MY METABOLISM!

You've probably heard people blame their weight issues on a slow metabolism, but what does that really mean? Is metabolism really the culprit when it comes to weight loss struggles? And, if so, is it possible to rev up your metabolism to burn calories more efficiently and get ripped quickly?

Yes, it is true that metabolism is linked to your weight. But contrary to popular belief, a slow metabolism is rarely the cause of excess weight gain. Although your metabolism influences your body's basic energy needs, it's the quality of your food intake and level of physical activity that ultimately determine how much you weigh.

Metabolism is the process by which your body converts what you eat and drink into energy. During this complex biochemical process, calories from your food are combined with oxygen to release the energy your body needs to function.

Even when you're at rest, your body needs energy for all of its elaborate and automated functions, such as breathing, circulating blood, adjusting hormone levels, and repairing cells. The number of calories your body uses to carry out these basic functions is known as your basal metabolic rate—also simply known as your metabolism. Several factors determine your individual metabolism, including:

- Your body size and composition. The bodies of people who are larger or have more muscle burn more calories, even at rest.
- Your sex. Men usually have less body fat and more muscle than women of the same age and weight, so they burn more calories.
- Your age. As you get older, the amount of muscle you have tends to decrease, and fat accounts for more of your weight, slowing down calorie burning.

Unfortunately, as much as we'd love a "magic bullet" to help us lose excess weight, the struggle with weight gain and obesity is a complex and multilayered challenge. Weight gain may stem from a combination of your individual genetic makeup, hormonal controls, diet composition, and the impact of environment on your lifestyle, including sleep, physical activity, and stress levels. All of these factors can result in an imbalance in the energy equation.

MY TOP TIPS FOR GETTING "TORN UP"

While you don't have much control over the overall speed of your metabolism, you absolutely can control how many calories you burn through the frequency and intensity of your physical activity and making more intentional lifestyle choices. Here are some of the primary methods that have kept me in good shape throughout my adult life:

- **REGULAR AEROBIC EXERCISE.** Walking, hiking, bicycling, and swimming are some of the best ways to burn calories. As a general rule of thumb, include at least 30 minutes of physical activity in your daily routine. If you can't set aside time for a long workout, try 10-minute chunks of high-intensity activity throughout your day.

- **LIFESTYLE ACTIVITIES.** Look for ways to walk and move around a few minutes more each day than the day before. Taking the stairs more often and parking your car farther away from the store are simple tricks to burn more calories. Even activities such as walking your dog, gardening, washing your car, and intense housework contribute to weight loss.

- **STRENGTH TRAINING/WEIGHT-BEARING EXERCISE.** Did you know that your body constantly burns calories, even when you're doing nothing? However, resting metabolic rate is significantly higher in people with more muscle mass. Every pound of muscle uses around six calories a day just to sustain itself, while each pound of fat burns only two calories daily. That seemingly incremental difference of four calories really adds up over time! After a session of intense strength training, muscles are activated all over your body, thereby raising your average metabolic rate. When you "get swole," as the bodybuilders like to say, you'll even start to burn calories in your sleep, thanks to all the extra lean muscle mass.

- **DRINKING WATER.** Your body needs water to process calories. If you are even mildly dehydrated, your metabolism can slow down. In one study, adults who drank eight or more glasses of water a day burned more calories than those who drank four. To stay hydrated, drink a glass of water or other unsweetened, natural beverage (like organic tea) before every meal and snack. Also, snack on organic, raw fruits and vegetables, which naturally contain water, rather than salty, dry, or dehydrated snacks that rob moisture from your digestive tract during processing.

- **NATURAL ENERGY BOOSTERS.** Green tea or oolong tea offer the combined benefits of natural caffeine and catechins, substances shown to rev up your metabolism for a couple of hours. Research suggests that drinking two to four cups of either tea may push the body to burn 17 percent more calories during moderately intense exercise for a short time. Also, superfoods such as maca powder, tribulus terrestris, and chia seeds have an innate capacity to increase energy and testosterone levels, thereby helping you work out and build muscle mass with more intensity and stamina.

- **SPICY FOODS.** Spicy foods have natural chemicals that can kick your metabolism into a higher gear. The effect is somewhat temporary, but if you eat spicy foods often, the benefits can add up quickly. For a quick boost, spice up your pasta dishes, rice bowls, chili, and soups with crushed red pepper flakes, chipotle, or cayenne!

- **SMALLER PORTIONS.** Studies have shown that snacking and eating smaller meals throughout the day has a positive effect on metabolism. Eating large portions of food per sitting can overtax your digestive system, thereby creating less efficiency for elimination and also depleting your energy stores. Conversely, eating smaller portions more often can support consistent weight loss. Try having a healthy snack every three to four hours to keep your metabolism cranking.

- **PROTEIN-RICH FOODS.** Your body burns many more calories as it digests protein than it does eating fat or carbohydrates. As part of a balanced diet, replacing some of your carbohydrate intake with protein-rich foods can actually boost your metabolism at mealtime. The key is to select alkaline, plant-based proteins that are highly assimilable, which are much healthier for your body. When you consume highly acidic, animal-based proteins, they come complete with high levels of cholesterol, artery-clogging fats, and, over time, result in a net loss of alkaline minerals in your body, most notably calcium.

IT'S UP TO YOU!

I hate to be the bearer of bad news, but there's just no easy way to lose weight. The most solid and reliable foundation for weight loss continues to be anchored in consistent physical activity, a positive, unstoppable mind-set, and a shift toward a healthy, clean, plant-based diet. Our knowledge is continually expanding about all of the mechanisms that impact human appetite, food selection, and how your body processes and burns food. The best way to find out what works for you is to engage in conscious experimentation with different foods, exercises, natural supplements, and mindfulness techniques until you crack the weight loss code.

And remember—what works for your individual body type, metabolism, and genetic structure is unique to you. It's not about comparing yourself to anyone else or their progress. It's about setting structured, achievable goals for yourself, experimenting with what works, asking for support from people you trust, and making a daily choice to be positively relentless in creating your ideal body and level of lifelong well-being. This process is a marathon, not a sprint, baby. Persistence and determination will get you results. Choose to focus on your daily progress, not perfection, and you'll be on track for long-term success!

MY TOP NUTRIENTS THAT SUPPORT WEIGHT LOSS

Calcium: Many studies now suggest that calcium is a major player in boosting metabolism and burning fat.

Capsicum: Not only is this great for your heart, but it also raises your body temperature, which in turn burns more calories.

Complex carbohydrates: Your body burns twice as many calories breaking these down than simple carbs, meaning you're burning fat as you eat!

Folic acid: Helps convert food into glucose, which turns into energy, helping you burn fat and stay slim.

Iron: Iron helps your red blood cells carry oxygen. Without enough iron, you'll feel tired, run-down, and exhausted, making it difficult to exercise. Since exercise is a key component of weight loss, iron is one of the most important minerals you can eat to lose weight.

Vitamin D: Every cell in your body needs D to function properly, including fat cells. Special receptors for D signal whether you should burn fat or simply store it; when D plugs into these receptors, it's like a switch that turns on the fat-melting mechanism.

MY TOP FOODS FOR HEALTHY WEIGHT LOSS

- almonds
- avocado
- black sesame seeds
- blueberries
- buckwheat
- cacao
- cantaloupe
- caralluma
- cayenne pepper
- chia seeds
- chile peppers
- coconut oil
- cold-pressed alkaline coffee
- flaxseed
- goji berries
- green beans
- green coffee bean extract
- green tea
- guarana
- hemp seeds
- honeydew melon
- jicama
- kale
- kiwi
- lentils
- maca powder
- medium-chain triglyceride (MCT)-rich oils
- oolong tea
- probiotics
- quinoa
- raspberry ketones
- red pepper flakes
- sea vegetables
- xylitol

RECIPES FOR WEIGHT LOSS

· · · · · · · · · · · · · · · · · ·

APPLE LEMON GINGER
CHIA CLEANSER

SERVES 1

WHEN IT'S TIME TO DETOX, YOU don't need to restrict yourself to a week's worth of green juice. Especially if you're new to cleansing, variety can help keep you dedicated to your regimen. The combination of apple, lemon, and ginger juice with chia seeds is great for alkalizing the body and helping you to eliminate toxins at the same time. Not only does this drink improve digestive functions, but it also has a thermogenic effect that helps activate the metabolism, making it a potent fat and calorie burner. Plus, it's easy to make and tastes yummy!

2 large apples, cored and quartered

1 large lemon, quartered

1½-inch piece ginger root, peeled

2 tablespoons chia seeds

½ teaspoon fulvic acid (optional)

1. Run the apples, lemon, and ginger root through a juicer and pour into a serving glass. Add the chia seeds to the juice and stir gently. Let rest for a few seconds until the seeds begin to absorb the juice and start to plump. Add the fulvic acid, if you're using it, and stir again. Serve immediately.

PINEAPPLE KALE
GREEN SMOOTHIE

SERVES 1

    NF

GREEN SMOOTHIES ARE NOT ONLY AN easy way to get your greens every day, but they happen to taste amazing when paired with the right balance of fruits and spices. This smoothie gives you a healthy dose of vitamin C from pineapple, assimilable protein from chia seeds, and vitamin K from kale. For a green, leafy vegetable, kale is unusually high in fiber. This helps create the bulk you need to keep you full for a good amount of time. Kale is also a great source of vitamin A and calcium. This is the kind of smoothie you can enjoy every morning. And I often do!

2 cups filtered water

1 cup fresh or frozen pineapple chunks

1 cup ice cubes

1 handful kale

1 tablespoon coconut nectar (optional)

½ teaspoon ground vanilla bean

Pinch ground cardamom

Pinch sea salt

1½ tablespoons chia seeds

1 Blend all ingredients in a high-speed blender for 40 seconds until smooth.

STRAWBERRY VINAIGRETTE
SALAD DRESSING

SOMETIMES YOU'RE JUST IN THE MOOD for a fresh, light salad dressing, and this vinaigrette features a sweet, strawberry taste with a tangy undertone of flavor. This dressing is full of antioxidants and omega fatty acids. It also features alkalizing ingredients such as lemon juice and apple cider vinegar. I especially love this dressing served over spicy organic greens like arugula, tatsoi, or watercress.

¼ cup filtered water

½ cup extra-virgin olive oil

½ cup coconut vinegar or apple cider vinegar

¼ cup fresh lemon juice

1 pound fresh strawberries

½ cup coconut nectar

3 tablespoons coconut sugar

1 teaspoon sea salt

Dash cayenne pepper

2 heaping tablespoons chia seeds

1 Add all ingredients to a high-speed blender, starting with the liquids first. Blend for 40 seconds until smooth. Serve over your favorite salad greens.

GREEN CURRY VEGETABLES
WITH JICAMA RICE

SERVES 4 TO 6

JICAMA IS A MEXICAN SWEET RADISH that can be processed into rice-size pieces for raw recipes like this glorious green curry dish. This fully raw recipe features tastes of sweet mango, crunchy bean sprouts, and a mellifluous mix of fresh mint and cilantro. I love warming this dish in the oven or dehydrator before serving to bring out the flavor even more. Oh, and leftovers the next day are divine. Even better, curry boosts your metabolism, helping you to burn calories, while the turmeric found in curry powder boasts a compound called curcumin, which is a potent anti-inflammatory.

GREEN CURRY SAUCE:

¼ cup grated fresh lemongrass

1 cup young Thai coconut meat

¼ cup raw cashews, soaked 2 hours

2 tablespoons fresh lime juice

3 tablespoons chopped jalapeno, seeded to taste

3 scallions, finely chopped

2 tablespoons ginger root, peeled and minced

¼ cup loosely packed fresh basil

2 to 3 teaspoons curry powder

1 teaspoon sea salt

5 dates, pitted and chopped

½ teaspoon cayenne pepper

¼ cup raw coconut water

VEGETABLES:

4 medium jicamas, peeled and chopped

1 ripe mango, peeled and cubed

1 red bell pepper, cored and cubed

¼ red onion, diced

1 handful fresh mint, torn

1 handful fresh cilantro, torn

½ cup bean sprouts

2 tablespoons black sesame seeds

½ cup chopped raw, dehydrated almonds

1. **To make the Green Curry Sauce:** blend all ingredients, except coconut water, in a high-speed blender until a smooth, thick, saucelike consistency is achieved. Gradually add coconut water and blend again to perfect the puree. Set aside at room temperature.

2. **To make the vegetables:** Process the chopped jicama root in a food processor until a ricelike consistency is achieved. Squeeze out the excess water in a cheesecloth or nut milk bag until the jicama rice is relatively dry. Set aside.

3. Combine all other vegetable ingredients in a mixing bowl, except the sesame seeds and almonds.

4. Mix the vegetables and jicama rice with Green Curry Sauce and top with sesame seeds, almonds, and a few sprigs of fresh mint and cilantro to serve.

CHIA SEED
PUDDING

OATMEAL CAN GET DOWNRIGHT AWFUL IF you eat it every morning for breakfast. Boredom sets in quickly, and then you might reach for things that aren't so good for you. (Strawberry Pop-Tart, anyone?) Leave it to the protein-rich delectability of this Chia Seed Pudding to rescue your taste buds from artificial breakfast Armageddon. This recipe gives you sustained energy to start the day with healthy omega fatty acids and the added bonus of rockin' regularity from 11 grams of plant-based fiber per ounce. Plus, you can make a batch and chill it overnight for a quick on-the-go breakfast option the next morning!

½ cup chia seeds

1½ cups hemp milk

3 tablespoons coconut nectar

1 teaspoon ground vanilla bean

1 teaspoon maca powder

¼ cup cacao nibs

¼ cup dried mulberries

¼ cup goji berries

¼ cup hemp seeds

¼ cup blueberries

¼ teaspoon ground cardamom

¼ teaspoon ground cinnamon

Pinch sea salt

1 Add the chia seeds to a mixing bowl and add the hemp milk. Stir the chia seeds vigorously as they soak up all the liquid. Wait about 10 minutes until you have a nice, thick consistency and then start adding the rest of the ingredients in the order listed. Mix all the ingredients together and serve.

COCONUT YOGURT
WITH FRESH FIGS & APPLES

SERVES 4 TO 6

IF YOU WANT TO HAVE A happy gut, you've got to have probiotics in your diet on a regular basis. They help boost your immunity, regularity, and digestive power. Yogurt is traditionally one of the best ways to get your daily dose of probiotics. This nondairy, coconut-based yogurt is just as creamy, tangy, and tantalizing as the traditional version made from cow's milk. Add your favorite fresh fruit, like figs and apples, to take it over the top!

4 young Thai coconuts

4 to 6 capsules of acidophilus probiotic powder

½ cup raw coconut water

3 limes, juiced and zested

⅛ cup coconut nectar

¼ teaspoon sea salt

¼ cup blueberries, reserved for garnish

¼ cup goji berries, soaked for 10 minutes, reserved for garnish

1 pint fresh figs, destemmed and halved, reserved for garnish

1 large apple, cored and sliced, reserved for garnish

1 Crack open the young Thai coconuts with a cleaver or coconut knife and scrape out the coconut meat with the back side of a spoon. Remove any shell pieces or hard particles and rinse with fresh water. Open the acidophilus capsules and empty the powdered probiotics into a small bowl. Blend the coconut meat, probiotic powder, coconut water, lime juice, 1 tablespoon lime zest, coconut nectar, and sea salt in a high-speed blender for 30 to 40 seconds until completely smooth.

2 Transfer the yogurt mixture to a medium mixing bowl. Cover the bowl with a kitchen towel and let the yogurt sit at room temperature for 2 to 4 hours to activate the probiotic cultures. Refrigerate for 30 to 60 minutes, depending on your desired consistency.

3 Remove the yogurt from the fridge and top with the blueberries, goji berries, figs, and apple. The yogurt will last for up to five days in a covered container in the fridge.

If fresh figs are out of season, use dried figs instead.

MELON KIWI
SMOOTHIE

SERVES 2

THIS IS ONE OF THE MOST water-dense smoothies you can enjoy. Melon fully digests in 15 to 30 minutes, making this an awesome weight-loss drink. The fiber gives you a feeling of satiety, not to mention that the flavor combination of sweet melon and sour kiwi is pretty darn delightful. Oh, and kiwi also has a superpowered nutrient called carnitine, which helps with fat burning. Jenny Craig needs to get in on this sweet smoothie action—stat!

2 cups cantaloupe or honeydew melon

2 kiwis, peeled

½ cup raw coconut water

4 teaspoons fresh lime juice

2 teaspoons grated ginger root

2 tablespoons fresh mint

1 banana, peeled

1 cup ice cubes

1 Blend all ingredients for 30 seconds in a high-speed blender and serve immediately. Garnish with a few fresh mint leaves.

WATERCRESS &
WATERMELON SALAD

THIS RECIPE WAS BORN FROM A desperate recipe brainstorming session where I had a funny thought: *What would happen if I put watermelon and watercress together?* And out came this salad. I love how the subtle sweetness of the watermelon plays off the spicy greens so beautifully in this dish. Watermelon is a wonder food for weight loss, being 92 percent water and loaded with potent antioxidants like glutathione and the detox diva of nutrients, citrulline. To bring this salad to the next level, make sure you find a good vegan cheese made from almonds, macadamia nuts, or cashews.

1 large head watercress, torn by hand

1½ cups watermelon, diced

1 cup cultured vegan cheese, cubed

2 tablespoons extra-virgin olive oil

1 lemon, juiced and zested

½ teaspoon sea salt

¼ teaspoon ground black pepper

1 Add all ingredients to a large mixing bowl and gently stir to combine well.

NACHO
CHEESY POPCORN

SERVES 4

THIS IS THE ULTIMATE HEALTHY POPCORN for movie night. The addition of vitamin B12–rich nutritional yeast, chili powder, cumin, and garlic makes this a cheesy, spicy snack that will attack your hunger and rev up your metabolism. I like sneaking this snack into the movie theatre. It's a way healthier, low-calorie alternative to the fatty, artificial popcorn you typically find at the concession stand.

2 tablespoons grapeseed oil

¾ cup unpopped popcorn seeds

¼ cup organic virgin coconut oil, melted

¼ cup nutritional yeast

1 tablespoon chili powder

1 teaspoon ground cumin

1 teaspoon garlic powder

½ teaspoon sea salt

1 Heat the grapeseed oil in a large saucepan over medium-high heat. Add the popcorn seeds and place the lid on the pan. Shake vigorously to coat the kernels with oil. When the corn starts to pop, shake the pan constantly until the popping stops, about 5 to 7 minutes. Remove the pan from the heat and pour the popped corn into a large mixing bowl.

2 Drizzle the melted coconut oil over the hot popcorn and sprinkle with the nutritional yeast, chili powder, cumin, garlic powder, and sea salt to taste. Stir thoroughly and serve immediately.

JASON'S TIP

For more spice and a bigger flavor kick, add cayenne pepper, curry powder, or a few shakes of hot sauce to the popcorn.

SUPERFOOD
SEAWEED SOUP

SEAWEED CAN BE A SCARY PROPOSITION if you've never tried it before. That's why it's important to create a good context for it—like this nourishing soup recipe. A variety of seaweeds adds alkaline minerals to the mix, while the cilantro and turmeric are great for detoxing heavy metals and preventing inflammation. And even more compelling: recent studies show that alginate in kelp can suppress the digestion of fat in the gut, which thereby reduces the amount of fat your body can absorb. This soup is a delicious example of food as medicine.

2 cups filtered water

1 cup fresh lemon juice

4 nori sheets, shredded into small pieces

½ cup whole-leaf dried dulse

½ cup whole-leaf dried kelp

3 tablespoons organic virgin coconut oil

1 large clove garlic

1 bunch cilantro

½ teaspoon sea salt

1 teaspoon turmeric powder

1 heaping teaspoon chlorella powder

Pinch cayenne pepper

1 avocado, pitted

1 Blend all ingredients in a high-speed blender for 40 seconds until smooth and creamy.

APPLE PIE
SMOOTHIE

THIS IS STRAIGHT-UP APPLE PIE IN a glass. The idea for this recipe came from my friend Michelle Marquis, The Alchemist Chef, when we were brainstorming some fantastic fall recipes. This smoothie is pretty dense and filling, which means it can also serve as a meal replacement. Even better, apples contain nondigestible compounds that promote the growth of beneficial bacteria in your gut associated with weight loss. No matter how you slice it, this sweet smoothie is a total home run.

1 apple, cored and chopped

1½ teaspoons ginger root, peeled and chopped

1 cup coconut milk

1 cup ice cubes

½ scoop vegan vanilla protein powder

2 tablespoons raw pecans

2 tablespoons golden flaxseed, ground

1 tablespoon coconut sugar

1 teaspoon lucuma powder

1 teaspoon ground cinnamon

½ teaspoon mesquite powder

Pinch ground cardamom

Pinch sea salt

2 tablespoons gluten-free granola, reserved for garnish

1 cinnamon stick, reserved for garnish

1. Blend all ingredients in a high-speed blender for 30 seconds and top with a sprinkle of granola. Garnish with a cinnamon stick.

4

EAT FOR

HAPPINESS

AND

GOOD MOODS

I'LL START THIS CHAPTER BY sharing one of my favorite Abraham-Hicks quotes: "There is no desire that anyone holds for any other reason than that they believe they will feel better in the achievement of it. Whether it is a material object, a physical state of being, a relationship, a condition, or a circumstance—at the heart of every desire is the desire to feel good."

The pursuit of happiness will take you down many roads, through many relationships, jobs, and life situations. However, we all know the feeling of being surrounded by material objects, people, and experiences that we at one time desired—only to feel isolation, disconnection, and a deep sense of longing. I know this feeling firsthand, and I can tell you that my struggle with clinical depression and daily mood swings were directly related to my lack of self-love, my inability to deal with negative emotions, and, most significantly, a few key nutritional deficiencies that threw my brain chemistry out of balance. In addition to learning new emotional healing tools, a gentle shift in my diet and optimizing my nutrition had tangible benefits for my mood and overall level of contentment.

Before I made these changes, I could feel that something was definitely "off," but I was too ashamed to ask for support. I thought I had to struggle with it alone and didn't want to burden anyone with my pain. As I dove into the research to look at the scope of depression in the U.S., I found I was definitely not alone in my struggle:

- 14.8 million American adults (about 6.7 percent of the U.S. population) ages 18 and older suffer from depression
- One in ten U.S. adults takes a pharmaceutical antidepressant medication
- Depression affects one in four American women in their 40s and 50s

Now, looking at those statistics, you may be thinking, *Wow, I didn't know it was THAT big of a problem!* But, if we're honest about it, mood swings and depressive states can strike us all . . . and for some of us, quite often. All it takes is one more domino to send the whole stack crashing down: your paycheck was late, the line at the DMV was way too long, or the distracted barista at Starbucks accidentally made your triple latte with whole milk when you *specifically* told her you wanted coconut milk. And then what happens? You fly off the handle like a frothing junkyard dog and act like it's the end of the freakin' world. Can you relate? I sure can. I've had plenty of those little irritating moments that feel like apocalyptic crises when in reality, they are just mirrors for something deeper inside of us that wants to be understood and healed.

GOOD FOODS FOR GOOD MOODS

If you've been feeling crappy, it's time to take a good look at your food choices to see how they are affecting your state of being. Are you craving a lot of sweets or starches? If your blood sugar is on a roller-coaster ride from eating too much processed sugar, refined carbohydrates, and artificial ingredients, you are more likely to feel imbalanced and cranky. You'll also feel off balance if you've started a super-restrictive crash diet; your GI tract will be in distress with intense hunger pangs.

Keeping your blood sugar steady and your GI tract running smoothly will do wonders for your overall health and moods. Plus, the key nutrients you get in certain foods can influence your brain's levels of feel-good neurotransmitters such as serotonin, GABA, and dopamine. Other critical nutrients can help prevent inflammation in your body so that your blood circulates well to all of your organs.

Here are my basic tips for how to improve your moods with foods, starting now:

Consume foods rich in vitamin B12 and folic acid. These two vitamins help to prevent mood disorders, central nervous system disorders, and dementias. The link between higher intakes of folate and a lower prevalence of depressive symptoms crosses cultures, too. A cross-sectional research study by the National Center for Global Health and Medicine in Tokyo confirmed this positive association in both Japanese men and women. Folic acid is usually found in beans, greens, and legumes. There are trace amounts of vitamin B12 in fortified nutritional yeast, spirulina, tempeh, blue-green algae, and chlorella as well.

Vitamin B12 is a by-product of bacteria and was once found in our water supply as well as on the plant foods we eat. Because we now chlorinate our water in municipal areas and because we don't pick our vegetables from the wild without washing them, it's much harder to obtain optimal levels of B12 strictly from plant-based food sources. In my opinion, just consume a high-quality methylcobalamin vitamin B12 supplement and call it a day!

Eat more fresh, organic fruits and vegetables. Fresh, organic (and especially locally grown) fruits and vegetables are packed with key nutrients, trace minerals, antioxidants, and phytochemicals that directly contribute to your overall health and mental well-being. In a population-based, cross-sectional study from the London School of Hygiene and Tropical Medicine, researchers found that the consumption of two or more servings of fresh fruits and vegetables a day was associated with an 11

percent higher likelihood of good overall functional health. People who ate the highest amount of fruits and vegetables felt much better about their state of health and well-being.

Choose selenium-rich foods. Selenium is a mineral that acts as an antioxidant in the body. What do antioxidants have to do with feeling better and minimizing bad moods? New research suggests that the presence of oxidative stress in the brain is associated with some cases of mild to moderate depression. One nested, case-controlled study by the organization Complementary Therapies in Medicine evaluated the depression scores of elderly people whose daily diet was either supplemented with 200 micrograms of selenium a day or a placebo. The group taking selenium had significant decreases in their depression symptoms.

Where can you find great sources of selenium? Whole grains! By eating several servings a day of whole grains such as oatmeal, whole-grain bread, and brown rice, you can easily get your daily dose. Just be careful if you're sugar sensitive, as these whole grains can be a hidden source. Other foods rich in selenium include beans, legumes, seeds, and nuts (especially Brazil nuts, which are also excellent for men's reproductive health and testosterone levels).

Consume omega-3 fatty acid–rich foods or supplements. Several recent studies have suggested that both men and women are at a lower risk of depression symptoms if they eat foods high in omega-3 fatty acids. Omega-3 fatty acids seem to have positive effects on depressive conditions, including postpartum depression. Plant foods rich in omega-3 fatty acids include hemp seeds, chia seeds, flaxseed, and various forms of microalgae, including marine phytoplankton, ocean algae, spirulina, and chlorella.

Take a daily dose of vitamin D. Does a little time in the sun seem to make you feel better? I know I feel a LOT better emotionally when I get a few minutes of direct sun on my skin every day. The sun's rays allow our bodies to synthesize and regulate vitamin D. Several correlated research studies from the Medical University of South Carolina showed an association between low serum levels of vitamin D and higher incidences of four mood disorders in women: PMS, seasonal affective disorder, nonspecified mood disorder, and major depressive disorder. Very few plant-based foods naturally contain high levels of assimilable vitamin D. I recommend you get your vitamin D from a variety of sources, including short periods of managed, direct sun exposure, natural vitamin D supplements, and fortified foods like whole-grain cereals, breads, organic fruit juices, and nondairy milks made from coconut, hemp, almond, or flax.

Eat dark chocolate for the win. Small amounts of dark chocolate can be a natural mood lifter, with raw cacao (unprocessed beans that are the primary component in chocolate) being the most potent option due to its high concentration of antioxidants and magnesium. Cacao has a powerful effect on your brain endorphins and helps you produce more phenylethylamine (PEA)—one of the brain chemicals that's released when you're in love! Not only that, cacao also seems to have a heart-healthy, anticlogging effect in our blood vessels. In one study from the Netherlands, Dutch men who ate one-third of a dark chocolate bar each day had lower levels of blood pressure and lower rates of heart disease. The chocolate also boosted their general sense of emotional well-being.

GENETIC FACTORS THAT MAY INFLUENCE MOOD

While nutrition clearly plays a big role in determining your mood, you may also have inherited certain mood disorders. New research is strongly demonstrating how genes influence our moods and other key personality traits. Some genes may program our brains to produce specific amounts of mood-enhancing chemicals.

But for some of us, genes can undersupply our neurotransmitters. This may be one reason why the same emotional traits seem to run in some families. If your mother always seemed anxious and worried and often poured herself a glass of wine, it should come as no surprise that you, too, might sometimes reach for a wine glass under intense emotional pressures. Parents who have low supplies of naturally stimulating and sedating brain chemicals can sometimes have depressed or anxious children who use food, alcohol, or drugs as substitutes for the healthy amounts of brain chemicals they so desperately need.

Prolonged states of chronic stress and anxiety can wholly deplete your neurotransmitters, which compromises your brain's ability to calm your nerves. This is particularly true if you have inherited marginal amounts of healthy brain chemicals to begin with. The emergency stores of precious brain chemicals can get used up if you call on them to calm yourself over and over again. Eventually, your brain can't keep up with the demand. That's why you may start to intuitively "help" your brain by eating foods with druglike effects that mimic the behavior of the depleted chemicals.

CHEESE: THE ULTIMATE FOOD ADDICTION

The steady use of druglike foods such as refined white sugars and flours, artificial ingredients, food additives (such as MSG), or alcohol or drugs can inhibit the production of your brain's natural pleasure chemicals and nullify healthy neurotransmitter function. In fact, one of the reasons that

Grilled Asparagus Sandwich with
Hollandaise Sauce (see recipe page 102)

dairy products are so damn addictive is that they contain naturally addicting protein fragments called casomorphins that derive from the digestion of a milk protein called casein. The distinguishing characteristic of casomorphins is their direct opiate effect in your brain. That's right; drinking milk and eating dairy products have a similar effect on your brain as using opium or heroin!

Like any other drugs, the more dairy products you eat, the more you become dependent on them for a feel-good high in your brain, leading to potentially massive withdrawal symptoms when you eliminate those foods from your lifestyle. Opioids are well known for their ability to produce euphoria, motivating some people to use them recreationally. All of these opiate-like substances can plug into your brain and actually fill up the empty places called receptors where your neurotransmitters should be plugging in. Your brain senses

that the receptors are already full, so it further reduces the amounts of neurotransmitters that it produces. As the amounts of these natural brain chemicals drop, more and more alcohol, drugs, or druglike foods are needed to fill newly emptied brain slots. This vicious circle ends when these substances you ingest are unable to do the trick any longer. Now your brain's natural neurotransmitters, functioning suboptimally, are completely exhausted, and you'll crave those mood-enhancing foods or drugs more voraciously than ever. So, you might want to think twice about that cheese and wine pairing. Recognizing that you may be self-medicating with food is the first step toward breaking your addiction and getting your brain back on a healthy track.

HOW TO DEAL WITH BAD MOODS

When you experience frequent negative emotions like depression, your entire world becomes clouded. It doesn't matter whether good things are happening in your life. It's as if a dark veil is cast over everything and you no longer appreciate the blessings you have. Beyond eating nutrient-dense whole foods and supplements, understanding your genetic predispositions, and avoiding certain foods, is there more you can do to manage your moods?

Practices such as keeping a gratitude journal, meditation, exercise, and psychotherapy can have dramatic benefits on your mood and help to increase feelings of appreciation and optimism—the belief that all is well. These practices can help remind you how great your life actually is.

In my own experience, I've found that a combination of these strategies and dietary tweaks helped to create significant changes in my mood and allowed me to shift into a more balanced, calm, and content state of being. I strongly feel that mood swings and depression must be consciously and consistently addressed at all levels of our existence: physical, mental, and spiritual.

MY TOP NUTRIENTS TO BOOST YOUR MOOD

Anthocyanins: Powerful antioxidants that may provide neuroprotective benefits such as bolstering short-term memory and reducing mood-killing inflammation.

Lycopene: Fat-soluble phytonutrient that helps protect vital brain fat. It actually stops the buildup of proinflammatory compounds linked to depression.

Omega-3 fatty acids: These help to form cell membranes, keep those membranes flexible, prevent "leakage" of neurotransmitters, and regulate the flow of hormones and other chemical messengers that affect our mood as well as our immune system.

Tryptophan: In addition to helping us sleep, tryptophan is needed to make serotonin, a neurotransmitter that regulates signals in the brain and therefore also our moods.

Vitamin B6: We already know that serotonin is important for fighting depression, but we need B6 to support its synthesis.

MY TOP FEEL-GOOD FOODS

- algae
- asparagus
- avocado
- beans
- blue or purple potatoes
- blueberries
- brown rice
- cacao
- celery
- chlorella
- citrus fruits
- coconuts
- coconut yogurt
- flaxseed
- fresh mint
- goji berries
- green tea
- kidney beans
- lemon
- mango
- marine phytoplankton
- pistachios
- probiotics
- pumpkin seeds
- rhodiola
- saffron
- spinach
- Swiss chard
- tomatoes
- valerian root
- walnuts

RECIPES
TO PROMOTE
GOOD MOODS

· · · · · · · · · · · · · · · ·

PASTA
MARINARA

KELP NOODLES ARE ONE OF MY favorite ingredients to use for raw "pasta" dishes. When you marinate them, their consistency comes surprisingly close to that of cooked spaghetti. For the marinara sauce, I sneak in some strawberries for a lingering sweetness, along with the classic flavors you know and love. And, as if the sauce wasn't boss enough, the tomatoes contain mood enhancers such as folate and magnesium as well as iron and vitamin B6, both needed by your brain to produce the important mood-regulating neurotransmitters dopamine, serotonin, and norepinephrine. This is a great first recipe to share with raw food rookies!

NOODLES:

2 bags kelp noodles, drained

¼ cup extra-virgin olive oil

¼ cup fresh lemon juice

½ teaspoon sea salt

MARINARA SAUCE:

3 small heirloom or roma tomatoes

¼ cup fresh lemon juice

1 tablespoon coconut aminos

3 tablespoons extra-virgin olive oil

3 tablespoons yellow onion, diced

4 cloves garlic, minced

½ cup fresh basil, packed

¼ cup fresh oregano, packed

¼ teaspoon sea salt

2 cups sun-dried tomatoes, soaked 30 minutes

6 to 8 fresh strawberries

1 **To make the noodles:** marinate kelp noodles with olive oil, lemon juice, and sea salt for 2 hours. Set aside.

2 **To make the marinara sauce:** blend the heirloom tomatoes in a high-speed blender until smooth. Add the lemon juice, coconut aminos, olive oil, yellow onion, garlic, basil, oregano, sea salt, sun-dried tomatoes, and strawberries. Blend until smooth.

3 Drain the excess marinade liquid from the kelp noodles, massage for 10 minutes, and place them in a medium mixing bowl. Combine well with the marinara sauce and serve immediately.

For a thicker sauce, use more sun-dried tomatoes and less blended tomato. For a sweeter sauce, use 1 to 2 more strawberries.

GRILLED ASPARAGUS SANDWICH
WITH HOLLANDAISE SAUCE

SERVES 4

THIS RECIPE IS ALL ABOUT THE juxtaposition of textures. The chewy, woodsy grilled asparagus is slathered in a tangy, light, dairy-free hollandaise sauce that creates a flavor explosion in your mouth. If you're prone to mood swings, asparagus is a must-have vegetable in your diet because it's packed with folic acid. Low levels of folic acid have been linked to depression, so you want to make sure you're getting plenty of it.

HOLLANDAISE SAUCE:

1 cup cashews, soaked 2 hours

2 tablespoons fresh lemon juice

2 heaping tablespoons nutritional yeast flakes

¼ cup extra-virgin olive oil

¼ teaspoon turmeric powder

⅛ teaspoon cayenne pepper

⅛ teaspoon holy basil powder

½ teaspoon sea salt

ASPARAGUS SANDWICH:

2 tablespoons organic virgin coconut oil

1 pound asparagus spears

4 gluten-free English muffins, halved and toasted

½ cup diced red bell pepper

¼ cup minced fresh parsley

⅛ cup hemp seeds

1. **To make the hollandaise sauce:** blend all sauce ingredients in a high-speed blender for 30 seconds until smooth and creamy.

2. Heat the coconut oil in a sauté pan and cook the asparagus spears for 5 to 6 minutes on medium heat until tender and slightly browned. Transfer to a plate.

3. **To assemble the sandwiches:** layer each English muffin with a generous amount of the asparagus spears, hollandaise sauce, red bell peppers, parsley, and hemp seeds. Serve immediately.

SPICY MANGO
KIWI PUDDING

SERVES 2

SOMETIMES I LIKE TO JUST THROW a bunch of fruit in the blender and see what happens. Hence, the genesis of this tropical fruit pudding. Mango contains vitamin B6, which promotes the production of serotonin. This hormone elevates your mood, so eating mango may help prevent depression and improve your feeling of general well-being. This creamy, spicy, and tart creation can be frequently enjoyed for breakfast, dessert, or as a quick pick-me-up snack.

1 cup raw coconut water

2 mangoes, diced

2 large kiwis, peeled and halved

1 lime, juiced

¼ habanero pepper

1 teaspoon arrowroot powder (optional)

1 teaspoon ground vanilla bean

1 Blend all ingredients in a high-speed blender for 40 seconds until smooth and creamy. Transfer to a covered container and chill in the refrigerator for at least 2 hours to thicken before serving.

If you can't find a fresh habanero pepper, feel free to add a dash of ground cayenne pepper to the mix.

SWEET CREPES WITH
STRAWBERRY TOMATO COULIS

IT SEEMS LIKE ALL I EVER want for breakfast are sweet things. There's something so sensual, satisfying, and splendid about crepes—they feel like they should be reserved for special occasions. This crepe recipe took me about 20 attempts to finally nail it. And the results are absolutely stunning. The inclusion of tomato in the strawberry sauce is hauntingly delicious, and you will be seduced by the perfect texture of these gluten-free crepes. Plus, strawberries contain anthocyanidins and anthocyanins—nutrients that help reduce stress and depression. C'est magnifique!

SWEET CASHEW CRÈME:

2 cups raw cashews, soaked for at least 1 hour

½ cup coconut nectar

1 teaspoon vanilla extract

¼ cup fresh lemon juice

¼ cup plus 2 tablespoons filtered water

½ teaspoon lemon zest

¼ cup plus 2 tablespoons organic virgin coconut oil, melted

CREPE BATTER:

1 cup gluten-free all-purpose baking flour

1 cup unsweetened coconut milk

4 tablespoons organic virgin coconut oil, divided

2 tablespoons coconut sugar

3 tablespoons golden flaxseed, finely ground

¼ teaspoon sea salt

1 teaspoon aluminum-free baking powder

½ cup filtered water

1 teaspoon vanilla extract

1 cup diced strawberries, reserved for garnish

1 cup crushed walnuts, reserved for garnish

STRAWBERRY TOMATO COULIS:

2 cups diced strawberries

1½ cups chopped tomatoes

5 tablespoons coconut nectar

1 tablespoon plus 1 teaspoon fresh lemon juice

Pinch sea salt

Using a very thin, wide rubber spatula will help immensely with getting the crepes out of the pan. Go slowly and take your time. Crepes don't like to be rushed. When using gluten-free flour, make sure it does not contain any added thickeners such as arrowroot powder, xanthan gum, or ground flaxseed. These will ruin the consistency of the crepes by making them too thick and the batter too viscous.

1 **To make the Sweet Cashew Crème:** blend all cream ingredients in a high-speed blender for 40 seconds until ultra smooth and creamy. Chill for at least 2 hours before serving.

2 **To make the crepe batter:** mix together the baking flour, coconut milk, 2 tablespoons of the coconut oil, coconut sugar, golden flaxseed, sea salt, baking powder, filtered water, and vanilla extract, preferably with a high-speed blender or hand mixer. Cover and refrigerate for 30 minutes. The batter will keep fresh in a covered container stored in the refrigerator for up to three days.

3 **To make the Strawberry Tomato Coulis:** combine all the coulis ingredients in a high-speed blender or food processor and pulse the mixture gradually until well combined, retaining a slight amount of chunkiness to the mixture. Set aside.

4 Heat the remaining 2 tablespoons of coconut oil over medium-low heat in a nonstick pan or crepe pan. If using an 8-inch pan, use ¼ cup of batter. If using a 9- or 9½-inch pan, use ⅓ cup of batter. Pour the batter into the pan and shake the pan immediately to spread the batter evenly. When the topside of the crepe is totally dry, starting to brown slightly around the edges, and producing little bubbles (after about 2 minutes), carefully flip the crepe with a thin spatula. The other side will need less cooking time, around 1 to 1½ minutes.

5 Carefully remove the finished crepe and transfer to a plate. Repeat until all of the crepe batter is used.

6 To assemble, fill each crepe with a large dollop of the Sweet Cashew Crème, spooning it lengthwise. Fold the edges of the crepe toward the middle, one at a time, and then flip the crepe over, with the top facing down on the plate. Spoon a generous amount of the Strawberry Tomato Coulis on top and garnish with diced strawberries and chopped walnuts.

ALKALIZING SUPERFOOD
GREEN SMOOTHIE

SERVES 2

MY GO-TO BREAKFAST EVERY DAY IS some version of this smoothie. It's loaded with a potent array of powerful superfoods to boost your mood and crank up your immunity. The addition of avocado adds a super-creamy texture while giving you the benefit of feel-good serotonin. Switching up your greens and fruits in this recipe is a good way to keep it fresh and interesting.

1¼ cups filtered water

2 pinches sea salt

⅛ cup shelled hemp seeds

¼ cup fresh diced mango

⅓ cup fresh blueberries

2 medium kale leaves, with stems

Small handful arugula

1 tablespoon coconut nectar

½ tablespoon green superfood powder

½ tablespoon tocotrienols

1 teaspoon maca powder

½ teaspoon shilajit powder

¼ teaspoon ground cinnamon

⅛ teaspoon ground vanilla bean

½ avocado, pitted

2 tablespoons goldenberries, soaked for 15 minutes

1 Blend the filtered water, sea salt, and shelled hemp seeds into frothy hemp milk in a high-speed blender for 30 to 45 seconds. Add the remaining ingredients and blend again until very smooth.

JASON'S TIP

Serve topped with raw, vegan granola; hemp seeds; or goji berries for a nice textural contrast and extra nutritional kick.

CHOCOLATE CHIP
MACADAMIA COOKIES

YOU CAN'T LOSE WITH STRAIGHT-UP, OLD-SCHOOL chocolate chip cookies. You win BIG by making them gluten free and adding heart-healthy macadamia nuts and shredded coconut. When your inner cookie monster comes out to play, feed him these puppies. They are a big hit with kids and partygoers alike. The combination of dark chocolate chips and whole grains creates a neurotransmitter party in your brain, where serotonin, tryptophan, and PEA are the guests of honor. A word of caution, though: be careful not to eat the entire batch of dough before it goes in the oven. Been there, done that.

1½ cups gluten-free oat flour

1 cup gluten-free all-purpose baking flour

1 cup coconut sugar

¼ cup ground golden flaxseed

¼ cup arrowroot powder

1½ teaspoons guar gum

1 teaspoon baking soda

1 teaspoon sea salt

2 tablespoons vanilla extract

4 tablespoons cinnamon applesauce

1 cup organic virgin coconut oil, melted

1 cup sugar-free vegan chocolate chips

½ cup raw macadamia nuts, crushed

¼ cup fine coconut shreds

1 Preheat the oven to 325 degrees Fahrenheit.

2 Add the oat flour, baking flour, coconut sugar, ground golden flaxseed, arrowroot powder, guar gum, baking soda, and sea salt to a large mixing bowl. Whisk until thoroughly combined.

3 Add the wet ingredients and mix together with a spatula until a thick dough forms. Add in the chocolate chips, macadamia nuts, and coconut shreds, and mix one last time.

4 Line a large baking sheet with parchment paper. Use a spoon to form discs of dough and place them on the cookie sheet about 1 inch apart. Bake for about 15 minutes or until golden brown. Let the cookies cool for about 15 minutes before eating.

JASON'S TIP

Serve these cookies with a cold glass of your favorite nondairy milk for some old-school milk n' cookies action!

FUDGE BROWNIES

THESE ARE THE BROWNIES THAT STARTED it all. These bodacious little bites were one of the most popular desserts in my early raw food classes and catering business. They are rich, gooey, smoky, sweet, and perfectly suited as a base for any nuts, berries, or superfoods you want to infuse them with. The raw cacao powder in these brownies is rich in tryptophan, a powerful mood enhancer. Tryptophan is crucial for the production of serotonin, which diminishes anxiety and has the same impact as love in our brain. Just a warning: you may want to get a padlock for the fridge after you make a batch of these babies!

BROWNIES:

1 teaspoon organic virgin coconut oil

8 cups raw pecans, preferably soaked and dehydrated first

1½ cups dates, pitted and packed

1½ cups raw cacao powder

½ tablespoon superfood greens powder

½ tablespoon maca powder

½ teaspoon sea salt

½ teaspoon ground cinnamon

¼ teaspoon ground vanilla bean

½ teaspoon shilajit powder (optional)

1 cup crushed raw pecans, reserved

½ cup dried cherries, reserved

FUDGE SAUCE:

2¾ cups coconut nectar

1 cup organic virgin coconut oil

1 cup raw cacao powder

¼ cup mesquite powder

¼ teaspoon sea salt

¼ cup raw cacao butter, liquefied

1 Coat a 13 x 9-inch baking dish with coconut oil and set aside.

2 **To make the brownies:** pulse the pecans into medium-size crumbs until mealy, using a high-speed food processor. (Be sure not to overprocess, as the pecans can break down easily and become pecan butter.) Slowly add the dates and process until very well combined. The mixture should be somewhat cakey—a slightly moist batter with a little texture. Add the raw cacao powder, superfood greens powder, maca powder, sea salt, ground cinnamon, vanilla bean, and shilajit powder, if using, and process until well incorporated.

3 Remove the brownie mixture from the processor bowl and transfer to the baking dish. Spread the mixture evenly into the baking dish and fold in the reserved pecans and dried cherries. Press the brownie mixture down with your palms to spread evenly. Chill in the refrigerator for 1 hour before serving.

4 **To make the fudge sauce:** add the coconut nectar and coconut oil to a high-speed blender and blend until very smooth. Add raw cacao powder, mesquite powder, and sea salt and blend again. Once an ultra-smooth consistency is attained, add the cacao butter and blend again.

5 Slice the brownies into 2 x 2-inch squares and serve with a generous drizzle of fudge sauce on top.

JASON'S
TIP

Instead of dried black
cherries, try goji berries
or goldenberries for an
extra superfood nutrient
kick. You could also
use dried pineapple or
mango for tropical tango
brownies. Experiment
and play with this recipe
to make it your own.

PANZANELLA
SALAD

THIS TERRIFIC TAKE ON THE CLASSIC Tuscan salad was the fulfillment of a fan request. I'd never really made a traditional "bread salad" before and was up for the new challenge. The texture is what really stands out in this recipe—how the crunch of the fresh vegetables plays so well with the sourdough bread. If you can find a dairy-free feta cheese, it really takes the complexity of the flavor over the top. High-carbohydrate foods like sourdough bread allow tryptophan to flood your brain, where it morphs into serotonin, a neurotransmitter that boosts your mood and curbs your food cravings.

½ loaf vegan sourdough bread, cubed

6 tablespoons extra-virgin olive oil, divided

1 large diced cucumber

2 pounds diced tomatoes

1 cup red onion

½ cup chopped Italian parsley

¼ cup fresh chopped mint

½ cup pitted green olives

1½ tablespoons capers

½ teaspoon dried basil

2 lemons, juiced and zested

One 6-ounce block vegan feta cheese, cubed

1 Preheat the oven to 425 degrees Fahrenheit.

2 Place the bread cubes in a glass or porcelain baking dish and cover with 3 tablespoons of the olive oil. Bake for 10 to 12 minutes.

3 Combine the cucumber, tomatoes, and red onion in a medium bowl. Toss with parsley, mint, olives, capers, basil, and lemon zest. Add the lemon juice and the remaining 3 tablespoons of olive oil and mix. Crumble the vegan feta cheese on top, add the toasted bread cubes, and toss once more. Serve immediately.

CINNAMON SUGAR
BUÑUELOS

I HAVE FOND MEMORIES OF MY mom making these buñuelos for me all the time as a child. I still adore the crispy crunch and sweet cinnamon taste, although now I make them with brown rice tortillas, which are much healthier than the version I grew up with. Brown rice helps to regulate your mood by boosting serotonin levels, while coconut oil's rich medium-chain triglyceride fats are used immediately by the body and brain to increase energy, aid in detoxification of the liver, fuel the brain's production of serotonin, and even improve metabolism. Now, if that don't make you feel good, I don't know what will!

2 large gluten-free brown rice tortillas

2 tablespoons organic virgin coconut oil, melted

⅓ cup coconut sugar

3 teaspoons ground cinnamon

¾ teaspoon sea salt

1 Preheat the oven to 325 degrees Fahrenheit.

2 Cut tortillas into 8 individual "pizza slices." Place them in a single layer on a cookie sheet lined with parchment paper. Coat tortillas with melted coconut oil. Sprinkle the remaining ingredients evenly on top and bake for 10 to 15 minutes until slightly golden brown and crispy.

DIRT PUDDING CUPS
WITH ORGANIC GUMMY WORMS

SERVES 2

THIS RECIPE IS A HEALTHY SPIN on an old-school childhood recipe—ironically, one that I never actually tried when I was a kid! Luckily, with the help of The Alchemist Chef, we reinvented it with creamy avocado chocolate pudding and "dirt" topping that has a haunting, smoky-sweet flavor. The unassuming black sesame seeds in the "dirt" are loaded with mood-boosting zinc, a mineral that has been shown to stave off depression and anxiety. No matter how old you are, these tasty treats will put a smile on your face.

PUDDING:

One 13.5-ounce can unsweetened coconut milk

½ cup coconut nectar

½ teaspoon vanilla extract

½ teaspoon sea salt

¾ tablespoon organic virgin coconut oil

½ cup raw cacao powder

2 ripe avocados, pitted

DIRT TOPPING:

1 cup raw pecans

⅔ cup black sesame seeds

¼ cup coconut sugar

½ teaspoon ground cinnamon

½ teaspoon sea salt

1 bag organic vegan gummy worms, reserved for garnish

1 **To make the pudding:** refrigerate the can of coconut milk for at least 24 hours to thicken. The coconut cream will separate from the water inside the can. Spoon out only the cream and transfer to a high-speed blender. Add the remaining pudding ingredients and blend for 30 seconds, until thick and creamy.

2 **To make the dirt topping:** add pecans, sesame seeds, coconut sugar, ground cinnamon, and sea salt to a food processor and pulse for about 12 to 20 seconds to create a dirtlike consistency, being careful not to overprocess.

3 In clear mason jars or short glasses, create layers of dirt and pudding by spooning the individual mixtures in, one on top of the other. Two to three layers will usually do the trick. Garnish with gummy worms and serve immediately.

SUPREME
VEGAN NACHOS

SERVES 4

NACHOS ARE THE KIND OF DISH that you have to approach with reckless abandon. You can't show up with some weak-ass toppings when it's nacho time. And this ultra-stacked recipe turns the nacho funk up to 11 on the taste dial! Raw walnuts are packed with a high amount of alpha-linolenic acid (ALA), a powerful omega-3 fatty acid that keeps you feeling chipper. Add that to the terrific cascade of delectable toppings and vegan cheese—and this plate is sure to please with ease. This is the ultimate dish for a Netflix night or game time.

3 cups raw walnuts

1½ teaspoons ground coriander

1 tablespoon ground cumin

¼ cup coconut aminos

¼ teaspoon ground black pepper

One 10-ounce package vegan nacho cheese

One 16-ounce bag tortilla chips

One 15-ounce can black beans, drained and rinsed

½ cup halved cherry tomatoes

½ cup salsa

½ cup guacamole

⅓ cup black olives, pitted and sliced

¼ cup jalapeno pepper, sliced

¼ cup radishes, sliced

½ cup green onion, sliced

½ cup cilantro, torn by hand

1 lime, quartered, reserved for garnish

1 Combine the walnuts, coriander, cumin, coconut aminos, and pepper in a food processor and pulse for 15 to 30 seconds or until desired texture is achieved. Set aside.

2 Melt the vegan nacho cheese in a small saucepot over medium heat, stirring frequently. Cook for about 2 minutes until fully melted and set aside.

3 Begin assembling your supreme vegan nachos by layering an extra-large plate with tortilla chips on the bottom, then melted vegan cheese, black beans, walnut mixture, and the remaining ingredients, finishing with fresh cilantro on top. Garnish with lime wedges and serve immediately.

Teese Vegan Nacho Cheese Sauce from Chicago Vegan Foods is my favorite choice for the cheese sauce in this recipe. You can find it at select health food stores or online.

5

EAT FOR

MORE ENERGY

WE HAVE A SERIOUS ENERGY CRISIS on our hands. And I'm not talking about peak oil or the fact that Tesla can't produce enough electric cars to meet demand. I'm referring to those all-too-familiar late-afternoon energy crashes that can have you pounding down a couple cans of Red Bull.

People are obsessed with gaining more energy throughout their day—and for good reason. The daily workload and stress level of most people are through the roof, and social pressure to keep up the pace can be intense. With family life, work responsibilities, hobbies, exercise, social media, and (if you're lucky) a fun social life—where the heck do you find the energy to show up and be fully present for all of your commitments?

As I've said before, I believe the key to a healthy life starts with adopting a mindset of treating your food as fuel for that glorious machine, your body. On the most fundamental level of being, food is fuel for your body, mind, and spirit. And experiencing consistently low energy levels is often a direct result of the quality, quantity, and intention of your daily food choices.

And yet, people are scrambling to squeeze every last drop of energy from their bodies and, in doing so, make less than beneficial choices. The number of hours they work per week has become a badge of honor

for many people to boast about. I'm not saying I'm against hard work. I understand and value how much energy it takes to hustle and be a success in this world, especially coming as I do from a low-income, blue-collar family in Detroit. But if all of your success, prosperity, and fame from the hard work, long hours, and determination comes at the expense of your long-term health, happiness, and contentment, then what the hell is the point? We need to stop the glorification of being busy and start taking better care of ourselves.

As a result of pushing ourselves too long and too hard without cultivating enough balance in our lives, the scope of our human energy crisis is almost out of control. A few key points about our self-appointed "fight against fatigue":

- 15 to 27 percent of Americans complain about long-term fatigue
- The Centers for Disease Control estimates that between 1 and 4 million people in the U.S. have chronic fatigue

- Chronic fatigue syndrome (CFS) occurs four times more frequently in women than in men, although people of either sex can develop it
- CFS occurs most often in people in their 40s and 50s, but people of all ages can get chronic fatigue

For consistent energy, it's important to pay attention to when you eat your meals throughout the day. And, believe it or not, it all starts in the morning.

BREAK(FAST) THE CYCLE

In the 1960s, influential nutritionist Adelle Davis popularized the mantra, "Eat breakfast like a king, lunch like a prince and dinner like a pauper." Why? Because fueling up appears to be more beneficial earlier in the day, when your body needs the most caloric intake for sustained energy throughout. What's more, skipping your morning meal may have more serious long-term effects on your health. Reporting in the American Heart Association journal *Circulation*, Harvard School of Public Health researchers studied the health outcomes of 26,902 male health professionals ages 45 to 82 over a 16-year period. They discovered that the men who skipped breakfast had a 27 percent higher risk of heart attack or death from heart disease than those who didn't. According to the scientists, skipping breakfast may make you hungrier and more likely to eat larger, more calorie-dense meals later in the day, leading to surges in blood sugar. Such spikes can pave the way for diabetes, high blood pressure, and high cholesterol levels, all primary risk factors that can potentially lead to a heart attack later in life.

Now, this doesn't mean you should go overboard with the mimosas and French toast at brunch! Eating a wholesome, balanced morning meal is important for setting your blood sugar pattern for the rest of the day. If you eat something with a good balance of fat and protein, your blood sugar will rise slowly and go down slowly. Choosing a breakfast made with refined sugar, like pastries or artificial coffee drinks, is the worst possible thing to do. You get a major insulin spike, and your blood sugar drops too low, so you inevitably get hungry again—and quickly. It's one of the reasons that so many people get into a vicious cycle of overeating junk food throughout the rest of their day.

LATE-NIGHT SNACK ATTACK

Calories get used no matter when you eat them, so it's technically okay to eat them late in the day if you absolutely have to. However, if you eat a really heavy dinner, you're not as likely to get rid of its calories before you go to sleep. What you don't burn off is more likely to be stored as fat, since you become less active toward the end of the day. Eating too close to bedtime also increases your blood sugar and insulin levels, causing you to have a hard time falling asleep. Therefore, as Davis recommended, your last meal should absolutely be the calorically lightest of the day, easy to digest, and ideally consumed at least three hours before you plan to fall asleep.

There's another reason that late-night eating isn't the best idea ever. As those midnight snacks send your blood sugar soaring, your levels of the hormone melatonin fall. Melatonin is supposed to help you feel tired and relaxed. A big boost of energy coming from your dinner can act as a short-lived stimulant, causing you to feel more awake immediately after a meal. Also, it's not a good practice to lie down and fall asleep immediately after a big meal (like those post-Thanksgiving naps on the couch), as it increases your chance for acid reflux and digestive distress.

There's no absolute, perfect formula for eating that can maximize your energy levels all the time, but paying attention to both what and when you eat is a fantastic place to start. Depending on your daily schedule, eating your meals at the exact same time every day may not be feasible. But I think it's a pretty safe bet that binge-eating a big-ass bowl of nacho chili cheese fries at midnight is probably not going to do wonders for your digestion, waistline, or energy levels.

HOW CELLS CONVERT NUTRIENTS INTO ENERGY

Complex organic food molecules such as sugars, fats, and proteins are rich sources of energy for cells because much of the energy used to form these molecules is literally stored within the chemical bonds that hold them together. Scientists can measure the amount of energy stored in foods using a device called a bomb calorimeter (which, coincidentally, is a kick-ass name for a punk band!). In this technique, food is placed inside the calorimeter and heated until it burns. The excess heat released by the reaction is directly proportional to the amount of energy contained in that food.

Cells need energy to accomplish the tasks of life. Beginning with energy sources obtained from their environment in the form of sunlight and organic food molecules, eukaryotic cells make energy-rich molecules via energy pathways including photosynthesis, glycolysis, the citric acid cycle, and oxidative phosphorylation. Any excess energy is then stored in larger, energy-rich molecules such as polysaccharides (starch and glycogen) and lipids.

Polysaccharide is a broad term for any sugar molecule that has a glycogen bond. Carbohydrates provide energy in the body and are the first thing burned when you exercise. Carbohydrates are often called the number-one energy source for your body. Also, fatigue seems to melt away when polysaccharides are eaten. Without carbohydrates, you would likely feel weak, dizzy, and have low blood sugar. Polysaccharides are praised for their long-lasting energy and low glycemic index. Many diets touting a low-carb approach are actually blaming the wrong nutrient. You need carbohydrates to live and for your body to perform its essential functions.

Polysaccharides also provide many other key benefits. First, they enhance your mood by increasing the amount of feel-good chemicals in your brain. They also support healthy blood sugar levels, which is very important for diabetics. Diabetics should supplement polysaccharides in their diet instead of simple carbohydrates that enter the bloodstream too quickly and cause an unsafe spike in blood sugar levels.

Polysaccharides also have a positive effect in your intestines when they are digested, improving intestinal health, helping to reduce certain cancers, and slowing things down so that energy is released slowly, stabilizing your blood sugar. Another benefit is that they promote cardiovascular health and immunity health and prevent many degenerative diseases (like heart disease). Liver function also improves when polysaccharides are ingested. In medicine, polysaccharides are used to heal common ailments, heal wounds, treat diarrhea, and even relieve heartburn symptoms.

THE CARBO-LOADING MYTH DEBUNKED

For years, endurance athletes in a multitude of sports have advocated the practice of "carbohydrate loading" right before a major race or competition. There is a degree of pretty solid science supporting this practice. By eating complex carbohydrates from natural, whole-food sources, your body can theoretically build up its glycogen reserves to use as sustained energy for competition day. However, the big question is whether or not these are quality carbohydrate sources and how efficiently your body can actually digest, assimilate, and utilize them as energy.

Complex, quality carbohydrates from whole plant foods should be at the center of these "high-performance" meals. During periods of intense training, at least 50 percent of your calories should come from carbs, as they are the main energy source for muscles. If you engage in high-intensity endurance training for more than 90 minutes a day, you absolutely need to load up on carbs and choose quality sources of them. Contrary to many dietary regimens, it's not about scarfing down gargantuan portions of pasta, but rather about consuming a healthy variety of natural, unprocessed foods that contain a great balance of essential carbs, vitamins, minerals, proteins, and antioxidants.

Many people don't realize it, but fruits are an excellent source of high-quality, assimilable carbs and contain key nutrients that your body needs to thrive as you push it hard. If you do happen to put off proper, balanced nutrition until the last minute prior to a competition, don't freak out and carbo-load the night before the race. Instead, eat a carbohydrate-rich breakfast or lunch the day before, which will give your body time to efficiently digest it, followed by a normal dinner and perhaps a healthy snack right before bedtime. Many people who do a massive carbo load the night before a competition end up in major gastrointestinal distress the next morning, which just makes competing at a high level of performance all the more difficult. You need to give your body time to digest, assimilate, and eliminate the food properly.

HYDRATION CELEBRATION

It's not all about the carbs or glycogen stores, though. The other key to giving your body energy for exercise is proper hydration. For each long workout, you need to make sure you're drinking back the weight you've lost in fluids. But be sure you're sipping over time, not guzzling a massive amount all at once. And don't wait until you exercise to properly hydrate. Drink a copious amount of water before and after your workout. Your muscles will need the steady hydration to recover from the strain and depletion.

Although I continue to refine my workout nutrition, I've definitely found a solid regimen when it comes to eating for sustained energy. I start my day by drinking at least 24 ounces of clean, filtered water (sometimes with fresh lemon juice or apple cider vinegar) first thing in the morning. (That's roughly two regular-size glasses of water.) When you wake up, your body is dehydrated and in a highly acidic state. The combination of filtered water and lemon juice or ACV both hydrates and alkalizes your body. After that, I eat a light breakfast, usually a bowl of chia seed pudding, quinoa with fresh fruit, or, most often, a superfood green smoothie loaded with a ton of antioxidants, protein, and complex carbohydrates.

No matter what I have for breakfast, I like to supplement it with easily digestible superfood ingredients and probiotics. If I need a super-high-octane energy boost, I'll reach for the matcha green tea, yerba mate tea, an acai smoothie with guarana, cordyceps mushrooms, an herbal energy drink mix, a handful of cacao nibs and goji berries, or colloidal PQQ (we'll learn more about the superpowers of PQQ later). Or, I'll just take all that stuff, throw it in my blender, and whip up some wonderful wizard workout fuel!

WHATEVER YOU DO . . . DON'T LET YOURSELF GET HANGRY

It's all too easy to skip meals, especially in the middle of a busy workday. I'm intimately acquainted with this bad habit, as I'm the first person to be underprepared at lunchtime. However, this habit of skipping meals can severely compromise your metabolism and lead to blood sugar crashes that may destabilize your mood (any of this sound familiar?). With my desire to create more sustainable solutions to my lunchtime snafus, I've come up with a reliable system to make sure I've got some nutritious and sustaining food on hand at all times.

I've found that keeping healthy snack foods in the glove compartment of my car is the best way to save myself from getting hangry in the middle of the day. *Hangry* (hungry + angry) is what happens when your blood sugar drops like a broken elevator and you become ravenously hungry to the point where your mood can become rather . . . shall we say . . . nasty. Being in a state of hanger can lead to a full-on rage in some cases, where you are bashing around, yelling at people, and frantically looking for something to shove in your gullet like a frothing wildebeest. Not a good look, honey.

Through a bit of trial and error, mixed with my own share of hanger attacks, I've found some great snacks: sprouted nuts, seeds, superfood trail mix, or vegan protein bars (*without* the chocolate coating; trust me on this one!). These are foods that can be preserved in a range of temperatures and won't go rancid or stale too quickly. If you don't drive a car, you can stash these foods in your office desk drawer or a tote bag. You'll also want to set a reminder or alert in your calendar for when the foods expire.

The next time you feel a food rage coming on and you remember there's a secret stash of good food waiting for you—it'll be like discovering an awesome Christmas present. Next thing you know, you're happy dancing instead of Hulking out.

UNDER PRESSURE

Our culture instills so many deep-seated beliefs about competition and performance that we often turn to pharmaceuticals to "keep up" with the workload and pace of life. Adderall, Ritalin, and other "smart drugs" have become insanely popular among college students and young professionals looking to consistently outperform their peers. These drugs are normally prescribed to treat attention deficit hyperactivity disorder (ADHD), but healthy people who want to get a leg up in school and work use them to improve focus, concentration, and memory.

Amphetamines, uppers, speed, cocaine, and any other energizing drug presents an inherent danger of overuse: as users develop tolerance to the drug, their dosage inevitably has to increase to maintain the same high as when they started using. Moreover, as users become more dependent on the release of energy brought about by the drug, their bodies become more uncomfortable and less able to produce natural energy on their own.

Energy pills and pharmaceutical drugs have never provided long-term solutions to any major physical crisis, much less a chronic energy deficit. We need to move beyond the "Band-Aid" mentality of just taking a pill and toward a conscious choice to relandscape our lifestyles and dietary choices as a society.

WOO HOO FOR PQQ!

Recently, a newly discovered nutrient with significant implications for mitochondrial vitality has come into vogue. First discovered by researchers in 1979, pyrroloquinoline quinone, or PQQ, was originally thought to be a B vitamin. Additional studies debunked the theory of PQQ being a legitimate vitamin, but its effect on mitochondrial function was wholly undeniable. In laboratory tests, dietary PQQ was observed to influence mitochondrial production in a profound way.

In 2010, researchers at the University of California at Davis released a peer-reviewed publication stating, "Bioactive compounds reported to stimulate mitochondrial biogenesis are linked to many health benefits such as increased longevity, improved energy utilization, and protection from reactive oxygen species. The ability of PQQ to stimulate mitochondrial biogenesis suggests that PQQ may be beneficial in diseases associated with mitochondrial dysfunction."

I regularly ingest a vial or two of PQQ prior to intense cardio or strength-training workouts and can attest to its energy-boosting powers and ability to increase my overall stamina.

FOOD IS YOUR FUEL FOR LIFE

Remember—food is your primary fuel source. Make sure it's high-quality, usable fuel that's appropriate for your fantastic, fleshy body machine. Feed it right, and it will provide you with trouble-free performance for decades to come!

MY TOP ENERGY-BOOSTING NUTRIENTS

B vitamins: Play an important role in cell metabolism by converting food into energy.

Coenzyme Q10: Important component in the oxygenation of blood cells that helps to relieve inflammation and promote energy conversion.

Medium-chain triglycerides: MCTs are fats with an unusual chemical structure that allows the body to digest them easily. Most fats are broken down in the intestine and remade into a special form that can be transported in the blood. But MCTs are absorbed intact and taken to the liver, where they are used directly for energy.

Selenium: Hormones actually play a big role in our energy levels. As it turns out, many of us are low in selenium, a nutrient responsible for regulating our thyroid hormones.

Tyrosine: Important amino acid that aids in the conversion of dopamine, the hormone that regulates our pleasure response, keeping us sharp and alert.

MY TOP ENERGY-BOOSTING FOODS

- acai berry
- asparagus
- astragalus root
- blue or purple potatoes
- blueberries
- cacao
- chai tea
- cherries
- chia seeds
- chiles
- cinnamon
- citrus fruits
- eleuthero root
- flaxseed
- garbanzo beans
- guarana
- licorice root
- maca powder
- masa flour
- matcha green tea
- quinoa
- raspberries
- rehmannia
- spinach
- sweet potatoes
- Swiss chard
- yerba mate

RECIPES
FOR
BOOSTING
ENERGY

···················

MAYAN CHOCOLATE COCONUT
MACAROONS

SERVES 4 TO 6

MACAROONS ARE ACTUALLY A DISTANT COOKIE cousin of the über-fashionable macaron, both with a fancy French pedigree to their name. This egg-free version features a diverse flavor profile with raw cacao, matcha green tea powder, goji berries, and the added kick of cinnamon, ginger, and cayenne. Along with the energizing properties of coconut and cacao, the matcha green tea powder is a natural source of sustained energy. The caffeine in matcha is unique in that the amino acid L-theanine works in synergy with it—giving you a big boost without the crash later in the day!

2 cups fine coconut shreds

½ cup cacao nibs

3 tablespoons raw cacao powder

1 tablespoon matcha green tea powder

1 tablespoon lucuma powder

3 tablespoons hemp seeds

3 tablespoons organic virgin coconut oil

½ teaspoon ground vanilla bean

¼ cup raw cacao butter, shredded

¼ cup coconut nectar

½ teaspoon sea salt

½ teaspoon ground cinnamon

Pinch powdered ginger

¼ teaspoon cayenne pepper

¼ cup goji berries

1 Combine all ingredients, except for the goji berries, in a high-speed food processor until the mixture is well incorporated, about 30 seconds. Check your macaroon consistency by taking a little bit of the mixture and smushing it together to see if you have a nice, sticky ball.

2 Add the goji berries and fold them into the mixture. Take a small spoonful of the macaroon mixture and roll into a ball with the palms of your hands. Repeat until you run out of mixture. Place the macaroons on a serving plate. Refrigerate for 1 hour, then enjoy.

JASON'S TIP

You can use 1 tablespoon of mesquite powder instead of lucuma powder if you want to give your macaroons an undertone of extra caramel flavor.

COCONUT CACAO
COOKIE DOUGH BALLS

COOKIE DOUGH IS ONE OF THOSE primal dessert urges that must be satisfied . . . or else! This mostly raw, dairy-free version comes chock-full of heart-healthy coconut shreds, a caramel undertone of flavor from lucuma, and magnesium-rich cacao nibs. The coconut oil contains MCTs; I've noted that unlike other saturated fats, MCTs provide an energy source for the body rather than being stored. The MCTs also help to boost thermogenesis and fat burning in the body. These mouthwatering balls are a healthy way to get your sweet fix and are a true people pleaser at parties!

3 cups fine coconut shreds, plus extra reserved for garnish

¼ cup plus 2 tablespoons organic virgin coconut oil

¾ cup lucuma powder

¼ cup plus 1 tablespoon coconut nectar

½ teaspoon ground vanilla bean

1¼ teaspoons sea salt

½ cup cacao nibs

1 Add the fine coconut shreds to a food processor. Turn the processor on and slowly add coconut oil, stopping to scrape down the sides of the processor bowl with a spatula as needed. Add the lucuma powder and coconut nectar and process. Add the vanilla bean and sea salt, pulsing until the mixture is incorporated. Transfer to a large mixing bowl and add the cacao nibs. Stir together and roll the mixture into balls. Plate on a serving dish and sprinkle with the reserved coconut shreds. Refrigerate for at least 30 minutes before serving.

SUPERFOOD
ACAI BOWL

SERVES 1 TO 2

THE DARK PURPLE ACAI BERRY IS one of nature's highest sources of antioxidants and boasts more protein than eggs. When frozen, the acai pulp serves as a delicious base for a superfood bowl. This version of the classic breakfast bowl is infused with other potent superfoods, including vitamin C–rich baobab powder and hormone-balancing maca powder. The taste is sweet, tart, fruity, and complex with a satisfyingly creamy texture.

6 ounces hemp milk

One 3.5-ounce pack frozen acai berry

1 tablespoon tocotrienols

1 tablespoon baobab powder

1 teaspoon maca powder

¼ teaspoon liquid stevia

2 teaspoons hemp seeds, reserved for garnish

3 tablespoons dried mulberries, reserved for garnish

1½ tablespoons cacao nibs, reserved for garnish

Handful fresh blueberries, reserved for garnish

1 Blend the hemp milk, acai, tocotrienols, baobab powder, maca powder, and stevia until the acai mixture has a sorbet-like consistency. Transfer the acai mixture to a serving bowl. Garnish with the remaining ingredients and serve immediately.

GRILLED PLANTAINS
WITH COCONUT WHIPPED CREAM

SERVES 2

IN PUERTO RICAN CUISINE, THE PLANTAIN is more than just a staple—it's a star! I love this recipe when I need a sweet fix but don't want something overwhelmingly sugary. The natural sugars of the plantain caramelize when you cook them, and the addition of the homemade coconut whipped cream makes this dish a piece of tropical heaven. Plantains provide essential minerals like magnesium and potassium, which support muscle function and aid in nerve transmission. Magnesium also helps you produce DNA and proteins, while potassium aids in carbohydrate metabolism. Thanks to my awesome vegan mom, Susan, for the inspiration and tutelage with this old-school energizing recipe.

One 13.5-ounce can unsweetened full fat coconut milk, refrigerated for 24 hours

½ tablespoon vanilla extract

¼ teaspoon liquid stevia

1 tablespoon organic virgin coconut oil

1 large green plantain, peeled and sliced into rounds

1   Remove the coconut milk from the fridge and scoop out the coconut cream that has separated to the bottom of the can into a bowl. Add the vanilla extract and stevia and whip by hand or use a hand mixer. Cover and refrigerate whipped coconut cream.

2   In a large skillet, heat the coconut oil over medium heat. Once the oil is melted, add the plantain slices. After about 3 minutes, flip the plantains and continue cooking them for another 2 to 3 minutes. When they look slightly crisp and golden brown, take them out of the skillet and set them on a paper towel to drain the excess oil.

3   Plate the plantains and top each with a dollop of coconut whipped cream.

FRUIT
PIZZA

THIS ONE IS FOR THE KIDS ... or for kids in adult bodies (hand raised). Honestly, you can be any age and you'll enjoy this colorful, fun, and energizing recipe. The fantastic array of fruit toppings is packed with vitamin C and antioxidants to keep your cells healthy, while the coconut sauce is bursting with energy-producing medium-chain triglycerides. This is one pizza that looks almost too pretty to eat. (Key word: *almost*.)

SAUCE:

2 cups raw coconut butter, loosely packed

1½ tablespoons vegan vanilla protein powder

Pinch sea salt

PIZZA:

2 gluten-free rice tortillas

1 tablespoon organic virgin coconut oil

⅓ cup sliced strawberries

⅓ cup diced pineapple

⅓ cup blueberries

½ cup tangerine wedges

1 tablespoon finely shredded coconut

2 to 3 tablespoons sugar-free vegan chocolate chips

1. Preheat the oven to 350 degrees Fahrenheit.

2. **To make the pizza sauce:** blend the coconut butter, protein powder, and salt in a high-speed blender for 40 seconds until very smooth and creamy. Set aside.

3. **To make the pizza:** gently brush each tortilla with coconut oil to coat the top. Place the oiled tortillas on a pizza stone or metal baking sheet and bake for 5 to 8 minutes. Flip tortillas and bake for another 5 to 8 minutes on the other side until crispy.

4. Remove the tortillas from the oven and top with sauce. Layer the remaining pizza ingredients on top to your desired amount. Serve immediately.

CREAMY
ORANGE JULIUS

SERVES 2

THE INFAMOUS ORANGE JULIUS IS, CUPS down, my absolute all-time favorite drink from childhood. I would ask my mom to make it for me all the time, especially when I was feeling sick. The creamy citrus flavor made me feel better and gave my immune system a boost. This healthy, nondairy version has the same ultra-creamy texture while kicking up the nutrition with omega fatty acids and protein from a variety of rad superfoods. As the hero of the recipe, the orange rations out energy steadily over time instead of giving you a quick sugar rush thanks to its vitamin C, potassium, and folate.

2 cups filtered water

⅓ cup macadamia nuts

⅓ cup hemp seeds

5 whole oranges, peeled

½ teaspoon ground vanilla bean

1 teaspoon maca powder

1 tablespoon baobab powder

1 teaspoon coconut sugar

1 tablespoon raw coconut butter

½ tablespoon organic virgin coconut oil

Pinch sea salt

1 cup ice cubes

1 Blend the filtered water, macadamia nuts, and hemp seeds in a high-speed blender for 30 seconds. Add all remaining ingredients to the blender and blend for another 30 seconds until frothy and creamy.

SUPERGREEN
SALAD DRESSING

THIS IS MY "KITCHEN SINK" SALAD dressing. I recall discovering this recipe several years ago when I threw some on-hand ingredients into a blender and slathered the result on some field greens. Victory! The dressing is ultra creamy thanks to the avocado, while the tangy lime juice, herbaceous cilantro, and sweet orange juice balance the flavor. Avocados, which are actually classified as a fruit, are rich in monounsaturated fat that is easily burned for energy. Due to this beneficial raw fat content, avocado enables your body to more efficiently absorb fat-soluble nutrients (such as alpha- and beta-carotene and lutein) in other foods eaten in conjunction. Think of it as the great unifying element in this delicious dressing.

1⅛ cups fresh orange juice

¼ cup plus 2 tablespoons fresh lime juice

1 small handful cilantro

1 green onion, chopped

1 tablespoon chopped shallots

½ small jalapeno, seeded

½ teaspoon sea salt

Pinch black pepper

3 cloves garlic, minced

½ teaspoon ground cumin

¼ teaspoon cayenne pepper

1 teaspoon coconut aminos

1 avocado, pitted

½ cup extra-virgin olive oil

1 Blend all ingredients in a high-speed blender, except for the avocado and olive oil. Slowly add the avocado and olive oil to emulsify for a thick, creamy consistency. Serve with your favorite organic greens.

To turn this recipe into a superfood soup, add some diced avocado, cucumber, red bell pepper, and hemp seeds on top!

GREEK
GARBANZO SALAD

SERVES 2

THIS LIP-SMACKIN' SALAD IS GREAT AS a super-quick lunch option. Early afternoon is usually my busiest time of day—and when my schedule is tight, I absolutely love this meal. You can eat it straight up, serve it over rice, stuff it in pita bread, or wrap it in a collard leaf. No matter how you decide to eat it, I think you'll enjoy the light flavor and dynamic texture. The groovy garbanzo beans are one of nature's best sources of folate, which helps red blood cell production and carries more oxygen to your muscles. In addition, they're mackin' out on manganese, which is an essential co-factor in enzymes that are important for energy production and antioxidant defenses.

1 head romaine lettuce, chopped

One 15-ounce can garbanzo
    beans, drained and rinsed

3 celery stalks, chopped

1 tomato, diced

3 tablespoons parsley,
    chiffonaded

2 tablespoons mint, chiffonaded

¼ cup green olives, pitted and
    sliced

3 scallions, minced

3 cloves garlic, minced

1 lemon, juiced and zested

3 tablespoons extra-virgin
    olive oil

Pinch sea salt

Pinch ground black pepper

½ cup vegan feta cheese,
    crumbled (optional)

1. Add all ingredients to a large mixing bowl and gently mix to combine well.

RISE & SHINE
ELIXIR

I'M NOT A BIG COFFEE DRINKER. Sure, I indulge in a cup of joe from time to time, but I prefer to use other methods to wake up in the morning. Enter the Rise & Shine Elixir. This hot beverage features the adaptogenic and hormone-balancing powder of gynostemma tea and a host of activating superfoods. Adaptogenic herbs like gynostemma help maintain the efficiency of the metabolic, neurological, immunologic, respiratory, and endocrine systems. The pumpkin seeds contain nearly half of the recommended daily amount of magnesium, which facilitates the creation of adenosine triphosphate (ATP)—the energy molecules of your body. This drink is dark, creamy, frothy, and surprisingly delicious. You can enjoy this elixir hot or even chill it in the fridge for an energy boost on a hot day.

3½ cups hot gynostemma tea

2 tablespoons black sesame seeds

3 tablespoons pumpkin seeds

3 tablespoons hemp seeds

1 teaspoon ground vanilla bean

2 tablespoons lucuma powder

1 tablespoon mesquite powder

1½ tablespoons tocotrienols

½ teaspoon ashwagandha powder

½ teaspoon reishi mushroom powder

½ teaspoon triphala powder

¼ teaspoon ground moringa leaf

1½ tablespoons vegan vanilla protein powder

¾ teaspoon liquid stevia, English toffee flavor

1 teaspoon fulvic acid

1½ tablespoons organic virgin coconut oil

¼ teaspoon sea salt

1½ tablespoons chia seeds

1. Blend all ingredients (adding the chia seeds last) in a high-speed blender for 30 seconds until smooth. Serve immediately. This elixir is amazing served hot, but it can also be served chilled.

QUINOA FALAFEL
WITH AVOCADO TAHINI SAUCE

SERVES 2

FALAFEL BECAME ONE OF MY STAPLE foods when I was a new vegetarian. With so many incredible Middle Eastern restaurants in my hometown, Detroit, it was easy to get. Instead of the deep-fried traditional version, I created this Quinoa Falafel recipe to enjoy the same crunch and satisfying taste while cranking up the protein content and digestibility. Quinoa is high in riboflavin (vitamin B2), which improves energy metabolism within brain and muscle cells. Just like chickpeas, quinoa is bursting with manganese, which helps to prevent damage of mitochondria during energy production as well as to protect red blood cells and other cells from injury by free radicals. You might need to double this recipe and make a second batch—they are that freakin' good!

AVOCADO TAHINI SAUCE:

½ cup filtered water

1 lime, juiced

1 avocado, pitted

¼ cup raw tahini

¼ cup cilantro

QUINOA FALAFEL:

One 15-ounce can garbanzo beans, drained and rinsed

1 onion, diced

2 garlic cloves, minced

1 tablespoon extra-virgin olive oil

⅓ cup cooked white quinoa

Pinch sea salt

1 tablespoon ground cumin

1 teaspoon ground golden flaxseed

2 tablespoons organic virgin coconut oil, reserved for frying

TOPPINGS:

Pinch ground black pepper

1 tablespoon hemp seeds

1. **To make the Avocado Tahini Sauce:** blend all sauce ingredients in a high-speed blender for 30 seconds until smooth. Set aside.

2. **To make the Quinoa Falafel:** combine all falafel ingredients in a food processor and pulse just a few times until you have a crumbly, doughlike consistency. Use a large spoon to parse out the dough and use the palms of your hands to roll it out, pressing each chunk of dough into a little hockey puck–shaped disk. Set aside.

3. Heat the coconut oil in a large skillet on medium-low heat. Add the falafels to the skillet and cook on each side, using metal tongs to flip them, for about 3 to 5 minutes or until golden brown and crispy. Remove from the heat and place the falafels on a paper towel to drain off any excess oil.

4. Serve with a dollop of sauce and top with ground black pepper and hemp seeds.

AS I WAS WRITING THIS COOKBOOK, it was pointed out to me that I had a glaring omission in my culinary repertoire. To my absolute shock, I had never created a savory pizza recipe from scratch before. Well, thanks to the awesome input of The Alchemist Chef, we concocted a magical masa harina crust with a bevy of fresh veggie toppings that absolutely sings with flavor. The crust is chewy, crispy, and dense and will hold up to sauce, vegan cheese, and whatever else you want to throw on it. No matter how you dress it, it's a tasty little canvas, compadres. The masa flour in the pizza dough is also much higher in carbohydrates and fiber than whole corn. Carbohydrates provide energy, while fiber helps control appetite and prevent constipation. Plus, the ground flaxseed in the mix contains *seven times* the potassium of bananas and more calcium than skim milk—both of which are magic minerals for more energy!

PIZZA DOUGH:

- 1½ cups masa harina
- 1½ tablespoons ground golden flaxseed
- 1 teaspoon fennel seeds
- 1 teaspoon fresh oregano, minced
- 1 teaspoon baking soda
- ½ teaspoon guar gum
- ½ teaspoon sea salt
- ¾ cup warm water
- 2 tablespoons extra-virgin olive oil
- 1 teaspoon apple cider vinegar

1 Preheat the oven to 400 degrees Fahrenheit.

2 **To make the pizza dough:** whisk all dry pizza dough ingredients in a medium glass or ceramic bowl. (Metal will interfere with the properties of the apple cider vinegar that make the dough rise.) Quickly add the wet ingredients, whisking at first and then using your hands to knead the dough. Separate into 4 equal parts and form into balls. With a wooden rolling pin, starting from the center and working your way out, roll into pies that are 5½ inches across and about ¼ inch thick. Transfer the pizza pies to an oiled cookie sheet or large pizza stone.

TOPPINGS:

¾ cup organic pizza sauce

¾ cup baby bella mushrooms, sliced

¾ cup cherry tomatoes, sliced

½ cup fennel bulb, sliced

6 large artichoke hearts, quartered

¼ cup sun-dried tomatoes, julienned

¾ cup vegan mozzarella cheese shreds (optional)

⅓ cup basil, chiffonaded, packed, reserved

¼ cup cilantro, minced, reserved

3 Brush the pizza pies with olive oil using a rubber pastry brush. Bake for 10 minutes. Remove from the oven and top with all of the toppings except the basil and cilantro, and bake for another 15 to 20 minutes until the pizza pie crusts are slightly crispy around the edges.

4 Add the fresh basil and cilantro and bake for 1 minute to keep the herbs fresh and flavorful.

6

EAT

FOR

DETOXIFICATION

DETOX ISN'T JUST FOR FORMER child actors or heavy-metal drummers. But seriously— you know what kind of detox I'm going to talk about here. Through a variety of natural ingredients, supplements, and healthy elimination modalities, you can remove harmful environmental toxins from your body . . . and have a fun time doing it!

Unless you've lived your entire life on a pristine desert island, you're going to need to detoxify your body at some point. Every day, you can accumulate a buildup of toxins from things like artificial food ingredients, pharmaceutical drugs, heavy metals, waterborne pollution, and crazy things like nuclear fallout. Now, this may sound like science fiction, but your body is being constantly bombarded with this stuff. All. The. Time. Prolonged exposure to toxins can create a serious overload of them in your system.

To achieve any level of longevity, you need to detox your body from these chemicals and eat the right foods to protect your cells from retoxing. Yes, *retoxing* is a real word—go ahead and check Urban Dictionary if you don't believe me. It's usually used to describe what happens when someone who finishes a weeklong raw juice cleanse to start the New Year immediately falls off the wagon with a deep-dish pizza and craft beer. That is the typical detox/retox cycle that, unfortunately, a LOT of people fall into.

Before I get into my recommended dynamic detox protocol and my personal cleansing regimen, behold the complex issue of chemical exposure:

- More than 6 million pounds of mercury and 2.5 billion pounds of other toxic chemicals are released into the environment in the U.S. each year
- 80,000 toxic chemicals have been released into our environment, and very few have been tested for their long-term impact on human health
- In 2007, Americans spent more than $28 million on detoxification products

So, even if you eat well, exercise, and keep your immunity strong, you may still be susceptible to the cacophony of chemicals in the food supply and the general

environment. To refer to the last century as the dawn of the industrial age is an understatement. Since 1965, more than 4 million distinct chemical compounds have been reported in scientific literature, and more than 6,000 new chemicals were added to this list between 1965 and 1978. As of 1981, of more than 70,000 chemicals currently in commercial production, 3,000 have been identified as being intentionally added to our food supply and 700 plus in our municipal drinking water alone. During commercial food processing and storage, up to 10,000 other chemical compounds can become an integral part of many common food products. Add to this an array of petrochemicals, industrial waste, medical and street drugs, radiation (X-rays, nuclear fallout), and gallons of pesticides, herbicides, and insecticides—and the result is a totally mind-blowing chemical avalanche!

There is currently a wealth of scientific evidence showing that thousands of drugs, preservatives, pesticides, and other pollutants remain stored in our bodies long after we are exposed to them. For example, we know that an organochlorinated pesticide such as DDT has a half-life of 20 to 50 years in the fat deposits of the human body. According to the U.S. Environmental Protection Agency, more than 400 foreign chemicals have been detected in human tissues: 48 were found in adipose tissue, 40 in women's breast milk, 73 in the liver, and more than 250 in the blood. As you'll see, this isn't anything we should take lightly.

HOW TOXINS AFFECT OUR HEALTH

So, in a nutshell, here's how you get sick . . . a toxin enters your body. And that's pretty much it. I'm kidding! But wait, there's more: the internal alarms go off, and your immune system's first defense is to excrete or expel the toxin. This is accomplished through perspiration, salivation, urination, and other disgusting bodily functions. In fact, often when you have a common cold, your body is actually just detoxifying and draining out nasty toxins. Those toxins may be viruses or other live organisms, or they may be chemicals that you got exposed to without even knowing it.

If you live in a densely populated metro area, your body is inundated with thousands of toxins from electronic devices, food, air, clothes, fragrances, pesticides, car exhaust—the list could probably go on forever. Fortunately, your body has the innate ability to get rid of most of this waste to prevent chronic buildup. Although your colon rids your body of excess waste, it's actually your liver that filters the toxins and sends them to your colon to leave your body. Your lymphatic system plays a role by bringing waste from other parts of your body to the elimination organs and creating ass-kicking T-cells to engulf the bad bacteria. But what happens if your colon gets clogged, your liver is overloaded, and your lymphatic system is backed up?

When your large intestine is not functioning, it congests your lymphatic system, forcing the waste to recirculate within your body. When your liver is clogged, it allows toxins to recirculate back into your body instead of filtering them out. Toxins can get into your bloodstream and cause inflammation in other parts of your body. As a result, your body resorts to another well-known organ to purge the waste: your skin. Acne, rashes, and eczema are signs that your body is trying to rid itself of toxins. Toxins can be stored in your body fat, preventing you from losing weight and fully detoxifying. Crohn's disease, irritable bowel syndrome (IBS), and candida overgrowth are conditions that can occur from a heavy toxic load.

If that toxin gets past this first line of defense due to either the strength or high quantity of the toxin or the weakness of your immune system, your body's second line of defense is launched into action. Here is where inflammation sets in. This is when you can be diagnosed with some kind of "itis" which, in simple terms, means "inflammation of." For example, tonsillitis is inflammation of the tonsils, colitis is inflammation of the colon, and dermatitis is inflammation of the derma, or skin.

If your immune system *still* can't handle the toxins, your body creates storage spaces outside of your cells in which to put the toxins. In this stage, your body does not allow the toxins inside the cells where they could do irreparable damage. These spaces also act as holding tanks so your body can deal with the toxic invasion incrementally. Symptoms of this incremental healing process are cysts, swellings, engorged fat cells, and benign tumors. Typical diagnoses are colon polyps, ovarian cysts, fibroid tumors, lipomas, and obesity, to name a few. Up to this point, the body has kept its organs and tissues safe.

Beyond this point is where the *real* problems begin. If the toxins are allowed to enter your cells, they may do irreparable damage to the chemical reactions that take place there and that allow the cells to do their jobs. They may also do damage to the DNA of the cells—their replicating factor—which leads to the creation of sick, malfunctioning organs. Examples are liver cirrhosis, heart attacks, impotence, Crohn's disease (a wearing away of the lining of the intestines), multiple sclerosis, Alzheimer's, and Parkinson's disease.

If these sick cells continue to replicate with no reversal of the situation, the likelihood of the cells turning cancerous is great. Therefore, the final manifestation of a toxic invasion that cannot be overcome by the immune system could be a serious disease with potentially life-threatening implications.

SPRING CLEANING FOR YOUR BODY

So, how do you start to overcome the toxic load? When it comes to detoxification and cleansing protocols, there are innumerable ways you can accomplish your goal of "cleaning house." It really starts with getting clear about what you want to detox from and the most safe, effective method of doing so. For example, a gallbladder flush is fundamentally and procedurally different from a liver detox or a chelation protocol for heavy metal toxicity. If you really want to know what kind of toxins are hanging around in your system, visit a naturopathic medical doctor who can run a full-panel test on your blood, urine, and/or saliva to determine your true toxic load.

There's certainly no "one size fits all" approach to detoxing and cleansing. It's really about doing your research and working with a doctor to determine what's really going on with your body. Without knowing it, picking an approach to cleansing and lifestyle modification is like throwing darts at a board with a blindfold on. You'll potentially waste a lot of time and hard-earned money with such a trial-and-error approach to your health.

I'm not going to cover the minute details and intricacies of each type of detox protocol, but I will offer you some fundamental cleansing tips and share some powerful natural foods and supplements that can support your detoxification and cleansing efforts.

Personally, I like to set an intention to cleanse seasonally. The change of seasons is a time of lots of shifts in the climate and the energies of the Earth. I'm a big advocate of eating local, seasonal foods year-round, as they tend to retain more flavor and nutrients when they are planted, grown, and harvested close by. Likewise, cleansing at the start of each new season can be a great way to give your body a much-needed reset and prepare your system to benefit from a whole new variety of foods.

TO LIVE LONG . . . GET YOUR SWEAT ON

If you want to effectively eliminate toxins from your body (especially heavy metals), it's a great idea to sweat 'em out. Far-infrared sauna therapy is a proven method for considerably raising the rate of energy expenditure in the body. It has also been used as an effective treatment for arthritis and inflammatory conditions. Heat from a far-infrared sauna increases your blood circulation and stimulates the sweat glands, releasing built-up toxins in the body. Daily sweating in one of these saunas can help detoxify your body as it rids itself of accumulated pesticide residues and highly toxic heavy metals (including lead, mercury, nickel, and cadmium) as well as alcohol, nicotine, sulfuric acid, and other organic and inorganic compounds. Saunas also stimulate cells to release toxins, which can then be eliminated by your liver and bowels.

Thanks to vastly improved technology, far-infrared sauna therapy is more beneficial for your health than a traditional sauna, as it uses a heat energy that penetrates deeper into your tissues, allowing an overall lower temperature to be used. I've used a far-infrared sauna for years and never once felt weak, sick, faint, dizzy, headachy, or uncomfortable with consistent usage of 15 to 25 minutes, three to four days per week.

SUPPORTING THE NATURAL CLEANSING PROCESS

One of the easiest ways to support your body's natural cleansing process is to drink more filtered water. As the adage goes, "Nature's solution to pollution is dilution." This definitely applies to the human body, as it's composed of 55 to 60 percent water. When initiating any kind of detox protocol, it's a fundamental cornerstone of the process to drink a lot of clean, filtered water—in particular, warm, filtered water with organic lemon juice—to facilitate toxin elimination.

If you are integrating a more powerful detox method like far-infrared sauna therapy, it's absolutely imperative to flush out toxins through your excretory system. Natural, organic liquids of all kinds are a great way to cleanse, whether you are doing fresh, raw juices; smoothies; broths; teas; filtered water; or a combination of those options. When you consume mostly liquids, you thereby eliminate a chunk of energy normally required for digestion of fiber and solid foods, which can range from 5 to 15 percent of your total energy. Think of this rest period from solid food as giving your body a much-needed break from the tiring task of digestion and reassigning its energy to detox and elimination duty.

It's important to note that protein and alcohol require the most energy to digest. This is why all effective detox protocols require you to give up all sources of animal protein and alcoholic beverages.

PLEASE DON'T PUNISH YOURSELF

One point about the mental side of cleansing: this is not an opportunity to punish yourself for the bad food choices you've made in the past or to unleash your cruel, authoritarian side. I've seen so many people become so unkind to themselves during a cleansing period. People are deeply emotionally attached to food, and when they take away what they're used to (or even depend on for comfort) for just a few days, some peeps start to absolutely freak out. This can start a vicious cycle of frustration and guilt.

My point is this: if you need to consume more liquids or even a bit of gentle, clean, plant-based solid foods to keep yourself sane and balanced, please do. The important thing during your cleanse is to have a clear goal and stick with the protocol. If things are not going as planned, give yourself permission to mindfully and gently adapt the cleansing program so you can finish it with sanity.

PRE-TOX AND POST-TOX PERIODS

Two big aspects of a cleanse program that people tend to overlook are the pre-tox period (how you prepare your body before a cleanse) and the post-tox period (how to come out of a cleanse and go back to eating solid, complex foods). Both of these periods are important. You never want to shock your body into or out of a detox protocol. You want to create a safe, gentle transition in and out of it to maximize the benefits.

Jumping from a Standard American Diet into an organic, raw vegan, 14-day juice fast is not a very wise idea. Crazily enough, I've heard of people doing it—and crashing really hard. If you did things that way, your body would likely release a massive amount of toxins in a very short time, causing a "toxic shock" to the body, which can actually do much more harm than good in the long run. The overload of toxins can get reabsorbed quickly if not eliminated properly. What I'm trying to say is: no deep-dish pizza-and-craft-beer binges leading up to a juice cleanse or detox program, got it? Good.

For both the pre-tox and post-tox periods, I encourage you to start eating more raw, clean, whole, unprocessed, plant-based foods. And by "clean," I don't mean foods that you've washed in the sink

(although I highly encourage washing all fresh fruits, veggies, and herbs!). "Clean eating" is a somewhat liberally defined term for a style of eating that's become really popular over the past five years thanks to several best-selling diet books.

I define "clean" foods as those that exist in a whole, minimally processed state, free of all artificial flavors, chemicals, additives, or unpronounceable ingredients. They are low in fat and calories and contain little to no oils, processed sugars, or refined salts. Clean foods require very little energy to digest and assimilate while allowing your body to process the nutrients with ease, grace, and efficiency. Sounds lovely, doesn't it? Examples of clean food recipes that I recommend for cleansing are: blended vegetable soups, fresh fruit salads, green smoothies, chia pudding, gluten-free grain bowls, and mineral-rich broths. Clean recipes are often easy and affordable and require little time to prepare and enjoy. I like to think about it this way: if the recipe has a ton of ingredients and takes a long time to prepare, you can bet your body is going to take a longer amount of time digesting it. This is not necessarily the approach you want when it comes to cleansing. Just keep your meals simple and easy to digest.

Now, there's no real rule of thumb for how long the pre-tox and post-tox periods should last. It's honestly an intuitive thing, mixed with some expert guidance from a trained professional whose advice you trust. Once you feel your body has adjusted to the cleaner foods, you can think about transitioning into a more expansive menu of blended foods and/or liquids exclusively.

MY PERSONAL SEASONAL CLEANSING PROTOCOL

My favorite kaleidoscope of clean foods and supplements for a seasonal cleanse looks a lil' somethin' like this:

- 16 to 32 ounces of fresh filtered water upon waking with organic lemon juice
- Raw organic green juice (minimum 64 ounces per day)
- Raw anti-inflammatory juice (usually a combo of pineapple, ginger, and turmeric root)
- Cleansing soup broth (usually made with mineral-rich seaweeds and a variety of medicinal mushrooms like shiitake, lion's mane, or reishi)
- Ground psyllium husk (to support bowel movements)
- A boatload of water throughout the day (generally 125 ounces or more)
- Far-infrared sauna therapy for a minimum of 15 minutes daily (until the sweat pours)
- Dry skin brushing with essential oils like lavender and eucalyptus
- Superfood greens supplement to maximize vitamin and mineral intake
- Plant-based probiotic to increase the amount of good bacteria in the digestive tract
- A whole lotta rest (the unreleased Led Zeppelin B-side)
- No work and no business deals, if possible

A point about the "no work, no business" recommendation in my protocol: I feel that it's important to minimize the major emotional stressors in your life while you are cleansing. You'll find a much deeper state of calm and, potentially, a more effective cleanse if you can stay at home, unplug the phone and the Internet, and just relax, homie. That's the part nobody really talks about during a true cleanse—but it's just as important to chill out and eliminate other toxins, like the emotional ones.

Seriously, as hard as it is to believe, the world won't end if you take a few days off to reset and recharge. It's crucial that you take this time to heal your body and renew your senses. Take some hot baths with magnesium salts, relax with some great music, meditate daily, and do your best to be very loving and compassionate with yourself. A proper cleanse isn't just about detoxing the chemical buildup on a physical level—it's also about detoxing from the negative thought patterns, belief systems, and myriad ways we hurt ourselves psychologically. It's an opportunity to cleanse your entire being on all levels of existence—mind, body, and spirit. To me, that's the real goal of a true cleanse and detox program: to take a clear, compassionate look at all kinds of crap in your life and then, effectively and lovingly, let go of it all!

PROGRESS, NOT PERFECTION

The post-cleanse period is a beautiful opportunity to re-create your relationship to food in new ways that serve your health and happiness for the rest of your life. The idea of "progress, not perfection" is a popular adage that perfectly applies to detoxification and cleansing. We are all works in progress, trying our absolute best to live in accordance with what works for our individual bodies and beings. Finding what works best for our constitution is a constant, lifelong experiment. Be willing to try multiple approaches and cleansing protocols before you find the one that's best for you and helps you achieve your aims.

APPETITE FOR REDUCTION

The detox recipes I've included in this chapter can be used in all areas of your cleansing protocol, depending on your goals and intentions. For instance, the noodle dishes, ice cream, popcorn, and salad can be enjoyed during either the pre-tox or post-tox periods, while the soup, smoothies, and juice can be helpful during your actual cleansing stage. Again, it's important to consult with a professional who's experienced in guiding clients through a structured cleanse protocol and who can help you co-create a program tailored to your specific aims. The recipes here all contain ingredients that may be beneficial in supporting your cleanse protocol. But even if you're not currently cleansing, they can be a delicious way to eat super clean throughout the year!

MY TOP NUTRIENTS TO HELP YOU DETOXIFY

Betaine: Said to promote the regeneration of liver cells and the flow of bile. It is also said to promote fat metabolism.

Caffeoylquinic acids: Also help to increase bile flow and to digest fat.

Choline: A water-soluble essential nutrient used in the synthesis of the constructional components in the body's cell membranes.

Glutathione and monounsaturated fatty acids (MFAs): Glutathione binds to heavy metals, while MFAs help to flush them out.

Methionine: Helps to regulate fat metabolism and increase bile flow, aiding the body in detoxing.

Sulfur: An essential element for all life, it is an important part of many enzymes and in antioxidant molecules.

MY TOP DETOXIFYING FOODS

- apple cider vinegar
- basil
- beets
- blue-green algae
- blueberries
- Brazil nuts
- cannellini beans
- carrots
- cherries
- cilantro
- cinnamon
- citrus fruits
- coriander seed
- daikon radish
- fennel
- garlic
- ginger root
- goji berries
- lemon
- milk thistle
- onion
- parsley
- pineapple
- sarsaparilla
- sea vegetables
- sesame seeds
- stinging nettles

RECIPES

FOR

DETOXIFICATION

....

PAPAYA
SWEET TART SMOOTHIE

SWEETARTS WERE ONE OF MY FAVORITE candies from childhood. Sometimes, I still get nostalgic for them. When that old-time craving hits, I make this smoothie. It's loaded with tons of antioxidants from the berry blend and amino acids from the chlorella and vegan protein powder, and somehow, someway, it magically tastes like that famous candy of yore after you blend it. It's pure alchemy in a glass, I tell ya. The real powerhouse of this recipe is the papaya and its seeds. The enzymes in the fruit have tremendous digestive benefits, while the seeds have been shown to be antiparasitic, antibacterial, and help to detox the liver.

3 cups raw coconut water

½ medium papaya, seeded, with seeds reserved

1 cup blueberries

1 cup raspberries

1 cup strawberries

1 tablespoon vegan vanilla protein powder (optional)

1 tablespoon chlorella powder

1 teaspoon baobab powder

¼ cup goldenberries

¼ teaspoon camu camu powder

½ teaspoon ground vanilla bean

1½ tablespoons hemp seeds

Pinch sea salt

1 tablespoon chia seeds

1. Blend all ingredients in a high-speed blender for 40 seconds until smooth and creamy.

TRIPLE BERRY
GELATO

INSTANT ICE CREAM IS A THING of beauty, especially when made with mixed berries. The sweet, tart balance of the berries in this recipe plays off the custard undertones of the lucuma and smokiness of the mesquite. The addition of coconut oil and vitamin E–rich tocotrienols creates the uber-creamy gelato texture. The powerful berries in this dessert are loaded with high levels of antioxidants, which can help cleanse your liver.

One caveat: If you have a regular, low-speed blender, I advise you not to attempt this recipe. Your blender is going to get a serious workout with this one. Hold on tight and use your tamper tool (if you use a VitaMix) or your Twister jar (if you use a Blendtec).

2 cups ice cubes

Two 10-ounce bags frozen mixed berries

2 tablespoons mesquite powder

2 tablespoons lucuma powder

1 teaspoon camu camu powder

¼ cup plus 2 tablespoons tocotrienols

Pinch sea salt

½ teaspoon liquid stevia

1 tablespoon organic virgin coconut oil

1 Blend all ingredients in a high-speed blender for about 45 to 60 seconds, until ultra smooth and creamy.

Top your gelato with goldenberries, goji berries, hemp seeds, or shredded coconut for an awesome mouthfeel and flavor!

KOMBUCHA
SMOOTHIE

KOMBUCHA IS A REALLY GREAT SUBSTITUTE for soda. This probiotic-rich, fizzy, tea-based beverage is fun to drink and makes a wonderful base for this unique smoothie. It also has some pretty stellar detox benefits, including alkalizing the body, detoxing the liver, and helping to reduce kidney stones. Throw in some tropical fruit and berries to crank up the vitamin C and antioxidants, and you get a bubbly, creamy, and delicious drink that breaks up the monotony of the same ol' smoothie every day.

2 cups of bottled or fresh-brewed kombucha

1 cup fresh or frozen pineapple, diced

½ cup strawberries, chopped

1 banana, peeled

2 tablespoons goji berries

1 teaspoon noni fruit powder

1 handful ice cubes

1 Blend all ingredients in a high-speed blender for 30 to 40 seconds until frothy.

THE
IMPASTA BOWL

SERVES 2

THIS RECIPE WAS BORN FROM A conversation about making fake pasta from vegetables; hence the name The Impasta Bowl (which also sounds like "the impossible" if you say it really fast!). As crazy as the name sounds, the dynamic flavor and freshness of this Asian-inspired noodle salad is even crazier. Carrots contain a unique kind of fiber that helps you detox excess bad estrogen and lower the number of endotoxins in your gut. The sweet, crunchy daikon radish goes a step further by helping to purge toxins from your liver, gallbladder, and kidneys. Now that's a seriously dynamic detox duo!

SAUCE:

1-inch piece of fresh ginger root, peeled and minced

1 large clove garlic, minced

1 large orange, juiced

1 tablespoon raw sesame oil

1 teaspoon coconut aminos

½ teaspoon red pepper flakes

¼ orange, zested

NOODLES:

1⅓ cup thinly sliced king oyster mushrooms

⅓ cup coconut aminos

1 tablespoon apple cider vinegar

1 large daikon radish, peeled

1 large carrot, peeled

1½ tablespoons diced scallions

½ cup cilantro, torn by hand

½ cup pea pods

2 large red cabbage leaves, reserved for plating

Sprinkle of black sesame seeds, reserved for plating

1 **To make the sauce:** whisk together all of the sauce ingredients in a medium mixing bowl until well combined. Set aside.

2 **To make the noodles:** combine the king oyster mushrooms with the coconut aminos and apple cider vinegar, allowing the mushrooms to marinate for at least 15 to 20 minutes.

3 Run the daikon radish and carrot through a spiralizer to create veggie noodles. (I find the texture of angel hair or spaghetti is best for this recipe.) Transfer the noodles to a large mixing bowl and add the scallions, cilantro, and pea pods.

4 Combine the sauce with the noodles and veggies, along with the marinated mushrooms and the mushroom marinade. Stir gently to combine well. Serve the finished noodles inside of a large red cabbage leaf with black sesame seeds on top.

CHEESY
CAULIFLOWER "POPCORN"

POPCORN IS USUALLY A GREAT OPTION for low-calorie snacking, but it's not always chock-full of nutrients. This innovative version pumps up the nutrition with vitamin B12, protein, and heart-healthy fats. The "popcorn" comes in the form of oven-roasted cauliflower florets. Speaking of cauliflower, this cruciferous crusader is high in phytochemicals called glucosinolates. These chemicals are broken down in the intestines to isothiocynates and indole-3-carbinol, compounds that regulate the body's detoxification enzymes and protect against cancer. The nutritional yeast adds a terrific cheesy flavor, and the spices round out a savory punch that will be a big hit for movie night or when the munchies strike.

2 large heads cauliflower, broken into popcorn-size florets

4 tablespoons organic virgin coconut oil

¼ cup plus 2 tablespoons nutritional yeast

1 teaspoon dried marjoram

1 teaspoon dried thyme

½ teaspoon onion or garlic granules

½ teaspoon black pepper, to taste

Pinch sea salt, to taste

½ teaspoon cayenne pepper (optional)

1. Preheat the oven to 450 degrees Fahrenheit.

2. Line two metal baking sheets with parchment paper and set aside.

3. Toss the cauliflower florets with the coconut oil in a medium mixing bowl. Add the remaining ingredients. Mix until coated and then spread evenly on the prepared pans. Bake for 45 to 50 minutes, tossing every 15 minutes. Remove from the oven and allow the "popcorn" to cool for a few minutes. Serve immediately.

JASON'S TIP

The cauliflower "popcorn" should be slightly crispy and caramelized but not burnt. Watch your cooking times carefully near the end to ensure the proper consistency and color. You can also prepare the "popcorn" in a dehydrator at 115 degrees Fahrenheit for 8 to 12 hours.

CILANTRO LIME
PUMPKIN PESTO PASTA

SOMETIMES YOU WANT A HEARTY BOWL of pasta, but not something that's going to make you feel like you swallowed a big-ass bowling ball. Instead of being a gut-buster like most noodle dishes, this pesto pasta is a true toxin-buster, with fresh cilantro, basil, and pumpkin seeds. Eating cilantro is an excellent way to help cleanse your body of toxic heavy metals like mercury, arsenic, and lead, which can accumulate in tissue and elsewhere as a result of repeated environmental and dietary exposure. These noodles are healthy, light, and surprisingly satisfying.

NOODLES:

- 4 quarts filtered water
- 2 tablespoons extra-virgin olive oil
- One 8-ounce box gluten-free angel hair pasta
- 1 cup black olives, pitted and quartered, plus more for garnish
- ½ red bell pepper, diced
- ¼ cup raw pumpkin seeds

PUMPKIN PESTO:

- 2½ cups fresh basil, tightly packed, plus more for garnish
- ½ cup cilantro
- ¾ cup extra-virgin olive oil
- 3 tablespoons fresh lime juice
- 1 tablespoon garlic, minced
- 2 teaspoons coconut aminos
- ½ teaspoon sea salt
- ½ teaspoon ground black pepper
- Pinch cayenne pepper
- ½ cup raw pine nuts, plus more for garnish

1 **To make the noodles:** bring 4 quarts of water to a rapid boil. Add the olive oil to the water. Add the angel hair to the water, return to a boil, and cook uncovered for 6 to 10 minutes until the pasta achieves an al dente texture. Drain in a colander. Transfer pasta to a large mixing bowl and fold in the black olives, red bell pepper, and pumpkin seeds. Mix well to combine and set aside.

2 **To make the Pumpkin Pesto:** Place all pesto ingredients in a food processor and process until semismooth with a little bit of chunky texture.

3 In a large mixing bowl, combine the noodles and Pumpkin Pesto and mix vigorously with a large spoon. Top with a sprinkle of chopped black olives, fresh basil, and pine nuts.

You can substitute spaghetti, glass noodles, or kelp noodles for the angel hair pasta in this recipe.

GINGER BORSCHT

SERVES 2

BORSCHT IS THE SOUP I ASSOCIATE most with my childhood. My Polish grandmother, Rose, perfected the dish long before I was born. Thanks to her, I have a myriad of delightful memories of all things beets! Grandma was as wise as she was beautiful, as beets are one of the most effective natural liver detoxifiers. Pectin, a fiber found in beets, allows toxins that have been removed from the liver to be flushed out of the system instead of reabsorbed by the body. This soup is a healthy take on my grandma's borscht with fresh ginger, garlic, and coconut milk. For a comforting, deeply nourishing soup, this one is tough to "beet."

1 cup low-sodium vegetable broth

1 cup coconut milk

1 teaspoon organic virgin coconut oil

¼ cup yellow onion, diced

2 cloves crushed garlic

2½ cups beets, peeled

¾ teaspoon sea salt

¼ teaspoon ground black pepper

½ teaspoon smoked paprika

1. Blend all ingredients in a high-speed blender for 40 seconds until smooth and creamy. Transfer to a medium saucepan and bring to a boil over medium heat. Reduce the heat and simmer on low for 15 minutes. Remove from the heat and serve.

JASON'S TIP

Top with vegan sour cream and minced scallions for extra creaminess and zingy flavor.

THE
ETHIOPIAN PLUNGER

SERVES 2

THIS SHAKE IS MY TAKE ON a traditional Ethiopian drink and is aptly named "The Plunger" because of its uncanny ability to get things, uh, moving swiftly in your digestive system. If you think I'm being ridiculous, well, I am—but it really works well as a powerful detox drink. The flaxseed provides a wonderful source of fiber that helps to bind and flush toxins from the intestinal tract. They're also a great source of health-promoting omega-3 fatty acids. This shake is a one-way ticket on the party train to Poopville.

1 teaspoon organic virgin coconut oil

¼ cup golden flaxseed

2 tablespoons maple syrup

2 cups filtered water

Pinch sea salt

1½ tablespoons chia seeds

1 cup ice cubes

1 Heat the coconut oil on low in a medium skillet and add the flaxseed. When the seeds begin to pop, remove from the heat and transfer to a high-speed blender. Add all remaining ingredients and blend on high speed for 30 seconds until smooth and frothy.

This shake is a great cure for constipation. Drink first thing in the morning to get things moving and grooving.

PINEAPPLE GINGER
GRAPEFRUIT JUICE

SERVES 2

(SF) (GF) (RA) (OF) (NF)

HOMEMADE, ORGANIC, RAW JUICE IS ONE of life's great little pleasures. Rather than going out and paying big bucks (up to $15!) for a cold-pressed juice at the juice bar, you can make awesome juices like this recipe for a fraction of the price. I love the perfect balance of sweet and tart flavors in this juice. The turmeric and pineapple both have anti-inflammatory and pain reduction benefits. The ginger root helps to crank up your agni, or digestive fire, which supports toxin elimination. This is the perfect recipe if you need a break from too much green juice on your cleanse.

4 cups fresh pineapple, chopped

1-inch piece ginger root, peeled

½-inch piece turmeric root, peeled

2 medium pink grapefruits, peeled and chopped

½ cup fresh mint leaves, destemmed

1 Juice all ingredients in a high-speed juicer and serve immediately.

MUSHROOM
DETOX SOUP

AS A FANTASTIC CLEANSING MEAL, THIS Mushroom Detox Soup is hard to beat. The fresh ingredients are easy to digest and come with a host of benefits. Ginger root reduces inflammation in the body and balances blood sugar. Its partner in crime, burdock root, is a potent blood cleanser and liver detoxifier. I love making this recipe after the hedonism of the holiday season to start the New Year in a healthy way, but you can enjoy the heck out of this powerful and delicious healing soup any time of year.

1 large onion, halved

2-inch piece ginger root, peeled

1 cinnamon stick

2 pieces whole star anise

½ teaspoon whole cloves

1 teaspoon whole coriander seeds

5 cups low-sodium vegetable stock or filtered water

2 teaspoons coconut aminos

2 cups carrots, peeled and chopped

⅓ cup burdock root, peeled and chopped

½ pound dried flat rice noodles

1 cup fresh shiitake mushrooms, thinly sliced

1 tablespoon sesame oil

2 cups bok choy, chopped and packed

2 whole scallions, minced, reserved for garnish

6 large dried shiitake mushroom caps, reserved for garnish

½ packed cup cilantro leaves, torn, reserved for garnish

1½ tablespoons fresh basil, torn, reserved for garnish

1 lime, reserved for garnish

1 Char the onion and ginger over an open flame (holding with metal tongs) or directly under a broiler until slightly blackened, about 5 minutes on each side. Rinse with water.

2 In a large pot, dry roast the cinnamon, star anise, cloves, and coriander over medium-low heat, stirring to prevent burning.

3 When the spices are aromatic, add the vegetable stock, coconut aminos, carrots, burdock root, and, charred onion and ginger. Bring the broth to a boil, reduce the heat, and simmer, covered, for 30 minutes. Strain and keep hot until ready to serve. While the broth is simmering, place the noodles in a large bowl and cover with hot water.

4 Let the noodles stand for 20 to 30 minutes or until tender but still chewy. (If soaking does not soften the noodles enough, blanch them in a pot of boiling water for a few seconds.) Drain.

5 Sauté the mushrooms in the sesame oil in a small saucepan. Lightly steam the bok choy.

6 Divide the noodles between two bowls. Arrange the mushrooms and bok choy over the noodles. Ladle about 2 cups of broth into each bowl. Serve with garnishes on the side.

MANGO LEMON PEPPER
KELP NOODLES

SERVES 2 TO 4

THIS IS A REALLY LIGHT, CRUNCHY, and delicious salad that is quite substantial. Kelp noodles are great—they provide a tasty alternative to cooked pasta in raw food recipes. And they're full of alginates, which are chemicals that bind toxic metals in the intestines, preventing their absorption. They're kind of like chelators but safer, as they allow the toxic metals to pass harmlessly out of the body. The mango lemon pepper sauce has a wonderfully subtle flavor and can pull double duty as a tasty salad dressing.

½ cup fresh mango, peeled and chopped

¼ cup raw tahini

1½ tablespoons ume plum vinegar

1 large lemon, juiced

2 tablespoons filtered water

1 large clove garlic, minced

One 12-ounce package kelp noodles, drained and rinsed

¼ teaspoon ground black pepper

1 handful of black olives, diced

1 Blend the mango, tahini, ume plum vinegar, lemon, filtered water, and garlic in a high-speed blender for 30 seconds until smooth and creamy.

2 Combine the mango lemon pepper sauce with the kelp noodles and mix with your hands to combine well. Serve the noodles topped with ground black pepper and black olives.

7

EAT

FOR

BRAINPOWER

YOUR BRAIN HAS A PRETTY IMPORTANT JOB. As the central processing center of the human body, the brain controls all essential functions. It is one of our most intricate, complex, and mysterious organs; in fact, its ultimate powers are still being researched and discovered.

What we DO know is that your brain thrives on specific nutrients that help it to function more effectively and perform optimally when you need it most. These days, your brain has more information to process, filter, and retain than ever. If you feel like your thinking is foggier and slower than usual, you're definitely not alone:

- Recent statistics show that up to 1 million Americans may deal with symptoms of chronic brain fog
- More than 16 million people in the U.S. are living with cognitive impairment and have trouble remembering, learning new things, and concentrating
- Major causes of cognitive dysfunction may result from the side effects of pharmaceutical drugs or problematic drug interactions
- Brain supplements are a billion-dollar industry in the U.S. alone

BRAIN-FRIENDLY NUTRITION

Keeping your brain healthy and well nourished is a goal that should be high on your personal health "to-do" list. There's a ton of evidence that suggests that what you do for your brain now can have a big impact on how it functions in the years and decades to come. Eating well in the present, along with other healthy lifestyle choices you make today, can keep your brain bopping and stave off age-related problems in the future, like cognitive decline and Alzheimer's disease.

When you feel mentally sluggish, foggy, unable to concentrate, and just plain tired, there's a good chance that what you have (or haven't) eaten may be the culprit. It's all too easy to be deficient in some of the nutrients that the brain needs to work at prime capacity, especially if you're dieting or constantly stressed-out or eating too much on the go. These nutritive deficiencies can affect you mentally, leading to a number of high-level cognitive problems and even to imbalanced emotional states such as anxiety and depression.

It's a good idea to become familiar with the brain-friendly nutrition provided by omega-3 fatty acids, B vitamins, vitamin D, and phytochemicals, which are plant-derived compounds that often act as antioxidants. These compounds provide a supercharged list of health benefits to your brain and body.

HEALTHY FATS ARE YOUR BRAIN'S BFF

To keep your brain happy, you need to feed it the right nutrients—and we know that the human brain loves healthy fats like the Cookie Monster loves chocolate chips! In fact, the average adult human brain is composed of about 60 percent fat. Specifically, omega-3 fatty acids (in particular, DHA and EPA) are absolutely essential for healthy brain function. Dietary docosahexaenoic acid (DHA) is needed for the optimum function of the retina and visual cortex, with visual acuity and mental development improved by extra doses of it. According to research from the Department of Neurology at Chi-Mei Medical Center in Taiwan, omega-3 fatty acids not only play a vital role in building our brain structure but also act as messengers that are involved in the synthesis and functions of brain neurotransmitters and in the molecules of the immune system. This is one reason why extremely low-fat diets can actually starve your brain of the essential nutrition it requires to function optimally.

Ironically, DHA is the most abundant omega-3 fatty acid in cell membranes in the brain, but the human body is not particularly efficient at synthesizing DHA.

Therefore, we are dependent on getting it from our food. It has been proposed that access to DHA during human evolution had a key role in increasing the brain/body-mass ratio—arguably a marker of our level of intelligence.

Over the past 100 years, the intake of saturated fatty acids, linoleic acid, and trans fatty acids has increased dramatically in Western civilization, whereas the consumption of omega-3 fatty acids has greatly decreased. Unlike omega-3 fatty acids, saturated fats and trans fats do more harm than good.

Let's take a closer look at these good guys, the omega-3s.

ONE ORDER OF OMEGA-3S, PLEASE

Omega-3 fatty acids help the brain communicate using the neurotransmitters serotonin and dopamine, powerful players in the regulation of mood. Another way omega-3s can help the brain is by enhancing the production of bone-derived neurotrophic factor (BDNF), which, through a cascade of events, ultimately stimulates the cell processes that are central in learning and memory. Finally, omegas can reduce inflammation in the brain, just as they do in the rest of the body.

So, what could possibly happen if your diet does not contain enough omega-3 fats? Since the body is not very good at manufacturing the chief omega fatty acid, DHA, it's possible to become extremely deficient in this compound. On the more severe end of the spectrum, DHA deficiency is associated with disorders like depression, ADHD, bipolar disorder, dyslexia, and schizophrenia. It can also lead to fatigue and problems with memory.

Another important omega-3 is alpha-linolenic acid (ALA), which is found in nonanimal sources like walnuts, flaxseed, soybean oil, spinach, and kale. Getting enough of this particular omega is not usually a problem for vegetarians. However, since the other omega-3s are mainly found in fish, high-potency natural supplements may be necessary for strict vegetarians and vegans. I found out that I was deficient in omega-3 fatty acids after seeing the results of my full blood panel test. Now I take a daily DHA and EPA supplement derived from third-party-tested ocean microalgae. The difference in my memory and overall brainpower has been noticeable!

"B" IS FOR BRAIN

The family of B vitamins, in particular B12, B6, and folate, are all important brain vitamins. B12 is required for a cell process called methylation, a basic chemical process that all cells, including brain cells, require to thrive. Many important processes in the nervous system require methylation: cell communication, the production of neurotransmitters that control many aspects of cognition; and the production of myelin, which acts as insulation for neurons to help them fire more efficiently (similar to how plastic coating on a wire improves its ability to transmit an electric signal).

Without enough B12, cell communication can be compromised at any age. Researchers at the University of Oxford's Oxford Project to Investigate Memory and

TURBOCHARGING YOUR BRAINPOWER!

- Add healthy fats like omega-3s and -6s to boost brainpower while cutting the bad fats like saturated and processed trans fatty acids that harm your brain.

- Eat moderate amounts of complex carbohydrates from whole grains and fruit to keep your glucose levels steady throughout the day.

- Eat lots of fruits and veggies with vivid colors for a full range of brain-healthy phytochemicals and antioxidants. Blueberries, strawberries, spinach, kale, oranges, sweet potatoes, eggplant, grapes, and raw cacao are examples of nutrient-rich foods.

- Drink coffee, tea, and red wine in moderation for added antioxidants.

- Take a high-quality natural B12 supplement.

- Eat healthy, plant-based proteins like tempeh, sprouted tofu, nuts, quinoa, lentils, hemp seeds, or chia seeds.

- Talk to a naturopathic medical doctor if you suspect you may be low in a nutrient. He or she can run a comprehensive blood panel test to determine if you have any deficiencies and make suggestions about how to get your levels up in a healthy and sustainable way.

Aging (OPTIMA) have found that B12 protects against age-related atrophy of brain cells and against damage to the brain's white matter (the tracts, or "wiring," of the brain that allow cells to communicate with one another).

Dr. David Smith, the founding director of OPTIMA, explains that without enough B12, the communication between different parts of the brain is less efficient. Eventually, after someone has been B12 deficient for a number of years, memory impairment sets in and gradually gets worse, leading to dementia.

Two other B vitamins, B6 and B9 (folate), are also essential for brain function, though we tend to hear less about them. Many foods are fortified with folate because of its role in preventing neural tube defects during pregnancy. Folate is also found in leafy greens, citrus fruits, peas, and beans. Vitamin B6 is found in the highest quantities in potatoes, bananas, chickpeas, and oatmeal. Vitamin B6 and folate work in conjunction with vitamin B12 by regulating a compound called homocysteine, which inhibits the methylation reaction, mentioned above, that is so important in the regulation of the nervous system.

If you have any concerns about your B vitamin levels, it is a good idea to get a comprehensive test of your blood panels.

THE POWER OF FLAVONOIDS

Phytochemicals are chemicals derived from plant sources that act as antioxidants by scavenging free radicals. There are a number of types of phytochemicals, but a familiar and key group is the flavonoids, which the scientific community and the public alike have embraced as necessary constituents for health and longevity.

Flavonoids take part in multiple cellular processes depending on the type of flavonoid. They are responsible for many aspects of our brain function. Researcher Fernando Gómez-Pinilla, Ph.D., studies the effect of nutrition on the brain at the University of California, Los Angeles. He explains that flavonoids play important roles in repairing damage in the brain. They do this by influencing how neurons "talk" to each other and by increasing levels of antioxidants and anti-inflammatory compounds that reduce damage to cells in the brain.

Some studies have found that extracts from blueberries, strawberries, spinach, and blackberries may reverse the normal cognitive changes and memory problems that accompany the aging process. They also appear to take part in cell functions that help the brain form memories in people of all ages. Flavonoids boost the brain's ability to form new neurons, prevent brain cells from dying, and enhance what researchers call "synaptic plasticity," the ability of neurons to form and reform connections with each another. These processes—particularly synaptic plasticity—are thought to be the basis for learning and memory.

There is also some evidence that flavonoids can not only stave off cognitive decline but also protect the brain from diseases such as Alzheimer's. This may be because the compounds protect against oxidative damage by hydrogen peroxide,

Spicy Tortilla Soup
(see recipe page 185)

which has been linked to the beta-amyloid plaques that characterize Alzheimer's.

Flavonoids (particularly the ones found in raw cacao beans) help boost blood flow to the brain. This may help protect against vascular diseases like stroke. The anti-inflammatory properties of certain flavonoids can also suppress inflammation in the brain, which helps reduce the risk of a variety of diseases. Parkinson's and Alzheimer's diseases may be a result of chronic inflammation, and certain flavonoids may offer protection against the kind of inflammation that accompanies them.

VITAMIN D TO THE RESCUE

In addition to its role as a promoter of bone and oral health, vitamin D serves important functions in brain health. This sunlight vitamin is synthesized in the skin when ultraviolet rays from the sun hit skin cells and is thought to protect the brain against cognitive deficits that come with age.

There are vitamin D receptors spread throughout many areas in the brain and the rest of the central nervous system. Vitamin D also influences certain proteins that aid in neuron growth and development, and it takes part in many other important aspects of brain function, like synaptic plasticity, learning, memory, the activity of neurotransmitters, and specific motor processes.

REFRAIN FROM JUNK FOOD FOR A HEALTHY BRAIN, DUDE!

While it's crucially important to add good, healthy fats (omega-3s and -6s) to your diet, it's also important to cut down on the bad fats and other substances that can negatively affect your brain health. Research by Terry Davidson, the director of American University's Center for Behavioral Neuroscience, shows that diets high in saturated fat and refined sugar impair your ability to learn and significantly reduce information retention. Other research has shown that simply eating too many calories can increase the amount of damaging molecules (like free radicals) that can build up in your brain. When these dangerous little particles become too numerous for your brain to remove, they can lead to problems in cognitive function.

You need to avoid eating foods high in refined, nutrient-stripped carbs and sugars. Complex carbs from whole grains and fresh fruit will help keep your glucose levels steady and fuel your brain throughout the day without the all-too-familiar crash that comes with processed grains found in white bread, cakes, candies, and cookies.

HURRY FOR THE CURRY

Curry powder usually contains turmeric, a golden-colored root that contains the anti-inflammatory antioxidant curcumin. Research has shown that curcumin may help inhibit the accumulation of destructive beta amyloids in the brains of Alzheimer's patients as well as break up existing plaques. Curcumin has even been shown to boost memory and stimulate the production of new brain cells. You can enjoy raw turmeric root or powder in a variety of recipes like smoothies, stir fries, curries, and nondairy milks.

The interesting thing about brain foods is that nature sometimes gives you clues to find the most beneficial sources of nutrients. For example, a halved walnut looks incredibly similar to a cross-section image of the human brain. It's no coincidence that walnuts contain a fantastic amount of brain-nourishing omega-3 fatty acids. Oh, nature, you're just so clever!

MY TOP NUTRIENTS TO BOOST BRAINPOWER

In addition to the other powerful nutrients I've previously detailed, DHA, B vitamins, vitamin E, and vitamin K are also supercharged brain boosters. However, here are a few new ones that may surprise you:

Carnosic acid: An antioxidant present in rosemary, it has neuroprotective benefits and mitigates the effects of oxidative stress.

Flavonoids: Powerful antioxidants that protect the brain against neurotoxins.

Nitrates: Improve blood flow to your brain.

MY TOP BRAIN-BOOSTING FOODS

- almonds
- ashwagandha
- avocado
- bacopa monnieri
- blue-green algae
- blueberries
- broccoli
- cacao
- cashews
- chia seeds
- curcumin
- eggplant
- flaxseed
- ginkgo biloba
- gotu kola
- hazelnuts
- hemp seeds
- macadamia nuts
- mucuna pruriens
- pecans
- pomegranates
- pumpkin seeds
- sage
- sesame seeds
- sunflower seeds
- tomatoes
- turmeric
- vacha
- walnuts
- whole grains

RECIPES
TO BOOST
BRAINPOWER

· · · · · · · · · · · · · · ·

AYURVEDIC
CHOCOLATE ELIXIR

SERVES 2

THIS IS CHOCOLATE MILK TO THE max. This elixir is loaded to the gills with a powerful blend of Ayurvedic herbs that help to boost brain function, detoxification, immunity, and cellular rejuvenation. In particular, the raw cacao powder contains powerful flavonols that can increase your cognitive function. With pumpkin and hemp seed oils, you also benefit from heart-healthy omega fatty acids. When a chocolate craving takes you to the brink, blend up a batch of this tasty drink!

¼ cup hemp seeds

3 cups filtered water

½ teaspoon ground vanilla bean

⅛ teaspoon sea salt

3 tablespoons raw cacao powder

¼ cup coconut sugar

1 tablespoon pumpkin seed oil

1 teaspoon hemp seed oil

1 tablespoon mesquite powder

1 teaspoon lucuma powder

1 tablespoon organic virgin coconut oil

1 teaspoon mucuna pruriens powder

1 teaspoon amla powder

1 teaspoon holy basil powder

1 teaspoon mangosteen powder

½ teaspoon shilajit powder

1 Blend the hemp seeds and filtered water for 30 seconds to make the hemp milk base. Add the remaining ingredients and blend for 30 more seconds until smooth and frothy.

PERUVIAN QUINOA STUFFED TOMATOES
WITH TOMATILLO SALSA

SERVES 4 TO 6

STUFFED TOMATOES ARE SOMETHING I'VE ENJOYED since childhood, when my mother would stuff everything from cabbage to bell peppers. This quinoa-stuffed tomato recipe features a deliciously nutty flavor and the subtle spice of tomatillo salsa. Roasting the tomatoes in the oven gives this dish a smoky undertone and brings out the flavor of all the vegetables. For all you brainiacs out there, you'll be happy to know that a cup of cooked quinoa offers 15 percent of the U.S. RDA of iron, which helps to deliver oxygen to the blood, boosting energy and brainpower.

STUFFED TOMATOES:

One 15-ounce can black beans, drained and rinsed

½ tablespoon balsamic vinegar

½ teaspoon sea salt, plus more for tomatoes

Pinch ground black pepper

2 cups cooked quinoa

⅓ cup red bell pepper, seeded and deveined, diced

2 tablespoons jalapeno pepper, minced (optional)

⅓ cup fresh cilantro, minced

½ cup corn kernels, cooked

¼ cup celery, finely chopped

2 garlic cloves, minced

¼ cup green onion, finely chopped

2 tablespoons fresh lemon juice

2 tablespoons extra-virgin olive oil

¼ cup pumpkin seeds

½ teaspoon ground cumin

⅛ to ¼ teaspoon cayenne pepper

8 medium-to-large whole red tomatoes

2 tablespoons nutritional yeast, reserved for baking

TOMATILLO SALSA:

½ pound fresh tomatillos (about 4 to 5 total)

½ large yellow onion, diced (about ¾ cup)

2 cloves garlic, minced

2 tablespoons fresh lime juice

¼ cup packed cilantro leaves, chopped

¼ jalapeno pepper, minced, about 2 teaspoons

½ teaspoon ground cumin

Pinch sea salt, to taste

Pinch black pepper, to taste

1 **To make the Stuffed Tomatoes:** preheat the oven to 450 degrees Fahrenheit. In a large mixing bowl, combine the black beans with vinegar, salt, and pepper. Add the quinoa, red bell pepper, jalapeno pepper if using, cilantro, corn, celery, garlic, green onion, lemon juice, olive oil, pumpkin seeds, and dry spices. Mix well to combine. Set aside.

2 Cut the upper part of the tomatoes horizontally and remove the tops. Gently scoop out all the pulp and seeds with a small spoon and discard. Sprinkle with salt and fill each tomato with a generous amount of the quinoa mixture. Sprinkle the top of each stuffed tomato with nutritional yeast. Bake the tomatoes in a lightly oiled 13 x 9-inch baking pan for 20 minutes.

3 Remove from the oven and serve immediately with fresh Tomatillo Salsa.

4 **To make the Tomatillo Salsa:** remove the husks from the tomatillos and wash with cool water. Cut into small pieces and add to a food processor with the onion and garlic. Process until very smooth. Add the lime juice, cilantro, and jalapeno, and process again until well combined. Transfer to a small saucepan. Season with cumin, salt, and pepper, and bring to a boil over medium heat. Cook, stirring occasionally, until most of the liquid has boiled off and it has a chunky consistency, about 15 minutes. Set aside and cool before using.

Feel free to use either a white quinoa or tricolor quinoa. The multicolored varieties tend to have a nuttier flavor and more dense consistency. The white quinoa tends to be lighter and fluffier. Regarding the tomatillo salsa: Tomatillos can stay fresh in a covered container in the refrigerator for up to one week. If you can't find fresh tomatillos in your area, you can always buy premade tomatillo salsa in a glass jar. There are many great brands available at your grocery store.

TEFF LOAF
WITH CRANBERRY GINGER SAUCE

SERVES 4

ONCE I REALIZED THAT I DIDN'T have a "meatloaf" recipe in my culinary arsenal, I didn't want to pull off a poor imitation of some 1970s vegetarian one from a dog-eared cookbook. Instead, I worked with this Teff Loaf that was shown to me by The Alchemist Chef. The dense, meaty texture of the loaf is perfectly accented by the sweet, tangy Cranberry Ginger Sauce. This is an iron-rich, nutritious alternative to the same ol' boring loaf. Speaking of iron, it helps to deliver rich stores of oxygen to your gray matter. I guess you could say teff is a pretty "def" brain grain.

TEFF LOAF:

6 cups chopped tomatoes, divided

2 teaspoons sea salt

3 cups filtered water

1½ cups teff grains

¼ cup fresh basil, packed

5 sprigs of thyme

5 sage leaves

3 to 4 cloves garlic

½ cup fresh spinach, packed

1 teaspoon extra-virgin olive oil, plus more for pan

CRANBERRY GINGER SAUCE:

½ cup fresh orange juice

1 large orange, zested

2-inch piece ginger root, grated

½ cup filtered water

½ teaspoon ground cinnamon

Heaping ¼ cup coconut sugar

2 cups fresh cranberries

¼ cup goji berries

⅛ teaspoon ground cloves

1 teaspoon fresh rosemary, minced, plus more for garnish

Pinch sea salt

1 **To make the Teff Loaf:** blend 3 cups tomatoes, salt, and filtered water in a high-speed blender. Transfer to a medium saucepan and add the teff grains. Bring to a boil. Cover and reduce the heat to a simmer. Simmer for 15 minutes, then mix. The consistency should be very thick but slightly runny. If there is still a lot of liquid, cover and cook for another couple of minutes.

2 Blend the remaining 3 cups of tomatoes, basil, thyme, sage, garlic, spinach, and olive oil in a high-speed blender or food processor until roughly chopped. Transfer to a small skillet and sauté for 3 to 4 minutes or until the garlic is translucent and the herbs begin to brown.

3 Add the tomato-spice mixture to the teff and mix well. Grease a standard loaf pan with olive oil. Transfer the teff loaf mixture to loaf pan and set aside for 10 minutes. The teff thickens quickly as it cools.

4 **To make the Cranberry Ginger Sauce:** combine all ingredients in a medium saucepan over medium heat. Once the mixture comes to a boil and the cranberries start to burst, reduce the heat to low and simmer for 15 minutes, stirring occasionally. As soon as the mixture thickens, remove from the heat.

5 Flip the cooled teff loaf onto a nice serving dish and top with cranberry sauce. Garnish with fresh sprigs of rosemary.

WRAPATOUILLE
WITH SOUR CREAM SAUCE

SERVES 6 TO 8

RATATOUILLE **BECAME A HOUSEHOLD NAME THANKS** to a certain cute cartoon rat. But the classic French Provençal stewed vegetable dish can be kind of cliché unless you funk it up a bit. This dish takes the veggies, adds a rich, creamy, dairy-free sour cream, and turns it into a sandwich wrap. The familiar, comforting flavor of this dish takes on a new life here. Eggplant takes the valedictorian award in this recipe, with its anthocyanin phytonutrient called nasunin. Nasunin is a potent antioxidant and free-radical scavenger that has been shown to protect the lipids (fats) in brain cell membranes from damage.

SOUR CREAM SAUCE:

1 cup raw cashews, soaked 1 hour

½ cup filtered water

¼ cup extra-virgin olive oil

2 tablespoons fresh lemon juice

2 teaspoons apple cider vinegar

¾ teaspoon sea salt

WRAPATOUILLE FILLING:

3 tablespoons extra-virgin olive oil

1½ cups yellow onion, sliced lengthwise

2 teaspoons garlic, minced

2 cups medium eggplant, peeled and sliced lengthwise

1 cup green bell peppers, sliced lengthwise

1 cup red bell peppers, sliced lengthwise

1 cup zucchini, sliced lengthwise

1½ cups cherry tomatoes, halved

2 tablespoons fresh parsley, chopped and divided

1 tablespoon fresh basil, chopped

1 teaspoon fresh thyme, chopped

½ cup marinara sauce

1 tablespoon balsamic vinegar

Pinch red pepper flakes

Pinch sea salt, to taste

Pinch black pepper, to taste

8 rounds whole-grain lavash or large rice tortillas, for serving

1 **To make the Sour Cream Sauce:** blend all ingredients in a high-speed blender for about 30 seconds until very smooth and creamy. If need be, scrape down the sides of the blender carafe with a spatula and blend again. Cover and store in the refrigerator.

2 **To make the Wrapatouille Filling:** heat the olive oil in a large sauté pan over medium heat. Cook the onions and garlic, stirring occasionally, until they are lightly caramelized, about 6 minutes. Add the eggplant and continue to cook, stirring occasionally, about 5 minutes. Stir in the bell peppers and zucchini, and continue to cook for an additional 5 minutes. Add the tomatoes, 1 tablespoon of parsley, basil, thyme, marinara sauce, vinegar, and spices, and cook for another 5 to 7 minutes. Mix well.

3 Scoop a large spoonful of filling onto a fresh lavash. Add a generous dollop of the Sour Cream Sauce and fold over both sides of the lavash wrap to close it. Top the sealed wrap with a small spoonful of the Sour Cream Sauce and sprinkle with the remaining 1 tablespoon of parsley. Serve immediately.

JASON'S TIP

The thickness of the vegetable strips is key to the proper mouthfeel of this recipe. Cut the strips to no more than ¼-inch matchstick size to fit well inside the wrap. The savory Sour Cream Sauce is extremely versatile while being tangy and light. You can also use it as a topping for cooked chili or soups or as a dipping sauce.

CREAM OF GREEN TOMATO
SOUP

THIS GREEN TOMATO SOUP IS BRIGHT, light, flavorful, and satisfying with fresh basil, rosemary, and gluten-free croutons. In terms of brainpower, tomatoes are one of the easiest and most economical ways to increase your intake of a brain-protecting class of plant nutrients called carotenoids. These molecules safeguard fat in the body, which is very valuable for brain function, since your brain is composed mostly of fat. Tomatoes are a particularly good source of two all-star carotenoids: lycopene and beta-carotene.

2 teaspoons extra-virgin olive oil, divided

5 medium green tomatoes, sliced into 1-inch-thick rounds

½ cup yellow onion, diced

½ cup green bell pepper, diced

2 cloves garlic, minced

2 cups low-sodium vegetable broth

2 cups filtered water

½ cup coconut milk

¾ teaspoon sea salt

¼ teaspoon ground black pepper

3 tablespoons tomato paste

1 tablespoon fresh basil, minced

1½ teaspoons fresh rosemary, minced

1 cup gluten-free herbed croutons, reserved for garnish

1 Preheat the oven to 400 degrees Fahrenheit.

2 Grease a glass baking pan with 1 teaspoon of olive oil and place the sliced tomato rounds on the pan. Flip the tomatoes to coat both sides with oil. Bake for 20 minutes, flipping halfway through. Remove the tomatoes from the oven and allow them to cool. When they're cool to the touch, slice off the skins, dice the tomatoes, and set aside.

3 Heat the remaining 1 teaspoon of olive oil in a 3-quart saucepan over medium heat. Add the onions, green bell pepper, and garlic. Cook, stirring occasionally, until the onions are translucent, about 5 to 6 minutes. Add the broth, water, coconut milk, salt, and pepper, and whisk in the tomato paste. Simmer, partially covered, for 15 minutes. Add tomatoes, basil, and rosemary, and simmer for another 5 to 8 minutes. Serve immediately with herbed croutons.

For a smoother texture, you can puree the entire soup, or puree half for a thick and chunky soup. This soup actually tastes great with a dollop of Sour Cream Sauce from my Wrapatouille recipe (see page 180).

CHOCOLATE PECAN
CRUNCHY BALLS

MAKES 9 BALLS

WHEN YOU'RE IN A PINCH FOR a quick and satisfying dessert recipe, these babies will deliciously save the day. There's something really addictive about the salty, sweet taste and gooey, crunchy consistency of these balls. I've never been able to stop at just one, and it's pretty awesome to watch them disappear so quickly at a party. Pecans have high levels of the antioxidant vitamin E that protects fat cells from oxidation, as well as choline, which ensures optimal brain function and boosts your memory. Raw cacao has been shown to increase levels of specific neurotransmitters in your brain that help promote a positive outlook, facilitate rejuvenation, and lift your spirit.

¼ cup raw pecan butter

1 teaspoon vanilla extract

3 tablespoons coconut nectar

Pinch sea salt

1 cup brown rice cacao crispies cereal

1½ tablespoons cacao nibs

1 Combine all ingredients in a large mixing bowl and mix well with a spatula. Form into bite-size balls on a serving plate or parchment paper. Put in the freezer for 10 to 15 minutes to firm up. Take them out and enjoy!

HEAVENLY
HEMP MILK

I LOVE HEMP MILK FOR SO many reasons. First, it's easy and affordable to make. Second, you don't have to use a mesh strainer or nut milk bag, as the hemp seeds leave no pulp. Third, you can make a big batch of it and use it for smoothies, sauces, oatmeal, or whatever your heart desires. And last, it's super nutritious, with protein and omega-3 fatty acids. Hemp's nutritional profile resembles that of eggs, and it is also a rich source of magnesium, iron, B vitamins, and zinc. Each of these nutrients is amazing for your brain. The protein content helps to fuel your brain and prevent fatigue, low mood, and sugar cravings, and the healthy fats also help to prevent depression.

6 cups filtered water

¾ cup hemp seeds

5 tablespoons coconut nectar

4 tablespoons raw coconut butter

1 teaspoon ground cinnamon

½ teaspoon ground vanilla bean

½ teaspoon sea salt

1 Blend all ingredients into frothy hemp milk in a high-speed blender for 40 seconds. Serve immediately.

JASON'S TIP

Use this hemp milk as a base for smoothies, ice cream, pie fillings, and even creamy soups.

SPICY
TORTILLA SOUP

THERE'S A CERTAIN VEGAN RESTAURANT CHAIN in Los Angeles that serves an epic tortilla soup . . . but only on Tuesdays. Ugh. So rather than remain beholden to Tortilla Tuesdays for my weekly fix, I created this deliciously spicy version featuring a mélange of fresh vegetables and crunchy sweet potato chips. It's oil free, low in sodium, and retains all the classic spiciness and hearty texture you'd expect from a proper tortilla soup. Warning: this is a seriously addictive bowl of soul. You'll probably want to double the recipe and hide it from your loved ones in a nondescript, unmarked container in the back of the fridge. Or, better yet, give 'em their own containers: tomatoes are chock-full of lycopene, a powerful antioxidant that protects against the kind of free radical damage to cells that occurs in the development of dementia, particularly Alzheimer's.

4 medium roma tomatoes, chopped

2 cups hot water

¼ cup diced red bell pepper

¼ cup diced carrot

2 tablespoons minced white onion

2 tablespoons cilantro

¾ sea salt

¾ teaspoon garlic granules

1 teaspoon salt-free herb seasoning

⅛ teaspoon smoked paprika

½ teaspoon fresh lime juice

⅓ cup vegan pepper jack cheese shreds (optional)

½ cup sweet potato tortilla chips

½ cup diced avocado, reserved for plating

⅓ cup minced cilantro, reserved for plating

1 Add all ingredients, except for the chips, avocado, and cilantro, to a high-speed blender. Before blending, cover with a kitchen towel to prevent hot liquid from escaping. Pulse until you have achieved a nice, slightly chunky consistency. Add the tortilla chips and pulse a few more times to crush them up. Serve in a large bowl and top with chopped avocado and cilantro.

PEAR APPLE
CRISP

FALL IS MY FAVORITE TIME TO make dessert. There's something so special about the crop of fruits that are in season that time of year. This dessert recipe is a perfect homage to two fantastic, fiber-filled fruits of fall: pear and apple. It's simple, satisfying, and sweet with a crazy, crunchy mouthfeel thanks to the gluten-free, oat-based crumble on top. Grab a glass of warm cider and dive right in, why don't ya? Plus, one medium pear contains 15 percent of your RDA of copper, a trace mineral that's essential for a healthy nervous system. In your brain, copper ions affect components that are responsible for making the neural synapses (junctions that allow your nerves to communicate) stronger or weaker.

FILLING:

3 to 4 cups sliced apples

3 to 4 cups sliced pears

1 tablespoon arrowroot powder

¼ cup maple syrup

¼ cup applesauce

½ orange, zested

½ teaspoon ground cinnamon

¼ teaspoon grated ginger root

¼ teaspoon sea salt

CRUMBLE TOPPING:

½ cup gluten-free oats

½ cup gluten-free all-purpose baking flour

¼ teaspoon sea salt

3 tablespoons maple syrup

3 tablespoons pumpkin oil

½ cup raw pecans, crushed

1 **To make the filling:** preheat the oven to 400 degrees Fahrenheit. Add all filling ingredients to a 3-quart glass baking dish and mix well. Bake for 30 to 40 minutes.

2 **To make the crumble topping:** add all ingredients, except the raw pecans, to a medium bowl and mix until clumpy. Mix in the crushed pecans.

3 Top the fruit filling generously with crumble topping. Bake for an additional 10 minutes. Remove from the heat, plate it up, and enjoy!

JASON'S TIP

Serve this crisp with a generous scoop of vegan vanilla ice cream for the best à-la-mode dessert ever!

EGGPLANT STIR-FRY
WITH FORBIDDEN RICE

SERVES 4

THIS RECIPE WINS THE DARKEST STIR-FRY Veggie Bowl Ever Award. If this dish was a car, the color would be purple on purple. The stir-fried eggplant finds its perfect match in forbidden rice: a dense, smoky rice that is full of flavor. Forbidden rice has a deep black or purple color, which is an indication of its high antioxidant properties. Anthocyanin antioxidants have been correlated with helping to prevent cardiovascular disease that can be caused by free radical damage while also improving brain function and reducing inflammation. I love this recipe not only for the fantastic color and awesome health benefits but also for the textural contrast of the soft eggplant, chewy rice, and crunchy vegetables.

1 tablespoon organic virgin coconut oil

1 teaspoon ginger root, minced

2 cloves garlic, crushed

½ cup yellow onion, diced

2 pinches crushed red pepper flakes

2 pinches sea salt

1 large eggplant, diced (about 6 cups)

½ cup water

3 tablespoons coconut aminos

1 tablespoon maple syrup

1 tablespoon mirin

1 tablespoon fresh lime juice

½ teaspoon sesame oil

1 teaspoon arrowroot powder

1½ cups snow peas, sliced

¼ cup scallions, diced

4 cups cooked forbidden rice, reserved for plating

¼ cup cilantro, minced, reserved for plating

1 Heat the coconut oil in a skillet over medium heat. Once the oil is warmed up to medium heat, add the ginger, garlic, onion, and red pepper flakes. Sauté until the onions are translucent, about 3 to 4 minutes, then add the sea salt and eggplant and cook for 5 minutes. Add the water to the skillet, allowing the water to slowly cook the eggplant, about 10 minutes. Reduce the heat to low.

2 Whisk together the coconut aminos, maple syrup, mirin, lime juice, sesame oil, and arrowroot powder in a separate mixing bowl.

3 When the eggplant is nice and tender, add the sauce to the skillet and cook for an additional 3 minutes. Add the snow peas and scallions. Cook for another 3 minutes. Plate the stir-fry on top of the forbidden rice. Top with minced cilantro and enjoy!

CHILI
CON "CARNE"

IT'S AMAZING THAT YOU CAN CREATE a similar taste and texture to ground beef with a few sunflower seeds, pumpkin seeds, and some key spices. This magical, meat-free chili is simple, satisfying, and delicious on its own or as a filling in a lettuce wrap. This dish is also loaded with vitamin E, protein, and magnesium. The hearty pumpkin seeds offer a double whammy for brainpower: zinc for memory and thinking skills, and omega-3 fatty acids EPA and DHA, which also aid with memory and retention in aging brains. Bring a pot of this to your local chili cookout and blow everyone's minds—literally!

½ cup raw sunflower seeds

½ cup raw pumpkin seeds

2 tablespoons coconut aminos

2 large tomatoes, finely diced

1 jalapeno pepper, seeded and minced

2 teaspoons extra-virgin olive oil

1 teaspoon ground chipotle pepper

½ teaspoon garlic granules

Pinch sea salt

1 cup parsley, minced

1. Add the sunflower seeds and pumpkin seeds to a food processor and pulse a few times for a chunky consistency almost like that of ground beef. Transfer to a medium mixing bowl. Add the remaining ingredients and stir to combine well. While delicious served at room temperature, the flavors of this chili will meld together even more after a few hours in the refrigerator.

8

EAT FOR

MORE
MUSCLE

"SO, UH, WHERE DO YOU get your protein, bro?" Hey . . . guess what? 1979 called. They want their painfully obvious question back. Sarcasm aside for a moment, it's actually never been easier to bulk up and create lean, strong, lifelong muscle with plant-based foods. And it's never been more delicious or exciting with a ton of scrumptious, protein-rich recipes at the ready.

No matter what you choose to eat to help pump you up, it's clear that peeps here in the U.S. are getting way too much couch time and not nearly enough crouch time:

- Less than 5 percent of U.S. adults participate in 30 minutes of physical activity each day
- Only one in three adults receives the recommended amount of physical activity each week
- Only 35 to 44 percent of adults 75 years or older are physically active, and 28 to 34 percent of adults ages 65 to 74 are physically active

Eating habits aside for a moment, you're probably not working out or exercising enough. I know life is busy—but that's not an acceptable excuse anymore. We're ALL busy these days. If you're spending 60 minutes of your day watching cat videos on YouTube or *Game of Thrones*, you can carve out that much time to exercise. It's all a matter of getting clear about your priorities in life. No matter what you choose to eat, you've got to move your body on a daily basis. It's critically important to do this for your long-term health, mobility, and vitality. And protein will help you get there.

WHAT IS PROTEIN, ANYWAY?

Protein is basically a composite of a variety of different amino acids. Your body uses protein to build and repair tissues. You also use protein to make enzymes, hormones, and other body chemicals. Protein is an important building block of bones, muscles, cartilage, skin, and blood. Your hair and nails are mostly made of protein as well. Protein makes up the enzymes that power many chemical reactions and the hemoglobin that carries oxygen in your blood. At least 10,000 different proteins make you what you are and keep you that way.

The Institute of Medicine recommends that adults get a minimum of 0.8 grams of protein for every kilogram of body weight per day (or 8 grams of protein for every 20 pounds). They have also set a wide range for acceptable protein intake—anywhere from 10 to 35 percent of calories each day. Beyond that, there's relatively little solid information on the ideal amount of protein in the diet or the healthiest target for calories contributed by protein.

Around the world, millions of people don't get enough protein. Lack of protein can cause growth failure, loss of muscle mass, decreased immunity, weakening of the heart and respiratory system, and eventual death.

GET SUPER LEAN WITH L-GLUTAMINE

Nutritionally speaking, there are 11 "essential" amino acids that make a complete protein. However, there are many more amino acids that are fundamental in muscle building and recovery. The most notable "nonessential" amino acid in terms of athletic benefit is L-glutamine (glutamic acid), which helps to repair your muscles after a strenuous workout. It is, in fact, the most common amino acid in your muscles, making up 61 percent of your skeletal tissue. It is also one of the 20 total amino acids encoded by human genes. It's not considered one of the 11 "essential" amino acids, but it is absolutely indispensable during times of athletic training. When your body is depleted of L-glutamine during intense workouts, muscle wasting can occur. This can result in fatigue and slower recovery time. Healthy doses of L-glutamine reduce

recovery time, thereby enhancing your strength program by helping to repair your muscles quicker.

Make no mistake, L-glutamine is not a miracle cure for laziness or a shortcut to build big, rippling muscles, but it definitely enhances the positive results of your workout by giving your body much-needed amino acids for lean muscle growth and healthy cell maintenance. By assisting in cell hydration, your cell volume is enhanced, again reducing your recovery time. Muscle damage caused by intense workouts or injuries can be repaired much more effectively where cell volume and hydration levels are high. Supplementing your intake of L-glutamine can also increase your levels of naturally occurring human growth hormone (HGH). Higher levels of HGH increase the speed of your metabolism, which allows for more efficient processing and assimilation of foods and quicker metabolizing of fats. In turn, this can result in fat reduction and lean muscle building.

VEGANS ARE NOT THE UNDERDOG

I'd like to invite you into an episode of *MythBusters* for a moment so we can address the biggest, most unsubstantiated lie about healthy vegetarians or vegans: that they're weak, undernourished, scrawny little hippies with the complexion of a white stucco ceiling who've never seen a weight bench or squat rack in their lives. Please allow me to flatten this tired, old myth like a stack of silver-dollar pancakes.

With the amazing nutritional knowledge, athletic science, and healthy, protein-rich foods available to us en masse, it's never been easier to build big ol' Popeye pecs with a plant-based lifestyle. In fact, it's substantially healthier in the long run to use natural plant proteins to build and maintain muscle mass, as they're the only proteins that don't come with the artery-clogging fat, high cholesterol, and damaging acidity of animal proteins.

One of the biggest benefits of protein-rich plant foods such as tempeh, tofu, seitan, beans, lentils, and quinoa is that they are alkaline-forming proteins. This means that they are much easier for the body to assimilate and digest without any negative effects on the pH balance of your blood. People who rely on whey protein, dairy products, and animal flesh for their protein sources are consuming far too much acidic protein, which can potentially result in a variety of major health issues, including osteoporosis, liver damage, and kidney failure. When your body is unable to efficiently process all the excess acidic protein, it dumps it down into your endocrine and excretory systems for processing and disposal. So many competitive bodybuilders have overtaxed their bodies from too much acidic animal protein that their organs start to fail them, most notably their kidneys. High-protein, animal product–rich diets and anabolic steroid use are the two primary reasons why bodybuilders can be at an increased risk for kidney disease.

WORKOUT VARIETY FOR LIFELONG VITALITY

In addition to healthy nutrition choices, the other pillar of your body temple is to consistently challenge your muscles with weight-bearing exercise. Whether you choose calisthenics, interval training, or good, old-fashioned weight lifting, you need to challenge your muscles to be strong, flexible, and lean for the rest of your life. Cardiovascular workouts like running and swimming do not provide enough resistance training to sustain lifelong muscle mass and strength. It's important to create a balance of aerobic training and anaerobic training.

Both anaerobic and aerobic workouts are useful in their own ways. Each creates a different body composition because of the variety of hormones released in the body. The style of athletic training you choose

largely depends upon what you are trying to accomplish with your body. High-intensity, strength-building anaerobic workouts burn mainly glycogen (sugar) while you are doing them. However, they create a unique hormone balance a few hours after you finish them. After you complete an intense anaerobic workout, your levels of testosterone, human growth hormone, epinephrine, and norepinephrine are elevated. This powerful hormone cocktail creates a phenomenal balance that favors muscle building and fat burning for several hours after your workout (assuming you combine this with great nutrition). If you are looking for increased lean muscle mass, anaerobic workouts are the best place to start. For most people, consistent anaerobic training creates a harder, more sculpted, muscular look to the body. A good example here would be the body of a sprinter or gymnast.

Researchers have been finding lately that the benefits of weight-bearing exercise continue well into old age. In one clever experiment, scientists at the Buck Institute for Age Research put 25 healthy older adults on a six-month weight training regimen that increased their muscle strength by 50 percent. The researchers measured the activity of genes in the muscles before and after the training. Before the training, the work of hundreds of genes involved in energy metabolism had diminished from those of young adults. After training, many had been restored to their youthful levels. The researchers concluded last year that the training had partly reversed the aging process.

If performed at a slow enough pace, aerobic workouts will burn fat for fuel once all of your glycogen stores (sugar) are depleted. Aerobic training methods will burn fat quickly for many people and are great practices to get lean. In addition, aerobic workouts are a wonderful way to build lung capacity and have demonstrated beneficial effects for heart health. However, there are two concerns with relying on this type of training exclusively. First, you do not get the same increase in muscle-building hormones as you do with anaerobic training. What's more, if done for long periods, cardiovasclar training has the potential to decrease your metabolism and melt away your muscle mass through down-regulating fat-burning and muscle-building hormones such as leptin, testosterone, and key thyroid hormones. Generally speaking, focusing exclusively on cardio workouts creates a leaner but softer appearance for your body with less muscle mass. A good example here would be the slighter frame of a long-distance or marathon runner.

THE GREAT BARLEY EATERS

The legendary Roman gladiators were subjected to strict training regimens, hours of physically exhausting tasks, and, as a reward, they battled each other to the death. And you thought your phys ed classes in high school were hellish! Interestingly, instead of eating a diet rich in animal-based protein like modern athletes do, recent evidence suggests that the gladiators did otherwise. Historic sources and ancient texts report that gladiators had their own unique diet comprising beans and grains, and they have been referred to as *hordearii* or "barley eaters." The phrase "barley eater" relates to the fact that gladiators were probably given grains of inferior quality. Research from MedUni in Vienna, which analyzed bones found in a 2nd-century Roman cemetery, has confirmed these claims. The findings also suggested that the gladiators' meals were washed down with a vinegar and plant ash drink to give them energy, a rudimentary form of ancient sports drink or "gladiator Gatorade," if you will.

THE INCOMPLETE PROTEIN MYTH

Back in 1971, a vegetarian manifesto called *Diet for a Small Planet* by influential author Frances Moore Lappé inadvertently started a nutritional myth that persists to this day. In the book, she states that vegetarians need to combine multiple plant ingredients like rice and beans to create complete proteins. Now, that made total sense considering the nutritional knowledge that was available at the time. Most beans are low in methionine and high in lysine, while brown rice is low in lysine and high in methionine. Mash 'em up, and whatcha got? Protein levels on par with those in meat. Not to mention one of the simplest, cheapest, and most eco-friendly meals in existence.

Lappé certainly meant no harm by her assertion, and her mistake was somewhat understandable. She was not a nutritionist, physiologist, or medical doctor. She was simply a sociologist trying to end world hunger. She realized that converting vegetable protein into animal protein created a ton of waste and deduced that if people just ate the plant protein, many more human beings could be fed. In a later edition of her book from 1991, she retracted her statement and basically said that in trying to end one myth—that world hunger was inevitable and unsolvable—she created a second one: the myth of the need for "protein complementing."

By correcting her original assertion, she clearly states that many plant foods typically consumed as sources of protein contain all of the essential amino acids and that human beings are virtually certain of getting enough protein from plant sources if they consume a sufficient variety and number of calories. Getting all of your essential amino acids, and therefore complete proteins, on a vegetarian or vegan diet is a piece of cake and does not require strict food combining principles. Plus, there are so many delicious vegan and raw protein powders on the market with more than enough protein per scoop to satisfy the requirements of most fitness aficionados.

What it really boils down to is this: you can get high levels of protein from a variety of sources, both plant and animal based. However, you want to ensure that your body maximizes the full spectrum of benefits from protein by consuming natural foods that are easy to digest and are readily available to rebuild muscle with no deleterious effects on blood or organ health. You want to maximize your nutritional gains and minimize your losses. The most sustainable way to accomplish this goal for healthy, lifelong fitness is to choose a protein-rich, nutrient-dense, highly alkaline, plant-based diet.

TESTOSTERONE: NATURE'S STEROIDS AND VIAGRA IN ONE!

Testosterone is the primary hormone involved in muscle building. It fuels our willpower, our sex drive, and our stamina. It's the thing that makes us want to make babies, conquer our enemies, and bang our chests like primordial beasts (sounds like a killer house party, right?). As men age, it's crucial to maintain healthy testosterone levels. As we learned earlier, a man's testosterone levels begin to decline at around 30 and continue to do so as he ages, leading to symptoms such as decreased sex drive, erectile dysfunction, depressed mood, and difficulties with concentration and memory. Typically, men lose about one percent of their testosterone per year after age 40. Luckily, there are some solid lifestyle strategies (and natural foods) to help keep testosterone flowing strong to fuel those biceps.

Dietary and exercise changes—particularly limiting high doses of sugar or fructose, eating healthy, plant-based saturated fats, and engaging in high-intensity exercises and strength training—can be very effective at boosting testosterone levels naturally. Other strategies to boost testosterone include optimizing your vitamin D and zinc levels, increasing your intake of branch-chain amino acids (BCAAs), and reducing stress.

If you're concerned about your testosterone levels, you'll want to get them tested. The test results from your doctor will most likely reflect "overall" testosterone—the combined total of all the forms of it that you have in your body, including molecules that are bound to sex hormone binding globulin (SHBG), those that are bound into a protein called albumin, and the "free" testosterone that isn't bound to anything. The molecules bound into either SHBG or albumin are not readily available to your body, so you could say that the bound testosterone is kept in a reserve or "bank." Your free testosterone circulates in your veins and can be instantly utilized by your body, which makes it very effective. Free testosterone is responsible for supporting all of the following functions: sexual stamina, increased muscle growth, rapid fat loss, deeper voice, aggressive behavior, energy, confidence, motivation, and just being an overall badass.

Here's the takeaway: your test results might show very high levels of total testosterone, but on average, your free testosterone makes up only around 2 percent of the total available for use while the rest is bound by SHBG or albumin. So, the real trick to having superhuman levels of free testosterone in your bloodstream is to lower your overall SHBG levels. This leaves you with less reserve testosterone; however, the higher level of free testosterone can be quickly used by your body in high-intensity situations.

To lower SHBG and increase free testosterone, I recommend consuming higher levels of boron, magnesium, zinc, omega-3 fatty acids, and vitamin D. Also, eating more complex carbohydrates from whole grains will help, as will eliminating your consumption of alcohol and over-the-counter drugs such as statins, beta-blockers, antifungals, antidepressants, and hair loss medications.

TOP TESTOSTERONE BOOSTERS

Now, to get really serious about increasing testosterone, there are some magical ingredients out there that can bump it up so you can pump it up. Personally, I've experimented with a variety of natural foods and supplements and found a pretty substantial increase from pumpkin seeds, Brazil nuts, pine pollen, maca powder, cistanche (that libido-boosting Chinese herb), PQQ, extra-virgin, raw coconut oil, a vegan protein powder with BCAAs, and tribulus terrestris (a potent Ayurvedic herb). These are all superfood supplements you can easily add into your smoothies, workout shakes, and tonics, or just take them straight up by the spoonful. However, it's really easy to overdo them if you start with too high a dose. I learned pretty quickly that moderate amounts turned me into a snarling beast. The feeling of invincibility and all-conquering vigor is great for the gym and the bedroom, but can quickly bleed over into a natural "roid rage" if your testosterone levels are boosted too quickly. I recommend that you engage in conscious experimentation and moderation with any kind of performance-enhancing natural products, preferably under the supervision of a natural-health professional or medical doctor who can accurately test your hormone levels.

HULK UP YOUR GAME WITH HUMAN GROWTH HORMONE AND FASTING

Human growth hormone (HGH) is a peptide that accelerates growth during puberty. After puberty, HGH plays a key role in muscle growth, fat burning, and libido. Along with the aforementioned testosterone, HGH is one of the most anabolic hormones in the human body. When both of these hormones are peaking, you'll likely experience optimal performance, strength, and vitality, especially if you're a guy.

Many bodybuilders inject themselves with testosterone and HGH because it's easily the fastest way to gain lean muscle mass and simultaneously burn fat in a short time. However, these steroids create a macabre array of side effects when taken in synthetic,

unnatural forms. What most people don't realize is that you can easily tweak these hormones naturally. They believe that you can't have a significant increase in either one of them without injections or steroids and that you'll just have to settle with your genetics. But I'm calling bullcrap on this one. In fact, there's one incredible and ancient way to boost your HGH naturally: fasting.

A landmark study from the Department of Internal Medicine at the University of Virginia Medical School demonstrated a direct correlation between intermittent fasting and a significant increase in HGH levels. Researchers worked with six perfectly healthy male subjects ranging from 21 to 36 years old who fasted for five days as their growth hormone levels were closely monitored. What they discovered was just incredible. HGH levels peaked to as high as 2,000 percent from the baseline right at the 24-hour mark of the first day!

In addition to intermittent fasting, there are specific foods you can eat to boost your HGH levels naturally. Personally, I'll fast on my rest days for up to 24 hours and eat specific foods on my heavy-lifting days at the gym to keep my HGH peaking. But first, here's a little secret: natural, melatonin-rich foods can help boost HGH by up to 157 percent! When I'm rockin' a pre-gym breakfast or post-workout meal, I eat foods like goji berries, raspberries, pineapple, fava beans, non-GMO tempeh, coconut yogurt, and raw, extra-virgin coconut oil (which also has the added benefit of fat-burning medium-chain triglycerides!).

It's a good idea to experiment with intermittent fasting and HGH-boosting foods for yourself, especially if one of your goals is to build lean muscle for a lifetime. Start slow, try new foods and different fasting periods, keep a journal of how your body feels and of fluctuations in your strength or energy levels—and you'll unlock the magic combination to unleash your inner Incredible Hulk in no time . . . but without the weird, fluorescent green skin!

MY TOP MUSCLE-BUILDING NUTRIENTS

Creatine: Helps to supply energy to all cells in the body, primarily muscle.

Essential amino acids: Amino acids are the building blocks for protein. Our bodies naturally synthesize most of our amino acids, but there are eight that we need to outsource through food, making them "essential."

Fiber: Muscle is lined with insulin receptors, and fiber helps to stabilize insulin response, making it easier to build muscle.

Vitamin K: Supports the function of amino acids (protein) during their conversion into muscle.

Zinc: Aids in the synthesis of DNA and protein activity, which are both essential for muscle growth and development.

MY TOP MUSCLE-BUILDING FOODS

- alkaline protein powders (made from amaranth, brown rice, chia, coconut, cranberry, hemp, pea, or sacha inchi)
- apples
- arnica
- bananas
- beans
- blue-green algae
- bok choy
- broccoli
- brown rice
- bulbine natalensis
- cashews
- cauliflower
- chia seeds
- chickpeas
- chlorella
- coconut oil
- coconut yogurt
- fava beans
- goji berries
- hemp seeds
- Jamaica dogwood
- kale
- lentils
- pineapple
- probiotics
- raspberries
- quinoa
- spinach
- spirulina
- sweet potatoes
- tongkat ali
- tribulus terrestris

RECIPES
TO BUILD MORE
MUSCLE

· · · · · · · · · · · · · · ·

HIGH-PROTEIN PROBIOTIC
SUPERFOOD SALAD

PEOPLE EXPECT HIGH-PROTEIN VEGAN MEALS TO be relegated to main courses, grain bowls, pasta dishes, or faux meats—rarely do people pump up a salad with protein-rich ingredients. Not only is the flavor of this recipe complex and dynamic, it's full of highly assimilable plant protein from hemp seeds, chlorella, and spirulina. Speaking of spirulina, it's composed of up to 71 percent protein, and has all essential amino acids, including muscle-building branch-chain amino acids (BCAAs). With this powerhouse dish, you've got salty, sweet, creamy, crunchy, and dense textures and flavors doing the taste bud tango. It's like you're the guest host of *Dancing with the Salad Stars*.

2 large handfuls arugula

3 tomatoes, diced

1 medium cucumber, diced

1 avocado, pitted and diced

¼ cup pumpkin seeds

¼ teaspoon sea salt

¼ cup pitted black olives

3 tablespoons extra-virgin olive oil

2 tablespoons hemp seeds

2 tablespoons spirulina powder

1 tablespoon chlorella powder

4 ounces cultured vegan cheese, crumbled (optional)

1 lemon, juiced

1 handful fresh basil leaves, torn by hand

1 Place all ingredients into a large salad bowl and mix well to combine.

JASON'S TIP

The best brand of vegan cheese I've found for this recipe is Dr. Cow Aged Cashew and Blue Green Algae. It's the closest thing I've found to dairy-free blue cheese.

BREAKFAST BOWL

SERVES 2

WHEN OATMEAL BOREDOM STRIKES, SEND IN the quinoa for breakfast duty. This protein-rich wonder is the perfect vehicle for a bevy of superfoods to help get your morning moving. Although technically a seed (most think it's a grain), quinoa contains a complete set of branch-chain and essential amino acids, making it a tissue- and muscle-building powerhouse. This dish is hearty, sweet, crunchy, and really easy to digest. It's also easily portable, so you can take it on the go—eat it in the car, at your desk, or right after your workout to "feed the beast."

1 cup dry quinoa

2 cups filtered water

¼ cup cacao nibs

¼ cup raw jungle peanuts

¼ cup goldenberries

½ teaspoon ground vanilla bean

1 teaspoon maca powder

1 tablespoon hemp seeds

¼ cup goji berries

¼ teaspoon mangosteen powder (optional)

1 teaspoon vegan vanilla protein powder

1 tablespoon organic virgin coconut oil

⅛ teaspoon sea salt

Coconut, hemp, or almond milk, to taste

Gluten-free granola, to taste, reserved for garnish

1 In a medium saucepan, add the quinoa and filtered water and bring to a simmer. Cook for 10 to 15 minutes, until all the liquid is absorbed. Fluff with a fork and set aside.

2 Transfer the cooked quinoa to a medium mixing bowl and combine with all remaining ingredients, except for the coconut milk and granola. Mix well. Top with coconut milk and granola to your liking.

BANANA BAOBAB
PROTEIN SHAKE

SF GF RA OF NF

THIS IS YOUR BASIC, SQUARE-ONE PROTEIN smoothie. It's quick, dirty, delicious, and sweet. Bananas give you a big dose of potassium, almonds provide a B-vitamin boost, and hemp seeds are packed with 11 grams of protein per three tablespoons. Plus, the baobab powder, made from a nutrient-dense African fruit, supplies your body with a slew of beneficial minerals including calcium, copper, iron, magnesium, and zinc. These minerals act both individually and synergistically to perform hundreds of beneficial tasks in your body. Blend this sucker up and suck it down like the magical monkey you are (a cute, furry, cuddly monkey, of course)!

4 cups almond milk

6 large bananas, peeled

¼ cup plus 2 tablespoons vegan vanilla protein powder

1 tablespoon baobab powder

3 tablespoons hemp seeds

¾ teaspoon stevia powder

1 teaspoon ground vanilla bean

2 tablespoons chia seeds

10 ice cubes

1 Blend all ingredients in a high-speed blender for 40 seconds until smooth and frothy.

BUCKWHEAT
BREAKFAST BARS

SERVES 4 TO 6

THESE BARS ARE BURSTING WITH BODACIOUS buckwheat and will be the blessing to cure your breakfast boredom, baby. I got burnt out on my same ol' morning smoothies one day and enlisted the help of The Alchemist Chef to help give birth to these bad boys. In addition to the protein-rich hemp and chia seeds, the buckwheat in this recipe boasts a powerful chemical called d-chiro-inositol, which increases sensitivity to insulin and normalizes glucose levels. This can help get more glucose, amino acids, and creatine into your muscle cells after training. These bars are awesome as a quick breakfast or satisfying snack during seriously busy days.

½ cup raw buckwheat groats, soaked

¼ cup chia seeds

¼ cup dried mango, chopped

¼ cup raw sprouted pumpkin seeds

2 tablespoons hemp seeds

2 tablespoons cacao nibs

2 tablespoons goji berries

½ cup dried figs, chopped

½ teaspoon sea salt

½ teaspoon ground cinnamon

1 cup raw sunflower seeds

½ cup coconut nectar

1 Add all ingredients, except sunflower seeds and coconut nectar, to a large bowl and mix until well combined.

2 Blend the sunflower seeds and coconut nectar in a high-speed blender or food processor for about 20 seconds or until you get a sticky, dense, buttery, and smooth paste.

3 Add sunflower–coconut nectar mixture to the buckwheat mixture and mix with your hands until evenly coated. Press into an 8 x 10-inch glass baking dish and refrigerate for 1 hour.

4 Using a knife and an offset spatula, cut into rectangular bars. You may also use a cookie cutter for fun shapes. The bars will last for up to five days in the fridge.

SPROUTED
QUINOA TABOULI SALAD

SERVES 2

TABOULI IS A MIDDLE EASTERN STAPLE that is usually made with bulgur wheat. By substituting quinoa and hemp seeds in the recipe, you have a gluten-free, super high-protein version that features all the fresh vegetables and herbs of the traditional version. This salad goes great with hummus, grape leaves, and veggie kabobs or can be eaten by itself for a quick lunch option.

2 cups dry quinoa, sprouted overnight

½ cup hemp seeds

½ cup extra-virgin olive oil

½ lemon, juiced

½ cup red onion, minced

1 medium cucumber, diced

2 cups tomato, diced

2 teaspoons sea salt

1 teaspoon ground cumin

¼ teaspoon cayenne pepper

1 cup minced parsley, plus more for garnish

½ lemon, cut into wedges, reserved for garnish

1 Cover the dry quinoa with water and soak overnight to sprout it. You will see little white tails on the quinoa seeds when they're sprouted. Drain the quinoa and transfer to a large mixing bowl.

2 Add the remaining ingredients and gently mix to combine well. Garnish with additional minced parsley and a fresh lemon wedge.

SOMETIMES YOU HAVE TO GET CREATIVE to disguise the good stuff, especially for kids. These bodacious bliss balls are basically protein-filled chocolate cannonballs thanks to spirulina, almonds, and pumpkin seeds. This supercharged snack is also full of B vitamins, omega fatty acids, and magnesium. These easy-to-make chocolate salty balls are the perfect portable meal replacement you can take to the gym, the office, or even on an impromptu road trip.

1 cup raw almonds

1 cup dates, pitted

¼ cup raw almond butter

¼ cup pumpkin seeds

¼ cup green raisins, soaked for 10 minutes

1½ tablespoons golden flaxseed, soaked for 10 minutes

1½ tablespoons raw cacao powder

1½ teaspoons spirulina powder

¼ teaspoon ground cinnamon

⅛ teaspoon ground cardamom

½ teaspoon vanilla extract

Pinch sea salt

1 Add the almonds and dates to a food processor and process to a mealy consistency. Transfer to a mixing bowl along with the rest of the ingredients. Mix with your hands until the ingredients are well combined. Divide into 9 or 10 pieces and roll into balls. Serve.

JASON'S TIP

If you want to get really fancy, you can roll your chocolate balls in shredded coconut or crushed nuts or top them with a pinch of sea salt. Put them in the refrigerator for at least 30 minutes to get extra firm. For some additional crunchiness, they can be baked at 300 degrees Fahrenheit for 15 to 20 minutes.

CAULIFLOWER PARSNIP MASH
WITH SWEDISH "NEATBALLS"

THIS DISH IS A HEALTHIER, MORE flavorful and complex version of the famous bargain meal you can find at the well-known discount furniture store from Sweden. The "neatballs" are made with seitan, a low-carb, high-protein "wheat meat" that lends a fantastic meaty texture and flavor. The cauliflower is rich in the mineral boron, which aids in building muscle and increasing free testosterone levels. When you taste the creamy, smooth texture and sweet flavor of the mash, you may never partake of regular mashed potatoes again.

CAULIFLOWER PARSNIP MASH:

2 medium heads of cauliflower, separated into 1-inch florets

4 medium parsnips, peeled and sliced into 1-inch pieces

2 cups low-sodium vegetable broth

1 bunch kale, roughly chopped

4 cloves garlic, minced

3 teaspoons fresh finely chopped thyme

¼ cup to ½ cup coconut milk

Pinch sea salt, to taste

Pinch black pepper, to taste

½ cup fresh finely chopped parsley

1 **To make the Cauliflower Parsnip Mash:** preheat the oven to 400 degrees Fahrenheit.

2 Combine the cauliflower, parsnips, and vegetable broth in a 13 x 9-inch glass baking dish. Cover with aluminum foil and bake for 30 minutes or until the vegetables are fork tender, tossing halfway through the cooking time.

3 Fill a medium saucepan fitted with a steamer basket with 2 inches of water. Add the kale to the basket and bring the water to a boil. Reduce the heat to low, cover the saucepan, and steam the kale for 10 minutes. When the kale is steamed, set it aside for plating.

4 Drain the cauliflower and parsnips and transfer to a food processor. Add the garlic and thyme and pulse a few times. Gradually add 1 tablespoon of coconut milk at a time and pulse until the consistency is very smooth, thick, and whipped. Season with salt and pepper to taste and garnish with fresh minced parsley. Serve over steamed kale.

SWEDISH "NEATBALLS":

1 tablespoon plus 1 teaspoon extra-virgin olive oil, plus more for the pan

1½ tablespoons ground flaxseed

⅓ cup warm water

Two 8-ounce packages seitan

½ cup raw walnuts

½ cup finely diced onion

2 cloves garlic, finely minced

½ cup bread crumbs

¼ cup finely chopped parsley

¼ teaspoon ground allspice

¼ teaspoon ground nutmeg

¼ teaspoon ground cardamom

¼ teaspoon ground pepper

1 teaspoon coconut aminos

MUSHROOM GRAVY:

1 tablespoon extra-virgin olive oil

1 cup finely diced onion

2 cloves garlic, minced

2 heaping cups diced crimini mushrooms

3 tablespoons coconut aminos

2 cups coconut milk

¼ teaspoon ground allspice

¼ teaspoon ground nutmeg

5 tablespoons spelt or gluten-free all-purpose flour

½ cup filtered water

Pinch sea salt, to taste

Pinch fresh ground pepper, to taste

5 **To make the Swedish "Neatballs":** preheat the oven to 400 degrees Fahrenheit.

6 Grease a 13 x 9-inch glass baking dish with olive oil. Whisk the ground flaxseed in warm water and set aside.

7 Pulse the seitan in a food processor until you achieve a ground-beef consistency. Add the walnuts and pulse to blend.

8 Heat 1 teaspoon of the olive oil in a large nonstick pan over medium heat. Cook the onions for 2 minutes, then add the garlic and sauté for another minute. Stir in the seitan and walnut mixture and sauté for another 3 to 4 minutes. Transfer to a medium mixing bowl and combine with the bread crumbs, parsley, spices, remaining 1 tablespoon of olive oil, coconut aminos, and ground flax-water mixture.

9 Roll into 20 to 24 small balls, making sure they are round, firm, and smooth. Transfer to the greased baking dish and bake for 20 to 25 minutes, turning halfway through until nicely browned. Serve with Cauliflower Mash and Mushroom Gravy.

10 **To make the Mushroom Gravy:** heat the olive oil over medium heat in a medium saucepan. Add the onions and cook for 5 minutes, or until they begin to soften. Add the garlic and mushrooms and sauté for about 3 minutes. Add the coconut aminos, coconut milk, allspice, and nutmeg, and bring to a high simmer but do not boil, stirring frequently.

11 Mix the flour and water in a small bowl to create a smooth paste. Slowly add to saucepan. Cook until thickened, about 3 to 4 minutes. Season with salt and pepper and then reduce the heat and cook for another 5 to 6 minutes. Serve with Swedish "Neatballs" and Cauliflower Mash.

JASON'S TIP

These neatballs are also great sliced and served cold as the filling in a sandwich.

CAULIFLOWER LENTIL TACOS
WITH FRESH GUACAMOLE

SERVES 4 TO 6

THIS DISH WAS THE ABSOLUTE MOST popular recipe from my TV series on Cooking Channel. People went absolutely nuts for these tacos, and it's easy to see why. The lentils and cauliflower team up to form the ground "meat" in this dish with authentic Mexican spices. In fact, lentils are a triple threat for fitness. They're packed with 18 grams of protein and 16 grams of fiber per cup along with low-impact, slow-digesting carbohydrates. The perfectly creamy guacamole and fresh fixings will make even the most ardent meathead do a straight-up double take after the very first bite.

GUACAMOLE:

6 ripe avocados, pitted and diced

1½ cups diced red onion

1 to 3 medium-size jalapeno peppers, to taste, stemmed, seeded, and minced

¼ cup plus 2 tablespoons fresh cilantro, finely chopped

¼ cup fresh lime juice

1½ teaspoons sea salt

¾ teaspoon ground cumin

Pinch ground black pepper, to taste

Pinch cayenne pepper, to taste (optional)

1½ ripe medium tomatoes, seeds and pulp removed, diced

CAULIFLOWER LENTIL TACO "MEAT":

1 cup green or brown lentils

3 cups filtered water

1 head cauliflower, stems and leaves removed, broken into 1-inch pieces

2 tablespoons extra-virgin olive oil

2 medium yellow onions, diced (about 1½ cups)

1 jalapeno pepper, seeded and minced

4 cloves minced garlic

4 teaspoons chili powder, divided

2 teaspoons ground cumin, divided

1 teaspoon ground coriander, divided

½ cup canned or homemade tomato sauce

1½ teaspoons salt, or to taste

½ teaspoon ground pepper, or to taste

One 5.5-ounce package organic taco shells

4 cups shredded romaine lettuce, reserved for topping

1 **To make the guacamole:** mash the avocados in a medium bowl until slightly chunky. Add the onion, jalapenos, cilantro, lime juice, salt, cumin, pepper, and cayenne, then mash the mixture some more.

2 Cover with plastic wrap directly on the surface of the guacamole to prevent oxidation. Refrigerate until chilled, about an hour. Just before serving, add the tomatoes to the guacamole and gently mix.

3 **To make the Cauliflower Lentil Taco "Meat":** rinse and drain the lentils thoroughly. Add the lentils to a medium saucepan. Add the filtered water and bring to a boil. Reduce the heat to low and simmer until tender, about 30 minutes. Drain.

4 Pulse the cauliflower into rice-size pieces in a high-speed food processor. Heat the olive oil in a large skillet over medium heat. Cook the onion and jalapeno until the onion is translucent, about 5 to 7 minutes. Add the cauliflower rice, garlic, 2 teaspoons of the chili powder, 1 teaspoon of the ground cumin, and ½ teaspoon of the ground coriander, and cook for 4 minutes. Stir in the tomato sauce and cook another 3 to 4 minutes or until the cauliflower is tender.

5 Add the cooked lentils, the remaining 2 teaspoons of chili powder, 1 teaspoon of ground cumin, ½ teaspoon of ground coriander, and the salt and pepper. Cook for an additional 3 minutes.

6 Scoop the Cauliflower Lentil Taco "Meat" into the taco shells and top with shredded romaine lettuce and a dollop of guacamole. Serve immediately.

With its hearty, chunky consistency, the Cauliflower Lentil Taco "Meat" can also be served as a side dish with refried beans, guacamole, or salsa.

ARROZ Y FRIJOLES. RICE AND BEANS. No matter what you call it, this old-school dish was a staple of my childhood and the simple, delicious Puerto Rican recipes my mom would make. This reinterpretation of the classic dish is a moving palette where you can use your favorite beans, fresh vegetables, and spices as you desire. As is, this recipe is pretty dynamite. Plus, it's a prime-time muscle builder. Beans are a highly nutritious source of both protein and fiber. Fiber is essential to maintaining a proper insulin response, which is critical to muscle growth, as it aids in the absorption and use of various nutrients and supplements. What's more, the average bean has 15 grams of protein per cup. Never ignore the power of the bean to stay lean and mean!

2 cups cooked brown rice

1 small onion, chopped

1 celery stalk, chopped

1 small green bell pepper, chopped

½ small jalapeno pepper, minced

1 tablespoon extra-virgin olive oil

1 clove garlic, minced

½ teaspoon chili powder

½ teaspoon ground cumin

¼ teaspoon sea salt

¼ teaspoon ground black pepper

1 large tomato, chopped

One 14-ounce can pinto or black beans, drained and rinsed

½ cup low-sodium vegetable broth

¼ cup fresh cilantro, minced

1 Cook the brown rice according to the directions on the package, as they may vary depending on the varietal. Sauté the onions, celery, green peppers, and jalapenos in a large saucepan over medium-high heat with olive oil. Cook until the onions are translucent. Add the garlic, chili powder, cumin, salt, and pepper, and sauté for an additional 1 to 3 minutes.

2 Add the tomato, beans, and vegetable broth. Bring to a boil and then reduce the heat. Simmer for 10 to 15 minutes. Turn off the heat and stir in the cilantro. Cover with the lid and let sit for 5 minutes before serving over a bed of brown rice.

ORANGE GLAZED
TEMPEH

I REALLY MISS THE TASTE OF orange chicken sometimes. Honestly, I do. The vegan version I used to order at Red Star Restaurant in my hometown, Detroit, was the bomb diggity, boy. Nothing better than eating a plate of that after band practice back in the day. I got a mad craving one day and decided to make my own healthy version with glazed tempeh. A 4-ounce serving of tempeh provides an average of 19 grams of super-digestible soy protein. Because tempeh is a fermented soy product, its enzymes are partially broken down, making it easier to metabolize. It does not produce the unpleasant gastrointestinal discomfort and gas that some other soy proteins sometimes do. The flavor of this dish is really yummy and hits that elusive sweet, savory, and crunchy spot that needs to be satisfied . . . or else!

3 cups cooked rice

1 teaspoon extra-virgin olive oil

2 cloves garlic, minced

1 teaspoon ginger root, peeled and minced

One 8-ounce package tempeh, diced small

1 cup fresh orange juice

2 teaspoons coconut aminos

2 teaspoons white vinegar

2 teaspoons maple syrup

½ teaspoon ground black pepper

1 lime, cut into wedges, reserved for garnish

¼ cup cilantro, minced, reserved for garnish

1 teaspoon black sesame seeds, reserved for garnish

1. Cook your favorite rice according to the directions on the box.

2. Heat the olive oil in a large skillet over medium heat. Add the garlic, ginger, and tempeh cubes and cook for 5 to 10 minutes, until the tempeh is slightly golden brown. Add the remaining ingredients; stir and cook for an additional 15 minutes or until most of the liquid is absorbed and a sauce remains on the tempeh.

3. Transfer the cooked rice to two small bowls and spoon a generous amount of the cooked tempeh on top. Garnish with the fresh lime, cilantro, and black sesame seeds.

BLACK BEAN
VEGGIE BURGERS

SERVES 8

CRAFTING THE PERFECT VEGGIE BURGER IS an art in itself. This bastion of health food has endured many iterations and variations over the years, and yet, I always go back to a familiar combination: black beans, quinoa, potato, corn, and carrot. These badass burgers are full of complete protein, B vitamins, vitamin A, and dietary fiber—all of which are essential for muscle growth and nutrient absorption. Not to mention, their dense, meaty texture and hearty flavor will have burger aficionados giving you serious props on these patties.

One 15-ounce can black beans, drained and rinsed

1 cup quinoa, cooked

1 carrot, peeled and grated

2 small potatoes, peeled and grated

½ cup corn kernels, cooked

2-inch piece leek, finely chopped

1 clove garlic, minced

1 teaspoon ground cumin

½ teaspoon ground paprika

⅛ teaspoon cayenne pepper

¼ teaspoon sea salt

¼ teaspoon ground black pepper

2 tablespoons extra-virgin olive oil

8 gluten-free hamburger buns

1 tomato, sliced into rounds, reserved for plating

½ red onion, sliced into rounds, reserved for plating

2 cups romaine lettuce, torn by hand, reserved for plating

½ cup ketchup, reserved for plating

¼ cup yellow mustard, reserved for plating

¼ cup vegan mayonnaise, reserved for plating

½ cup pickle slices, reserved for plating

1 Transfer about a third of the black beans to a large bowl and lightly mash with a fork. Add the quinoa, carrot, potatoes, corn, leek, garlic, cumin, paprika, cayenne, sea salt, and black pepper, and mix well. The bean mixture should be somewhat sticky. Divide the bean mixture into 8 pieces, roll into balls, and flatten to make patties.

2 Heat the olive oil in a nonstick frying pan. Fry the patties, flipping occasionally, until cooked through with a nice brown coloring on both sides, about 3 to 4 minutes on each side.

3 Serve patties on burger buns topped with tomato, onion, romaine lettuce, ketchup, mustard, mayonnaise, and pickles.

 JASON'S TIP

Top with sliced avocado for some healthy fats, or give your burger an extra kick with some pickled jalapeno peppers!

9

EAT

FOR

IMMUNITY

GERMS, BACTERIA, AND VIRUSES ARE everywhere—planes, trains, and automobiles; escalators; babies; hotel room phones; remote controls—you name it. One thing's for sure: you're always eligible for a license to ill in the modern world. From flesh-eating viruses to nuclear fallout to the common cold, the world is full of malicious maladies that can potentially annihilate you, if not render you snot nosed and fully horizontal for days on end.

Okay, so maybe I'm being a bit dramatic. But really, how do you combat these potential threats to your vitality on a daily basis?

The good news is that you have a powerful defense system inside of you that's perfectly designed to protect you and keep your body in a balanced state of homeostasis. Yes, your immune system is like nature's NORAD missile defense system, launching rockets of white blood cells to annihilate marauding toxins, viruses, and pathogens. Here's the key, though: your immune system needs your help to function at the peak of its powers. And how to create a killer immunity arsenal is what this chapter is all about!

Now, I know what it's like to get the faintest hint of a sniffle and run out to snag some Sudafed at the drugstore. But, if medications and pharmaceuticals were the answer, how is it possible that people spend billions of dollars on drugs and still get sick? People aren't finding solutions—they're just waiting around for the next time they get sick. Check it out:

- Seasonal cough and cold medication generates $8 billion annually
- U.S. adults get an average of two to four colds every year
- Young children suffer from an average of six to eight colds per year

Be honest—how many times a year do YOU get sick? I don't mean seasonal allergies—I mean a full-on cold, flu, or other common debilitating sickness, like food poisoning. If you're getting sick multiple times a year, then it's time to get the full download about your immune system and how you can supercharge its performance. Because taking a week off from work or school, slurping down a bowl of canned chicken noodle soup, and dosing yourself on a bottle of NyQuil ain't doing the job anymore. But, honestly, did it ever?

YOUR IMMUNE SYSTEM IS PRETTY BADASS

Your immune system is just like any other bodily system. In order for it to function at full capacity all the time, it needs the right kind of fuel to boost its superpowers. One of the keys to supporting your healthy immune function is to know which foods and nutrients to consume. For example, if you're looking to ward off viruses, something like olive leaf extract is great. If you want to manhandle marauding microbes, then raw coconut oil is your frontline warlord. For general immune boosting throughout the year, high doses of vitamins C and D will rock out and knock out a common cold. Much like the entire theme of this book, it's critically important to select the right ingredients to accomplish the goal of keeping your immune system humming along. In simple terms, we can look at this approach in two distinct ways: learning what to eat to keep your immunity consistently strong to ward off potential sickness and the correct protocol to follow when you're already feeling like a pupu platter and want to feel better fast.

Most people find that the wintertime is when most maladies strike. But it is possible to shield yourself to some degree with strong immunity. Keeping your immune system running efficiently is a matter of consistently good lifestyle choices and eating a balanced intake of the proper nutrients that ensure that your body gets rid of toxins.

GET YOUR LYMPHATIC SYSTEM BACK IN THE FLOW

Your lymphatic system can be compared to the 405 Freeway in Los Angeles. When it's congested, nothing moves. The same thing can happen in your body. Your lymphatic system affects every organ and cell in your body. This highly important but little-known circulatory system is the body's primary waste elimination system. Your lymph system helps to eliminate toxins and keep things flowing in your body via lymphatic drainage. It contains more than 600 collection sites called the lymph nodes and has a network of collecting vessels more extensive than the venous system.

When the lymph fails to function properly and the collecting terminals become blocked, it's like a bottleneck. The lymph starts backing up, creating a toxic, oxygen-deprived environment conducive to degeneration and disease. The clear lymph fluid becomes sluggish or even stagnant, changing from a waterlike consistency to one more like milk, then yogurt, then cottage cheese. Sounds gross, right? Unfortunately, toxic lymph fluid can be stored for a long time in your system. This is not a healthy condition. Thickened, gel-like, stagnant lymph fluid overloaded with toxins is the ideal environment for the onset of numerous illnesses.

Moving this stagnant lymph flow is a major key to rejuvenation. Improving the flow, which is an essential component of the immune system, enhances your body's natural healing ability to clear up illness. A healthy lymphatic system can absorb and discharge unwanted body fat, carry away excess body fluids and toxic wastes, and aid in healing challenges associated with the muscular, circulatory, respiratory, digestive, endocrine, and nervous systems. Again, your lymphatic system affects every organ and cell in your body. It is the transportation highway of your immune system, and keeping it clear is like getting a free pass in the carpool lane!

Many factors can contribute to blockages of the lymph system, including chronic constipation, physical and emotional life stresses, environmental toxins, heavy metals and chemicals, inflammation, infections, injuries and surgery (scar tissue and adhesions), bruises and traumas, food allergies, highly acidic diets, tight clothing, lack of exercise, hormonal imbalances, structural misalignment, normal aging processes, and genetic predispositions. Yes, even unexpressed emotions such as anger, fear, or resentment can become toxic to the lymph system. Artificial and restrictive clothing (such as polyester blouses and tight bras and jeans), air-conditioning, and even antiperspirant deodorants prevent excretion and natural cleansing of toxins. Your skin is the largest eliminative organ, and about one-third of your system's toxins are excreted through it, coming to about a pound a day. Blocking the flow of this natural design with antiperspirants works against both the lymphatic and immune systems.

There are many conditions that sluggish lymph circulation can lead to that may be improved by lymphatic treatment. These include but are not limited to: colds, sinus problems, allergies, menstrual cramps, cellulite, chronic pain, arthritis, digestive disorders, ulcers, wrinkles, acne, mental confusion, and emotional disorders. Most physical and emotional challenges can be aggravated by blockage of the lymph flow.

It's clear how poor lymphatic function can contribute to a wide range of dysfunction and lack of vitality. But what can you do to remedy the situation? To keep your lymph glands grand, techniques like daily dry skin brushing, jumping on a rebounder (small trampoline), and eating a superhydrating, alkaline, plant-based diet are perfect daily activities to keep your lymphatic system healthy. A regular yoga practice has also been shown to promote long-term lymphatic health. If more severe lymphatic blockages happen, you may need to seek the help of a trained professional who is skilled in lymphatic drainage massage.

HALLELUJAH FOR HYDRATION

The benefits for the immune system of drinking a ton of clean, filtered, mineral-rich water cannot be understated. When I say "a ton," what I really mean is at least one 16-ounce glass of water per hour of waking activity. Generally speaking, that should be enough to keep yourself well hydrated without overwhelming you. Some doctors and wellness experts recommend more (especially during a cleansing or detoxification

protocol), but I want to keep it realistic and well within the range of consistent execution. Drinking a lot of water will keep your digestive tract clean and your bowels regular. Chronic dehydration is one of the most underdiagnosed conditions and can result in fatigue, muscle pain, cramping, migraine headaches, and constipation.

Regarding strong immunity, keeping yourself hydrated helps to flush out daily toxins and keep your colon healthy. A point about drinking filtered water: many home or under-sink filtration systems (like those that use multistage reverse osmosis) will remove toxins such as chlorine, pesticides, organochlorines, and heavy metal residues from your water. However, they also strip your water of essential trace minerals that your body needs. You can remineralize and alkalize your water by adding a few drops of ocean trace minerals and a capful of organic apple cider vinegar to each glass that you drink.

THE POWER OF PROBIOTICS

Inside your body, there live billions and billions of intelligent, sentient little organisms. It may sound like creepy science fiction stuff, yet your body is teeming with tiny little life forms called bacteria. Most of them are very pleasant and helpful, while some of them can be downright nasty and pathogenic. After you finish shuddering about your body playing host to billions of little buggers, allow me to put your mind to rest with this: you can actually "train" bacteria to be your friends and support your health! To maintain a strong immune system, you have to work on having a healthy gut. Healthy intestinal flora help to boost your immune system by keeping your gut healthy, your digestive system protected, and your foods processed and eliminated efficiently without toxic buildup. How do you keep the good gut flora up and the bad flora down? By eating healthy, probiotic-rich foods.

To keep the "friendly" gut bacteria doing the happy dance (and reproducing like randy little rabbits), eat probiotic-rich and fermented foods daily. Before you wince and complain about them smelling funky or tasting too sour, you've probably already tried familiar probiotic-rich foods like yogurt or sauerkraut. There's also delicious, refreshing beverages such as kombucha, coconut kefir, rejuvelac, and kvass that are bursting with beneficial bacteria. Fermented savory foods such as kimchi, natto, tempeh, and certain varieties of pickles offer tasty, flavorful additions to your recipes while packing a potent probiotic punch. You can also take probiotic supplements, whether in capsule or liquid form. Supplements are an easy way to get your daily dose, though they're not nearly as delicious or versatile as probiotic-rich foods.

Fermented foods, with their plethora of friendly bacteria, have a centuries-old reputation as health foods in many different cultures. New research substantiates the claim that the bacteria found in naturally fermented foods can strengthen the immune system and ward off infection, not just in the digestive tract, but throughout the entire human body. Recent research published in the *Journal of Science and*

Medicine in Sport found that New Zealand athletes had about 40 percent fewer colds and gastrointestinal infections when they took a probiotic compared to when they took a placebo. Other research has found that probiotic supplements may greatly lower the risk of an antibiotic-resistant superbug, Clostridium difficile, which is increasingly common in nursing homes and hospitals and named by the Centers for Disease Control as an "urgent threat" in their 2013 report on antibiotic-resistant infections. C. difficile can cause severe diarrhea and life-threatening inflammation of the colon.

However, probiotics may not be safe in people who are severely immuno-compromised. Make sure to speak with your doctor if you want to use a probiotic to ward off antibiotic-associated GI troubles. If you're just trying to ward off whatever nasty stuff is floating around, I suggest you try a vegan probiotic supplement containing the following strains for maximum benefit: Saccharomyces boulardii, Lactobacillus acidophilus, Lactobacillus gasseri, Bifidobacterium bifidum, and Bifidobacterium longum. Whichever probiotic supplement you choose, it needs to be handled correctly and possibly refrigerated, as high temperatures kill some probiotic organisms.

KICK OUT THE GERMS, MOTHERLOVERS!

That phrase is not only a clever homage to one of my favorite Detroit rock bands of all time (the MC5), but also a rallying cry when you're sick. After your immune system has been compromised and some icky germ, virus, bacteria, or parasite has stormed the gates, what the heck can you do to feel better? Well, you may already be susceptible to getting sick. Some people are simply prone to higher levels of illness. According to research, many people's immune systems are functioning at only around 50 percent of their full capacity. Science has shown that nutrient-dense foods packed with antioxidants have the power to double your immune system's function so you can keep disease and illness at bay. What's more, as you age, toxins (from both the environment and your diet) build up in your body. By the time you're in your 40s, daily stress, hormonal shifts, and years of toxic buildup create a scenario in which you can get sick easier and more often.

By eating nutrient-dense, plant-based foods, you'll scrub out and destroy the toxins that cause illness and help your body activate its own cleaning system to provide higher levels of immunity. You can renew your energy, lose weight, put an end to sick days, and potentially increase your longevity.

EATING HABITS OF HEALTHY, ILLNESS-FREE PEOPLE

It's easy to deduce that if you successfully avoid illnesses and disease, the greater your chance of living longer. If we take another look at the eating habits of centenarians and cultures with the longest lifespans, we find one culinary commonality that helps to boost their immunity: plant-strong, nutrient-dense diets. Dissecting their eating habits, we can glean a solid approach for our own lifestyle.

We can boost our immunity by eating foods with the most vitamins, minerals, and phytochemicals (plant compounds such as antioxidants, including beta-carotene, vitamin C, folic acid, and vitamin E), and the least amount of calories. Caloric restriction is a cornerstone of longevity-promoting diets. Phytonutrient-rich foods include colorful fruits and vegetables such as dark, leafy greens, tomatoes, peppers, and berries. Dark, leafy greens contain lymphocytes that aid digestion, and dark berries contain anthocyanins and bioflavonoids that protect your heart and ward off cancer. Fruits and vegetables are rich in nutrients like vitamins C and E, plus beta-carotene and zinc.

It's a good idea to go for a wide variety of brightly colored fruits and vegetables, including citrus fruits, kiwi, apples, red grapes, kale, onions, spinach, sweet potatoes, and carrots. Other foods particularly good for your immune system include fresh garlic and medicinal mushrooms like shiitake, maitake, reishi, or chaga, all of which can help fight viruses and bacteria. If you happen to come down with a cold or the flu, a big bowl of antioxidant-rich, immune-boosting garlic and mushroom soup may help your immune system even better than Mom's old-school chicken noodle soup!

Avoid eating nutrient-stripped, fast-absorbing foods such as trans fatty acids, refined sugar, and white flour. These highly processed foods create a massive glucose response in your bloodstream and spike your insulin levels. This spike promotes fat storage, weakens your immune system, and increases your risk of cancer. By eating slow-absorbing foods, your body is able to properly absorb essential nutrients and use them to fight disease. Slow-absorbing foods include nuts, seeds, legumes, and beans. The sterols and stanols in nuts and seeds actually help pull bad fats out of the body, allowing good fats to be absorbed to lower your "bad" LDL cholesterol and increasing your brain function.

It's also important to vigorously masticate on a daily basis. Chewing your food properly facilitates the release of important nutrients and your own powerful enzymes that protect your cells. The average person chews each bite of food as few as 15 times. Try adding 10 more chews to every bite. Studies show that people who chew more often also consume 10 percent less food. It requires more presence and focus when you eat, which can also result in a higher level of gratification and appreciation for your food!

HOW YOUR LIFESTYLE AFFECTS YOUR IMMUNITY

Your lifestyle also has a huge impact on how well your immune system protects you from germs, viruses, and chronic illness. Replacing bad habits with healthy new ones can help keep your immune system kicking serious ass. Here are some good life habits that many of us overlook. I can definitely relate to a few of these . . . can you?

- Not slacking on good sleep: You may have noticed you're more likely to catch a cold or other infection when you're not getting enough sleep. Not getting enough sleep can also lead to higher levels of stress hormones like cortisol. Although researchers aren't exactly sure how sleep boosts the immune system, it's clear that getting enough sleep—between seven and nine hours—is key for lifelong good health.

- **Exercising daily is essential:** Try to get regular, moderate exercise, even a daily 30-minute walk. It can help your immune system fight infection. Exercise can also boost your body's feel-good chemicals, reduce your stress hormones, and help you sleep better, all of which your immune system loves.

- **Reduce your stress or face the mess:** Everyone experiences stress in life. The key is how you respond to it. If stress continues for long periods unabated, it makes you much more vulnerable to illness, from colds to serious diseases. Chronic stress exposes your body to a steady stream of stress hormones that suppress your immune system and deplete your body of essential vitamins and minerals. I recommend meditation, at least 15 minutes a day to start. Turn off your cell phone, eliminate all distractions, find a calm place in the house, and just be still in a comfortable position.

- **Maintain strong personal relationships:** Connecting with other people is a wonderful way to reduce stress and eliminate feelings of isolation. Strong relationships and a supportive social network are good for you (and I don't just mean on Facebook). Although there are many other things that affect your health, making meaningful connections with people is always a good idea.

- **Lighten up and laugh more:** Laughing is really good for you. It curbs the levels of stress hormones in your body and boosts white blood cells that help to fight infection. Just anticipating a funny event can have a positive effect on your immune system.

From eating the right foods to reducing your stress to getting your gut healthy—there are so many ways to give your immune system a boost. One thing's for sure: it needs your support to kick some ass. When you empower your body's front line of defense with the right ammo to ward off the yucky stuff, you'll have a much better chance of rockin' to a ripe old age with serious spunk and vigor. So start eating clean, remember to laugh a lot, let go of negative emotional baggage, surround yourself with positive peeps, get your gut health going strong, and baby, you can kiss all those sick days good-bye!

MY TOP IMMUNE-BOOSTING NUTRIENTS

When we consider that 80 percent of our immune system is found in our gut, it's safe to say that essentially all nutrients are required for optimal immunity, including everything listed in this book thus far. However, here are a few that shine brighter than the rest:

Chromium: Mostly thought of as a blood sugar regulatory mineral, recent research shows chromium can enhance the ability of white blood cells to respond to infection.

Copper: A diet deficient in copper may affect the human immune system, reducing the activity of some cells that attack invading bacteria.

Dimethylglycine (DMG): This amino acid is said to support our immunity, especially against harmful foreign invaders.

Probiotics: Probiotics are healthy groups of bacteria. Our immune systems are made mostly of bacteria. When we eat junk foods, we are literally killing these live cultures in our guts and thus depleting our immune systems. Consuming foods high in probiotics helps to rebuild our internal microflora and support our immune system.

Vitamin C: In addition to being a powerful antioxidant, vitamin C also plays an important role in connective tissue in our bones. The stronger these tissues are, the more they can resist attack from microbes.

MY TOP IMMUNE-BOOSTING FOODS

- acai berry
- acerola
- almonds
- apples
- aronia berry
- astragalus
- cabbage
- camu camu berry
- cherries
- chlorella
- citrus fruits
- colloidal silver
- echinacea
- elderberry
- ganoderma
- garlic
- ginger root
- goji berries
- goldenseal
- holy basil
- kakadu plum
- mushrooms (in particular, shiitake, reishi, chaga, and cordyceps)
- oregano oil
- parsley
- pineapple
- probiotics
- raspberries
- rose hips
- spinach
- sprouts
- sweet potatoes
- turmeric root
- watercress
- watermelon

RECIPES
TO BOOST
IMMUNITY

······················

HIGH C
SMOOTHIE

SERVES 2

WHEN IT COMES TO IMMUNITY, VITAMIN C is on the front line of protection. When you start to feel a little ill or that dreaded scratch in the back of your throat, it's time to strike quickly. This smoothie is bursting with bombtastic amounts of immune-boosting natural vitamin C to keep you healthy and ward off illness. Now that's worthy of a high note!

1 cup fresh orange juice

½ cup goji berries, plus a few reserved for garnish

½ cup young Thai coconut meat

2½ cups fresh or frozen mango

1 tablespoon baobab powder

1 tablespoon ground vanilla bean

1 tablespoon camu camu powder

Pinch cayenne pepper

⅛ teaspoon sea salt

⅛ teaspoon liquid stevia

1 Blend all ingredients in a high-speed blender for 30 seconds until creamy and smooth. Pour into drinking glasses and garnish with some reserved goji berries.

AYURVEDIC
COCONUT CREAM SPREAD

SERVES 2

COCONUT OIL IS BETTER THAN BUTTER. There, I said it. With a host of metabolism-boosting, antimicrobial, and antiviral properties, it may be the most potent and medicinal oil on the planet. This recipe serves as an awesome spread for sandwiches, a dip for crudités, or even a salad dressing. The turmeric and holy basil help to fight inflammation while boosting your immunity and calming your nerves.

½ cup organic virgin coconut oil

½ teaspoon sea salt

¼ teaspoon turmeric powder

Pinch holy basil extract powder

¼ teaspoon cayenne pepper

Pinch coconut sugar

1 Mix all ingredients vigorously in a mixing bowl with a wooden spoon or whisk. Serve on bread, crackers, nut loaf, or muffins.

INDIAN
BERRY CHUTNEY

SERVES 4

CHUTNEY IS A TRADITIONAL INDIAN CONDIMENT made from fruit and spices. It's typically used in conjunction with spicy foods, as the light sweetness of the fruit helps to balance the taste of intensely spicy dishes. This version uses tart goldenberries and sweet mulberries to pump up the vitamin C content and add assimilable iron, which is essential for healthy blood.

1 cup goldenberries, soaked for 1 hour

1 cup mulberries, soaked for 1 hour

¼ cup yellow onion, diced

1 teaspoon ginger root, minced

1 teaspoon jalapeno, seeded and minced

¼ cup cilantro, minced

1 clove garlic, minced

1 tablespoon extra-virgin olive oil

¼ teaspoon ground cumin

Pinch sea salt

1 Add all ingredients to a food processor and pulse until chunky.

This chutney is ultra versatile! Serve it with a side of papadum chips or over quinoa, curried vegetables, samosas, sandwiches, or even pizza.

SPICED
ORANGE APPLE
CIDER

SERVES 2

WHEN AUTUMN ARRIVES, IT'S TIME FOR copious amounts of hot cider. I was lucky enough to grow up in Southeastern Michigan, where there are many cider mills to visit and one can partake in a fresh cup of this beautiful beverage. The addition of orange adds a sweet and tart undertone to the flavor, while the cinnamon and clove keep it authentic and heartwarming. I look forward every year to drinking this glorious concoction nestled up to a warm fireplace. Plus, it's popping with vitamin C to ward off any potential maladies that are all too common when the temperatures drop.

2 cups hot water

2 apples, cored and peeled

¼ large orange, peeled

2 tablespoons coconut nectar

1½ teaspoons ground cinnamon

¼ teaspoon ground cloves

Pinch sea salt

1 Add all ingredients to a high-speed blender. Cover the lid with a kitchen towel to prevent hot liquid from escaping. Blend for 40 seconds until smooth and frothy. Pour the cider into mugs, garnish with a cinnamon stick, and serve immediately.

GOLDEN
TURMERIC MILK

TURMERIC ROOT IS ONE OF THE most potent anti-inflammatory ingredients in the world. Combined with the other Ayurvedic and Indian spices in this recipe, it's a very calming, restorative, and balancing beverage that can be enjoyed year-round (and not just after yoga classes!). Oh, and don't worry about the golden milk mustache. It looks good on ya, babe.

2 cups raw coconut water

1½ cups coconut milk

4 to 5 inches turmeric root, sliced

2½ inches ginger root, sliced

1 teaspoon ground cinnamon

¼ teaspoon ground cardamom

¼ teaspoon ashwagandha powder

¼ teaspoon holy basil extract powder

½ teaspoon turmeric powder

1 tablespoon organic virgin coconut oil

2 tablespoons coconut nectar or ¼ teaspoon liquid stevia

1 Combine all ingredients in a medium saucepan. Bring to a rolling boil and whisk for a few minutes to combine. Remove from heat and cover for about 10 minutes, allowing the herbs and roots to steep. Strain into a high-speed blender using a fine mesh strainer. Discard the turmeric and ginger root. Blend for 30 seconds until smooth and creamy. Pour the milk into your favorite mug and enjoy.

CREAM OF MUSHROOM
SOUP

SERVES 2 TO 3

ONE OF MY FAVORITE APPETIZERS AT Thai restaurants is coconut soup. There's something magnificent about the creamy broth and spicy, sweet taste that lingers throughout the meal. This version leans toward an Eastern European influence as well, with its smoked paprika and the addition of fresh parsley. The result is a comforting, smooth, and rich soup that leaves you satiated and slim. The magical, medicinal mushrooms—maitake and shiitake—both possess antiviral, anticancer, and immune-enhancing properties.

1 tablespoon organic virgin coconut oil

⅓ cup red onion, diced

3 cups maitake or shiitake mushrooms, thinly sliced

1 tablespoon coconut aminos

3 cups coconut milk

¼ teaspoon ground black pepper, or to taste

1 teaspoon smoked paprika, plus more for garnish

1 tablespoon minced parsley, plus more for garnish

1 tablespoon extra-virgin olive oil

1 Melt the coconut oil in a saucepan over low heat. Add the red onion and sauté until just slightly translucent, about 5 to 6 minutes. Keep on a low temperature to avoid browning the onions. Add the mushrooms and coconut aminos. Cook for an additional 10 to 15 minutes, until mushrooms are super soft. Add the coconut milk and stir continually over low heat until you get a gentle, rolling boil. Reduce the heat and stir in the pepper, paprika, parsley, and olive oil. Transfer to your favorite soup bowl and top with more parsley and a dash of paprika.

SUPERFOOD
LEMONADE

YOU MIGHT WANT TO SET UP a lemonade stand on the corner of your block after you taste this one. It's not exactly what you've been used to in the past, with the creamy lucuma and malty maca powder. Combined with the immune-boosting powers of tart camu camu and tangy goldenberries (both high in vitamin C)—this IS a pretty fancy lemonade. Heck, that just means you can charge a lil' extra at the stand!

6 cups filtered water

4 to 5 lemons, peeled and seeded

2 teaspoons stevia powder

1 teaspoon camu camu powder

1 tablespoon maca powder

1 tablespoon lucuma powder

¼ cup goldenberries

3 tablespoons organic virgin coconut oil

½ teaspoon sea salt

1 cup ice cubes

1 Blend all ingredients in a high-speed blender for 40 seconds until frothy and creamy.

GRAPEFRUIT
SPINACH SALAD

SERVES 2

THIS TANGY, SWEET, AND SAVORY SALAD is perfect when you're sweating bullets and want something cooling and crunchy. The dressing has a delicious, tangy undertone that goes great with the spinach and snap of the raw pecans. Grapefruit is a classic immune booster with loads of vitamin C and seeds that are actually antiviral (so leave them in). Speaking of spinach, it's packed with antioxidants and beta-carotene, which help to increase the infection-fighting abilities of your immune system. It's a refreshingly simple salad that won't let you down at a dinner party. Peeps always love this one.

DRESSING:

¾ cup grapefruit, peeled and chopped

1 teaspoon maple syrup

¼ cup frozen strawberries

2 tablespoons extra-virgin olive oil

1 teaspoon Dijon mustard

2 teaspoons poppy seeds

⅛ teaspoon arrowroot powder

1 inch orange rind

1 inch grapefruit rind

SALAD:

1 large grapefruit, peeled and chopped, plus more for garnish

1 pound baby spinach

½ cup raw pecans, crushed, for garnish

1 **To make the dressing:** blend all dressing ingredients in a high-speed blender for 30 seconds until smooth. Set aside.

2 **To make the salad:** combine the grapefruit and spinach greens in a large mixing bowl. Pour the dressing on top and toss until evenly combined. Plate the salad and top with crushed pecans and additional diced grapefruit.

INCREDIBLE
IMMUNITY TONIC

WHEN I GET TO RAID THE proverbial superfood medicine chest, this is the kind of recipe that results. There are so many immune-boosting, detoxifying ingredients and antioxidants in this recipe, you could probably fall into a vat of toxic waste after you drink it and come out relatively unscathed. I don't recommend you try that, however.

2 cups raw coconut water

3 navel oranges, peeled

2 teaspoons fresh lemon juice

¼ teaspoon camu camu powder

½ teaspoon turmeric powder

2 teaspoons schisandra powder

1-inch piece fresh ginger root, peeled

Dash cayenne pepper

½ teaspoon fulvic acid

½ teaspoon MSM powder

½ cup fresh or frozen blueberries

¼ teaspoon liquid stevia

One 6-inch piece of aloe vera leaf, filleted

1 cup ice cubes

1 Blend all ingredients in a high-speed blender for 30 seconds until smooth and creamy. Serve.

GLORIOUS
GREEN JUICE

SERVES 2

THIS JUICE TASTES SWEET AND SPICY, with an awesome flavor balance between the apples, ginger, and watercress. It has huge levels of antioxidants, iodine, folate, and vitamin C—all great for boosting immunity and for gentle detox support. In fact, this is a phenomenal juice to add to your cleanse protocol. This juice is great for adrenal, liver, and skin rejuvenation. For people who are brand-new to the green juice craze, this recipe is the perfect place to start.

1 large bunch watercress

½ medium bunch curly parsley

2 cups sunflower sprouts

1 large green apple, sliced

3 medium gala, fuji, or pink lady apples, sliced

5-inch piece ginger root, peeled

1 small lemon, peeled and quartered

1 Run all ingredients through a juicer, alternating ingredients as you put them in for maximum extraction. Serve immediately.

Using a slow juicer will help you extract more nutrients and juice from the greens and fruit. Also, if you find this juice too spicy, leave out the ginger or reduce the amount of watercress.

POTATO LEEK & PURPLE CORN
CHOWDER

SERVES 2

ANTIOXIDANTS AREN'T JUST FOUND IN DARK berries. Purple corn and potatoes also feature the cell-protecting benefits of phytonutrients. By combining the two in this creamy, chunky chowder, we bump up the nutrition and add dynamic flavor. The addition of chickpea miso makes this soy free, thanks to the suggestion from The Alchemist Chef. The deep, rich, dark purple flavor, though, is what makes this soup truly special.

3 tablespoons extra-virgin olive oil

1 large leek, sliced into half moons

2 quarts low-sodium vegetable broth, divided

5 garlic cloves, minced

5 medium purple or red potatoes, diced

3 tablespoons coconut sugar

½ cup purple corn powder

3 bay leaves

1 tablespoon truffle salt

2 tablespoons chickpea miso

Dash ground white pepper

1 sprig fresh dill

1 Heat the olive oil in a large saucepan over medium heat. Add the sliced leeks and sauté 5 minutes, until they're light and golden brown.

2 Heat 1 quart of the vegetable broth in a medium stockpot over medium heat and bring it to a simmer.

3 Add the garlic and potatoes to the saucepan and sauté for another 5 minutes until softened. Add the coconut sugar to the saucepan and stir it as it starts to slowly caramelize.

4 Transfer the vegetables to the stockpot. Cover with a lid and simmer on low heat for 20 to 25 minutes.

5 Add a ½ quart of the vegetable broth to the same saucepan you used to cook the potatoes and 2 veggies. Increase the temperature to high heat to bring the broth to a rolling boil. Add the purple corn powder. Whisk the roux mixture vigorously, as it will start to thicken quickly.

6 Gradually add the remaining ½ quart of vegetable broth as the roux begins to thicken. Simmer for 10 to 15 minutes until you have a dense, gravylike consistency. Transfer the roux to the stockpot to create a chowder. Simmer for 3 minutes, adding the bay leaves, truffle salt, and miso.

7 Transfer half the chowder to a blender. Make sure your blender lid is secure, and cover it with a folded towel to protect yourself from the hot steam and liquids. Press down on the lid while blending to prevent any liquid from spilling. Blend for about 15 to 20 seconds. Carefully take off the lid and pour the mixture back into the stockpot.

8 Serve in soup bowls and top with ground white pepper and dill.

10

EAT FOR

STRONG BONES

CONTRARY TO POPULAR BELIEF, building strong bones isn't just about the calcium. Antithetical to celebrity advertisements promoting dairy milk for strong bones, the keys to lifelong bone health do not come oozing out of a swollen cow udder or from toxic, chemical calcium supplements. Building strong bones comes down to three basic things: exercises that build bone density, having the correct intake of healthy nutrients that build strong bones, and eating an alkaline vegan diet to prevent the depletion of calcium and critical minerals in your body.

When it comes to lifelong bone health, pretty much everything you've been told by the mainstream media is either completely false or intentionally misleading. Let me break this down for you, because the information I'm about to share with you is too legit to quit!

If consumption rates of milk and dairy products are so high, then why do the statistics reflect that bone health today is the complete opposite? If you've ever had a family member or friend with bone-health issues, it may have a direct correlation to their dietary choices. Millions of people are now experiencing serious bone fractures and symptoms of osteoporosis, especially later in their lives:

- Osteoporosis is estimated to affect 200 million women worldwide

- Nearly 75 percent of hip, spine, and forearm fractures occur among people 65 years old or older
- By 2050, the worldwide incidence of hip fractures in men is projected to increase by 310 percent, and in women, 240 percent

So wipe off your milk mustache and let's get ready to rumble!

NO BONES ABOUT IT—YOU NEED TO START YOUNG

The unfortunate reality is that most people don't start thinking about the health of their bones until midlife or later, by which time it can be too late to do very much to protect against serious bone loss and resulting fractures. Researchers who study bone health state that we should start thinking about long-term bone health starting in childhood and continuing through adolescence, when the body builds most of the bone that must sustain it for the remaining years of life.

Once peak bone mass has been reached, any further gains are relatively minimal, so our younger years are the best time to pay attention to our bone development. By age 20, girls have gained between 90 and 96 percent of their peak bone mass. For boys, peak mass occurs a few years later, in their mid-20s.

About 26 percent of total adult bone mass is accrued in the two years that bone mass increases the most: age 12.5 in girls and 14.1 in boys. The amount of bone added during those 2 years is about the same as what is typically lost in the 30 years between ages 50 and 80. The best available evidence strongly indicates that increasing peak bone mass in childhood by just 10 percent could delay the onset of osteoporosis, especially in postmenopausal women, by about 13 years.

Although nothing can be done about the three factors with the greatest influence on bone mass—gender, age, and genetics—two others factors under our control can make the difference between crippling fractures in midlife and escaping the effects of osteoporosis. Those factors are how many bone-building nutrients we consume and how often we engage in supportive, weight-bearing exercise.

CALCIUM: HERO OR CULPRIT?

We're all familiar with the mantra "calcium builds strong bones." Indeed, calcium does play a role in bone health. But this blockbuster bone builder doesn't have a shot at the gold without some key supporting players. There are other, even more vitally important nutrients that you need to consume regularly if you want to keep your bones unbreakable like Bruce Willis. Okay, maybe not unbreakable, but pretty damn strong.

Believe it or not, calcium supplements can do way more harm than good, depending on the source they are derived from. Almost half the population of the U.S. (almost 70 percent of adult women) uses dietary supplements containing calcium. In general, we absorb less than half of the calcium we ingest. Some researchers warn that calcium supplements are responsible for an increase in calcification. In this process, calcium causes constipation and builds up in the body in soft tissues where it can harden, or calcify. Sites of calcification include artery walls, kidneys, gallbladder, muscles, and breast tissue. For instance, a low-quality form of coral calcium can create calcification in your body and is highly detrimental in the long run. You want to focus on high-quality, assimilable calcium from food sources (not supplements) and increase your intake of vitamin D and magnesium—which are the REAL stars.

MAGNESIUM: THE MASTER MINERAL

Why is magnesium referred to as "master mineral" for our health? Most people think that calcium is THE most important factor in bone health. However, research demonstrates that vitamin D is a major player, and magnesium is absolutely necessary to convert that vitamin D into its active form so that it can turn on the calcium absorption in your body. Magnesium stimulates the hormone calcitonin, which helps to preserve bone structure by drawing calcium out of the blood and soft tissues and back into the bones. This action helps lower the likelihood of osteoporosis, some forms of arthritis, heart attack, and kidney stones. So, if you're taking lots of calcium and not much vitamin D or magnesium, you are highly susceptible to these conditions.

Healthy amounts of magnesium have been shown to help prevent heart disease and stroke, ward off diabetes, improve elimination of toxins, act as a natural laxative, increase muscle flexibility, and increase blood alkalinity. The highest alkaline, plant-based food sources of natural magnesium are chlorella; spirulina; AFA algae; pumpkin seeds and oil; dark, leafy green vegetables like kale and collard greens; and bitter greens like dandelion. The number-one source, however, is raw cacao. Kapow!

In addition to its magical ability to draw calcium back into your bones, magnesium is a fantastic nutrient for sound sleep, relaxation, and maintaining a balanced mood. However, a true bone-building, box office blockbuster wouldn't be complete without our crowd-pleasing co-stars, vitamins D and K.

OMG, D AND K, FTW!

Vitamin D3 is one of the most useful nutritional tools we have at our disposal for improving overall bone health. This vitamin is unique because, intrinsically, vitamin D3 is in the form of cholecalciferol. However, vitamin D3 acquires hormone-like powers when cholecalciferol is converted into calcitriol by the liver and kidneys. As a hormone, calcitriol controls phosphorus, calcium, bone metabolism, and neuromuscular function. Vitamin D3 is the only vitamin that your body can manufacture from direct sunlight exposure (UVB rays). Yet, with most of us spending too much time indoors and extensively using sunscreens due to concern about skin cancer, we are now a society with millions of individuals deficient in this life-sustaining, bone-building, and immune-modulating vitamin.

Vitamin D3 is actually an oil-soluble steroid hormone that forms when your skin is exposed to UVB radiation from the sun. When UVB rays hit the surface of your skin, your skin converts a cholesterol derivative into usable vitamin D3. It takes up to 48 hours for this form of vitamin D3 to be fully absorbed into your bloodstream and elevate your overall vitamin D levels.

One of the best-known and long-established benefits of vitamin D3 is its ability to improve bone health and the health of the musculoskeletal system. It is well documented that vitamin D3 deficiency causes osteopenia, precipitates and exacerbates osteoporosis, causes a painful bone disease known as osteomalacia, and increases muscle weakness, which increases the risk of falls and fractures. Vitamin D3 insufficiency may alter the regulatory mechanisms of parathyroid hormone (PTH) and cause a secondary hyperparathyroidism that increases the risk of osteoporosis and fractures.

Vitamin D3 is generally found in dairy products and is manufactured in the body from healthy sun exposure. However, dairy products are much too acidic to be considered healthy for the human body and can strip your bones of calcium due to their acidic nature. You can easily get a healthy daily dose of vitamin D3 by lying out in the sunshine, allowing the sun's rays to make contact with your naked skin. Or, if you want to get a little exercise at the same time, take a 15-to-30-minute walk with your skin exposed. I'm not saying totally naked here, but liberally expose your arms and legs to the sun. If you live in a climate where sunshine is not regularly abundant, you can use a natural, plant-based, transdermal vitamin D cream or take a high-quality oral supplement.

Vitamin K may very well be "the next vitamin D" as research uncovers a growing number of benefits the nutrient offers. However, most people are far too deficient in vitamin K to reap its maximum benefits. Vitamin K comes in two forms: vitamin K1 and vitamin K2. Among the many types of vitamin K2, MK-7 is a newer agent with more practical applications because it stays in your body longer. In 2008, a German research group discovered that vitamin K2 provides substantial protection from prostate cancer, which is one of the leading causes of cancer death among men in the United States. Preliminary findings also suggest that vitamin K can help protect you from brain disease. Vitamin K is also seen to contribute to bone health. To raise your vitamin K1 levels, you should eat more organic, green, leafy vegetables. It is also important to balance your vitamin D and calcium levels when taking vitamin K, as these three nutrients work together.

Interestingly, the highest known source of highly assimilable vitamin K2 comes from a somewhat obscure traditional Japanese food called natto. Natto is made from ultra-fermented soybeans that are cultured with a unique spore that creates two benefits: high amounts of bone-building vitamin K2 and the potent enzyme nattokinase, which has been shown in research studies to decrease the amount of arterial plaque in the heart, thereby staving off some danger of atherosclerosis. Natto is definitely a unique, acquired taste; the experience is somewhere between really potent fermented cheese and soft, sticky tempeh. Personally, I'm hooked on natto and serve it with green onions, sliced avocado, and barbeque sauce on toast for a nutritious flavor explosion!

EAT ALKALINE AND YOU'LL BE FINE

When your body is in homeostasis, it is in a state of optimal balance. All systems are working effortlessly and in a state of harmonic cooperation to keep your body functioning properly. Examples of homeostasis include the regulation of temperature and the balance between acidity and alkalinity (pH). It is a process that maintains the stability of the human body's internal environment in response to changes in external conditions.

When your body becomes too acidic from stress, negative emotions, or eating too many acidic foods, you are in a state of imbalance and potential disease. In particular, when your blood becomes too acidic, you could die in a matter of minutes unless an alkaline mineral buffers the acidic pH of your blood. So, who gets the call from the body to come in as the cavalry? It's calcium to the rescue!

Whew—isn't it nice to know that our bodies have such a sophisticated system of balance to prevent us from a gruesome and untimely death? Indeed—except for the fact that the body pulls the calcium from its most abundant source: your bones. So, you see, if you eat too many highly acidic foods like meat, cheese, milk, eggs, processed flours, white sugar, refined vinegars, and artificial preservatives, your body quickly becomes acidic and therefore a breeding ground for potential disease and loss of bone density.

This is precisely why drinking animal milk is such a nutritional contradiction. Yes, animal milks do contain calcium. However, because your body has to buffer the increased acidity by leaching alkaline calcium from your bones, there is never, ever a net gain in your calcium levels. In fact, consuming acidic foods for long periods of time always results in a net calcium loss. That's why the developed nations that consume the most dairy have the highest incidence of osteoporosis and bone fractures. For example, in the United States alone, osteoporosis and low bone mass are a major public health threat for more than 52 million women and men over the age of 50, and, if current trends continue, the figure could climb to more than 61 million people by 2020.

PERFECT PLANT-BASED MILKS

Luckily, there are much healthier, more alkaline, nondairy milks on the market now made from nutrient-dense ingredients such as coconut, hemp, rice, almond, and quinoa. Based on the research, I think it's safe to say that plant-based milks are the better, more sustainable choice for long-term bone health.

As a final statement to drive this point home, nobody I know finds the notion of drinking rhinocerous, giraffe, hippopotamus, or zebra milk acceptable—so why do we somehow think it's proper, beneficial, or healthy for the human body to consume cow, goat, or horse milk? In fact, we are the only mammalian species that systematically seeks out, corporatizes, and consumes the milk of ANOTHER species. Quite simply, from a biological perspective, milk from animals is meant for only one group of recipients: their own babies.

HIT THE WEIGHTS, QUASIMODO

Exercising is one of the most basic and effective ways to maintain bone density and stave off osteoporosis throughout your life. After all, the old Hunchback of Notre Dame look is not going to be in vogue anytime soon.

Exercise affects your bone strength in two primary ways: bones respond to the pressure of gravitational forces like those experienced when walking, running, or jumping, and in reaction to the stress exerted by muscle contraction. There are two types of exercises that are important for building and maintaining bone density: weight-bearing and muscle-strengthening exercises.

Weight-bearing exercises include activities that make you move against gravity while staying upright. Weight-bearing exercises can be high impact or low impact in nature. High-impact weight-bearing exercises help to build your bones and keep them strong. (Note: If you have broken a bone due to osteoporosis or are at risk of breaking a bone, you may need to avoid certain high-impact exercises, so you should check with your doctor before doing any of them.) Examples of high-impact weight-bearing exercises are dancing, aerobics, plyometrics, hiking, running, jogging, jumping rope, tennis, and stair climbing.

Low-impact weight-bearing exercises can also help keep bones strong and are a safe alternative if you cannot do high-impact exercises. Examples of low-impact weight-bearing exercises are those done on elliptical machines and stair step machines, low-impact aerobics, and fast walking.

You should aim to do a weight-bearing exercise routine for 30 minutes a day. You can do one 30-minute session or break it up into multiple sessions throughout the day. The benefits for your bones are the same.

Muscle-strengthening exercises include activities where you move your body, a weight, or some other resistance against gravity. These are also known as resistance exercises and include weight lifting, calisthenics (body weight exercises), using elastic exercise bands or weight machines, and other functional, structured movements like yoga and Pilates. However, certain yoga poses may not be safe for people with osteoporosis or those at increased risk of broken bones. For example, exercises that have you bend forward at extreme angles may increase the

chance of breaking a bone in the spine. A physical therapist or certified yoga teacher should be able to help you learn which poses are safe and appropriate.

Muscle-strengthening exercises should be done two to three days a week minimum. Start with small amounts at a time—no more than 45 minutes total per day (which is also optimal for a healthy hormone cascade). Try to alternate the training of complementary body parts—i.e., chest and arms one day, back and abs another day, and legs exclusively on another.

STARTING YOUR NEW STRENGTH PROGRAM

If you haven't exercised regularly for a while, check with a medical doctor or health care professional before starting a new exercise routine, especially if you have health problems such as heart disease, diabetes, or high blood pressure. If you're at high risk of breaking a bone, you should work with a physical therapist to develop a safe and sustainable exercise program. Once you have a solid program planned out, be sure to start slowly. If you've already broken any bones in your spine, be very careful to avoid activities that require reaching down, bending forward, rapid twisting motions, heavy lifting, and those that increase your chance of a fall. As you get started, your muscles may feel sore for a day or two after you exercise. If soreness lasts longer, you may be working too hard and need to ease up. Exercises should be done in a full, pain-free range of motion.

Someday, when you're older and (maybe) a little more gray, the difference between being the world champion of shuffleboard and picking yourself up off the floor with a bad fracture will be your overall bone health. Your posture, spinal health, and mobility are dependent on you actively protecting and maintaining your bone density as the years roll on. 'Cause honestly, it's so much cooler to be a 90-year-old badass judo master than to be confined to a bed with mind-numbing daytime talk shows on loop. I mean, have you SEEN daytime TV lately? Spare yourself the impending horror and keep your skeleton strong—starting today!

MY TOP BONE-BUILDING NUTRIENTS

Boron: A mineral used for building strong bones and treating osteoarthritis. It's found in many food sources.

Chromium: Helps to keep insulin activity in the body efficient, an effect that may be bone-protective by promoting the production of collagen and by moderating bone breakdown.

Folic acid: Directly associated with bone mineral density (BMD) levels.

Magnesium: The "master mineral" that contributes to the structural development of bone and is required for the synthesis of DNA, RNA, and the antioxidant glutathione. It also plays a role in the active transport of calcium and potassium across cell membranes.

Silica: Works in conjunction with calcium to maintain bone strength.

Strontium: Known as the "bone maker," this compound has a powerful effect on bone health, and it's found abundantly in many leafy, green vegetables.

Vitamins D and C: While these two also promote other aspects of health, when they are combined they become incredibly effective in helping to build strong bones.

MY TOP BONE-BUILDING FOODS

- almonds
- asparagus
- bananas
- bok choy
- broccoli
- brussels sprouts
- cashews
- cauliflower
- collard greens
- comfrey
- dark green, leafy vegetables
- fortified cereals and nut milks
- green beans
- horsetail
- kale
- non-GMO soy products (tofu, tempeh, miso, natto)
- nut-based yogurts and cheeses
- okra
- onions
- oranges
- papayas
- peanuts
- peas
- prunes
- pumpkin seeds
- raisins
- sesame seeds
- spinach
- strawberries
- sunflower seeds
- sweet potatoes
- tomatoes
- white beans

RECIPES FOR STRONG BONES

....

GREEN BEAN
CASEROLE

EVERY YEAR FOR THANKSGIVING, I SOMEHOW get put on "green bean duty," which involves cleaning, stripping, and halving ten pounds of beans for the holiday feast. Inspired by the epic vegan celebrations with my family, this delectable dish has the classic flavor combination of garlic, mushrooms, green beans, and crispy onions that you can enjoy year-round. Green beans are your bones' best friend, with solid amounts of vitamin K. Adequate vitamin K consumption improves bone health by acting as a modifier of bone matrix proteins, improving calcium absorption and reducing urinary excretion of calcium.

2 cups green beans

1½ baby bella mushrooms, thinly sliced

5 cloves garlic, minced

1 tablespoon extra-virgin olive oil

Pinch cayenne pepper

Pinch ground black pepper

¾ cup low-sodium vegetable broth

Pinch sea salt

1 tablespoon dry white wine

¾ cup coconut milk

1 tablespoon chia seeds

2 slices gluten-free bread, lightly toasted

One 12-ounce bag toasted onion rings or crispy onions

1 tablespoon organic virgin coconut oil, plus more for pan

1 Preheat the oven to 425 degrees Fahrenheit.

2 Boil 2 quarts of water in a large pot. Add the green beans and cook for about 6 minutes. Avoid overboiling your beans. Drain the green beans and pour cold water over them to stop them from cooking.

3 Add the mushrooms, garlic, and olive oil to a large sauté pan. Sauté on high heat for about 5 minutes. Add the cayenne pepper and black pepper and cook until the vegetables are slightly soft.

4 Add the vegetable broth, salt, white wine, coconut milk, and chia seeds to the sauté pan. Lower the heat, add in your green beans, and continue cooking for about 10 minutes.

5 Add the gluten-free bread, toasted onion rings, and coconut oil to a high-speed food processor. Process for 10 seconds. Grease a large baking pan with coconut oil. Transfer the mushroom sauce mix and green beans to the baking pan. Top with your bread crumb mixture and bake for 15 to 20 minutes.

CURRIED BROCCOLI
WITH GRILLED TEMPEH

TEMPEH IS ONE OF MY FAVORITE plant-based meat substitutes. This splendid, fermented soy cake has a nutty flavor and a meaty consistency. I love to use it as a substitute for chicken in my recipes, like this killer curry dish. The tempeh provides protein and alkaline calcium, while broccoli is kickin' it with copious amounts of vitamin K—all three nutrients are the bomb for your bone health. This creamy, spicy, and filling recipe is one of my all-time faves. Enjoy!

3 cups cooked basmati brown rice

1 tablespoon organic virgin coconut oil

One 8-ounce package tempeh

2 tablespoons toasted sesame oil

1 tablespoon minced garlic

1 tablespoon ginger root, peeled and minced

1 medium yellow onion, thinly sliced

2⅓ cups coconut milk

2 tablespoons coconut nectar

1⅓ tablespoons coconut aminos

1⅓ teaspoons curry powder

½ teaspoon ground cumin

½ teaspoon turmeric powder

¼ teaspoon crushed red pepper flakes

2 cups fresh broccoli florets

1½ teaspoons chopped fresh cilantro, plus more for garnish

1 tablespoon black sesame seeds, to garnish

1 Cook the basmati brown rice according to the directions on the box, as they may vary depending on the varietal. Heat the coconut oil in a medium sauté pan or skillet. Add the tempeh and gently grill until golden brown, 5 to 7 minutes on each side. Remove the tempeh from the pan and dice into ½- to 1-inch cubes. Set aside.

2 Place the sesame oil in a medium saucepan over medium-high heat. Add the garlic, ginger, and onion, and stir frequently, cooking for 5 minutes. Add the grilled tempeh, coconut milk, coconut nectar, coconut aminos, curry powder, cumin, turmeric, red pepper flakes, and broccoli. Reduce to a low heat and simmer for 15 minutes more. Add the chopped cilantro. Spoon the curry mixture over the cooked brown rice and garnish with cilantro leaves and black sesame seeds.

JASON'S TIP

You may use other flavors of marinated tempeh for a different taste and texture.

KALE APPLE
QUINOA BOWL

KALE IS ONE OF THE HEALTHIEST green, leafy vegetables you can eat, but some people aren't sold on the slightly bitter taste and crunchy texture. With this bowl, you combine kale with the nutty taste of quinoa and the sweetness of apples. It's an ultra-simple yet deeply satisfying combo that will have you callin' for the kale again and again. Kale is full of two big-time bone builders: vitamin K and calcium. Studies show that calcium absorption from kale is far superior to that from milk. That's because, unlike other greens like spinach, kale has almost no oxalates that impair absorption.

1 teaspoon organic virgin coconut oil

½ bunch kale, chiffonaded

¼ teaspoon sea salt, divided

2 apples, cored and diced

2 cups cooked quinoa

1 tablespoon hemp seeds

1 Heat the coconut oil in a medium skillet. Add the kale and cook for about 3 to 4 minutes over medium heat. Add ⅛ teaspoon of the sea salt, stir, and transfer to a bowl and set aside.

2 Add the diced apples to the same skillet and cook for about 2 minutes, stirring frequently. Remove from the heat.

3 Plate your quinoa first, then add the kale and top with diced apples. Top with the remaining ⅛ teaspoon of salt and the hemp seeds.

CREAMY
CAULIFLOWER BISQUE

SERVES 4 TO 6

WHEN YOU NEED A DENSE, CREAMY, comforting soup, make this Cauliflower Bisque. There's something very "homemade" about the flavor of this soup, which is punctuated by tarragon, herbes de provence, and a host of vegetables. This dish tastes like it's made with real cow's milk, which is a testament to the magical creaminess of the cauliflower and fat-burning coconut oil in this recipe. Cauliflower is full of plentiful amounts of vitamin C, which serves a dual purpose. It acts as an antioxidant as well as a vitamin, stimulating the production of bone-building cells (osteoblasts) while suppressing the cells that destroy bone (osteoclasts). It is also vital to the production of collagen, a protein-based connective tissue in bones and cartilage.

½ head large cauliflower, cut into florets

2½ cups vegetable broth, divided

1 cup filtered water, divided

1 tablespoon fresh lemon juice

1 teaspoon sea salt, divided

1½ tablespoons organic virgin coconut oil

1 large carrot, diced

1 large celery stalk, diced

½ yellow onion, diced

3 cloves garlic, minced

½ teaspoon dried herbes de provence

¼ teaspoon dried tarragon

¼ teaspoon onion granules

½ cup sunflower seeds, plus more for garnish

¼ cup pepitas (pumpkin seeds), reserved for garnish

1 tablespoon pumpkin seed oil, reserved for garnish

1. Place the cauliflower, 1¼ cups vegetable broth, ½ cup water, lemon juice, and ½ teaspoon sea salt in a large stockpot. Bring to a boil, then lower the heat, cover, and simmer for 15 minutes.

2. Heat the coconut oil in a large skillet over medium heat. Cook the carrot, celery, and onion along with the remaining ½ teaspoon of sea salt until the vegetables are soft, about 15 minutes. Add the garlic and cook an additional 5 minutes or until the vegetables are beginning to brown. Stir in the dried herbs and onion granules and cook a few minutes longer. Add the sautéed vegetables to the cauliflower mixture and stir to combine. At this point, the cauliflower should be very tender. If not, continue to simmer the soup until it is. Once the cauliflower is cooked through, turn off the heat and let the soup cool.

3. Blend the sunflower seeds and the remaining vegetable broth and water in a high-speed blender until the mixture is smooth. Add the soup to the blender and puree until very smooth and creamy. Pour the finished soup into bowls and garnish with sunflower seeds, pepitas, and pumpkin seed oil.

If you're using a traditional upright tabletop blender, be careful about adding hot soup to your blender carafe. Blend no more than 2 cups at a time. Make sure the top of the blender carafe is secured properly and cover it with a kitchen towel to prevent spillage.

BUFFALO CAULIFLOWER BITES
WITH CASHEW DILL
DIPPING SAUCE

SOMETIMES, IT CAN BE A DAUNTING proposition to make healthier versions of traditional American bar food. This Buffalo Cauliflower Bites recipe nails the same flavor and crazy crunch appeal of the old-school meat-based version—with a lot fewer calories and way less fat. As mentioned before, cauliflower is full of vitamin K, which improves calcium absorption and overall bone strength. Whether it's a karaoke contest, game night, or a birthday party—this recipe is a finger-lickin' people pleaser through and through.

BUFFALO CAULIFLOWER BITES:

- 1 teaspoon organic virgin coconut oil
- 1 cup coconut milk
- 1 cup gluten-free chickpea flour
- 1 large head cauliflower, broken into medium-size florets
- ½ cup apple cider vinegar
- 1 tablespoon chili powder
- 1 tablespoon garlic powder
- 2 teaspoons sweet paprika
- ½ teaspoon smoked paprika
- ½ teaspoon onion powder
- ½ teaspoon cayenne pepper
- 1 teaspoon sea salt
- 1 tablespoon extra-virgin olive oil, plus more for the baking dish
- 2 teaspoons maple syrup
- 2 tablespoons filtered water, plus more if needed to thin
- 2 teaspoons arrowroot powder
- 4 stalks celery, cut into sticks, reserved for plating

CASHEW DILL SAUCE:

1¼ cups raw cashews, soaked for 1 hour

½ cup filtered water

¼ cup extra-virgin olive oil

2 tablespoons fresh lemon juice

2 teaspoons apple cider vinegar

2 teaspoons nutritional yeast

1 teaspoon dried dill

¾ teaspoon sea salt

1 **To make the Buffalo Cauliflower Bites:** preheat the oven to 450 degrees Fahrenheit. Lightly oil a baking sheet with coconut oil. Whisk together the coconut milk and flour until well combined. Dunk the individual cauliflower florets into the flour mixture, transfer to the oiled baking sheet, and bake for 20 minutes.

2 Combine the apple cider vinegar, spices, olive oil, and maple syrup in a small saucepan. Bring to a simmer, then reduce heat to medium low and cook for 5 to 7 minutes, or until the mixture starts to thicken. Whisk in the water and arrowroot powder. Simmer for an additional 1 to 2 minutes and then remove from the heat. Add additional water to thin as needed.

3 Coat cauliflower florets with the sauce mixture and bake for an additional 8 minutes.

4 **To make the Cashew Dill Sauce:** blend all ingredients in a high-speed blender for 30 seconds until very smooth and creamy. If need be, scrape down the sides of the blender carafe with a spatula and blend again. Serve immediately with the Buffalo Cauliflower Bites and garnish with fresh celery sticks.

CHOCOLATE
KALE CHIPS

KALE CHIPS HAVE BECOME ALL THE rage as one of the top healthy snack foods. And yet, plenty of people still haven't tried them. For the skeptics and nonbelievers . . . just slather them in gooey chocolate, throw 'em in the oven, and you'll be instantly converted. The crunchy texture and sweet taste will win you over instantly. This is the ultimate way to sneak more healthy greens into a child's diet. And it'll help kids build strong bones for a lifetime! One cup of kale has an astounding 1,300 percent RDA of vitamin K. In conjunction with vitamin D, it regulates osteoclast production, making it a super important part of building and maintaining healthy bone mass.

½ cup cashews, soaked in water for 1 to 2 hours to soften

¾ cup coconut sugar

4 tablespoons maple syrup

⅓ cup raw cacao powder

1 teaspoon ground vanilla bean

½ teaspoon ground cinnamon

2 tablespoons organic virgin coconut oil

Pinch cayenne pepper

1 large bunch of curly kale, thoroughly washed and big stems removed

1 teaspoon hemp seeds

¼ cup extra-fine shredded coconut flakes

1 Preheat the oven to 300 degrees Fahrenheit.

2 Blend all ingredients, except the kale, hemp seeds, and coconut flakes, in a high-speed blender until the mixture is smooth to create a chocolate sauce.

3 Add the kale to a large bowl and top with chocolate sauce. Fold in the hemp seeds and shredded coconut flakes. Toss vigorously with your hands to coat the leaves evenly.

4 Transfer the coated kale to a parchment-lined cookie sheet and bake for about 20 minutes. Flip the kale leaves and bake for another 5 to 10 minutes. Watch the kale chips very closely, as they may burn quickly if left in the oven a few moments too long. Remove the kale chips from the oven when crispy and serve immediately.

If you have a dehydrator, you can transfer the chocolate-covered kale to two Teflex-lined dehydrator sheets and dehydrate at 118 degrees Fahrenheit for about 5 hours. Then flip the kale chips, or just shake them around, and dehydrate them for another 4 to 5 hours or until very crispy.

COLLARD GREENS

SERVES 2

TRADITIONALLY A STAPLE INGREDIENT IN SOUL food, collard greens are intrinsically healthy for you. Unfortunately, they're often made with dangerously unhealthy additions like bacon grease that are heavy in saturated fat and cholesterol. By taking out the junk and adding some slick superfood ingredients, these classic collard greens become the perfect sidekick to baked sweet potatoes, bean salads, black-eyed peas, nut loaf, veggie burgers, or barbequed veggie skewers. Collard greens are a venerable caped crusader for strong bones, helping to build bone matrix proteins, improve collagen production, and increase calcium absorption.

1 tablespoon extra-virgin olive oil

1½ cups yellow onion, diced

4 cloves garlic, minced

1 pound collard greens, chopped

3 cups low-sodium vegetable broth

1 tablespoon coconut sugar

1 tablespoon liquid smoke

1 tablespoon blackstrap molasses

¼ to ½ teaspoon sea salt, or to taste

Pinch ground black pepper

Pinch cayenne pepper

2 large tomatoes, seeded and diced

2 tablespoons hemp seeds, reserved for garnish

1 Heat the olive oil in a large saucepan over medium heat. Add the onions and garlic and cook for 3 to 5 minutes or until slightly translucent and golden brown. Add the chopped collard greens and vegetable broth until the greens are three-quarters covered by the broth.

2 Add the coconut sugar, liquid smoke, molasses, salt, pepper, and cayenne pepper. Cover and bring to a simmer. Cook until the greens are tender, about 40 minutes.

3 When you plate up your greens, top them with the diced tomatoes and raw hemp seeds.

These collard greens taste insanely good with my Butternut Squash Mac n' Cheese recipe (see page 302).

THE
BURGERRITO

SERVES 2

LUNCH IS ALWAYS THE MOST CHALLENGING meal of the day for me. As I often find myself with limited time midday, I reach for the saving grace of The Burgerrito (aka the Burger Burrito). The Red Pepper Tahini Sauce is light, creamy, and zesty, which pairs well with whatever veggie burger you choose to use. Throw it all in a wrap with fresh veggies and sprouts . . . and you'll see what a quick, satisfying lunch is all about! A large red bell pepper provides more than 50 percent of your RDA of manganese, a mineral that helps develop strong bones and connective tissues. Bell peppers provide a source of vitamin C, or ascorbic acid, which helps your body make collagen, a protein that holds your bones, skin, tendons, ligaments, and connective tissues together.

RED PEPPER TAHINI SAUCE:

1 red bell pepper, diced

1 zucchini, diced

3 sprigs green onion

1 habanero pepper

¼ cup raw tahini

1 tablespoon coconut aminos

Dash smoked paprika

Pinch black pepper

Pinch sea salt

3 lemons, juiced

BURRITO FILLING:

2 gluten-free tortillas

2 teaspoons organic virgin coconut oil

2 veggie burger patties

¼ cucumber, julienned

1 red bell pepper, seeded and julienned

½ carrot, julienned

1 avocado, pitted and julienned

1 head of baby lettuce, torn by hand

1 bunch sunflower sprouts

1 **To make the Red Pepper Tahini Sauce:** blend all sauce ingredients in a high-speed blender for 40 seconds until smooth and creamy.

2 **For the burrito filling:** warm the gluten-free tortillas over an open flame with metal tongs until they are warm and pliable. Heat the coconut oil in a large skillet over medium heat. Grill the veggie burger patties for several minutes until slightly browned and warmed through.

3 Cut the patties in half and place inside the tortillas. Stack the remaining fresh vegetables, lettuce, and sunflower sprouts on top of the patties. Drizzle a generous amount of Red Pepper Tahini Sauce on top and fold each tortilla to close. You may need to use toothpicks to secure your Burgerrito.

EDAMAME
HUMMUS

THERE ARE ABOUT 10 MILLION RECIPES for chickpea hummus (give or take), so I thought it would be interesting to give edamame a chance to shine here and "take a dip." This hummus is similar to the traditional version, as it includes the same spices and ingredients to make the base. The flavor of the edamame lends a nutty, fresh taste and protein-dense texture to the hummus. What's more, edamame is one of the most well-rounded bone builders around. It contains manganese, vitamin K, potassium, and magnesium. Yowzah! Manganese helps in building strong bones while vitamin K plays a role in adding to bone density. Both potassium and magnesium contribute in preventing the onset of osteoporosis. Its isoflavones also assist in maintenance of the bone density due to estrogenlike properties. Enjoy this spread with vegetable crudités or as a base for a wrap. You and your guests are sure to enjoy this light, tangy, oil-free alternative to your regular old hummus!

1½ cups shelled edamame

¼ cup raw tahini

3 tablespoons fresh lemon juice

¼ cup filtered water

1 clove garlic, minced

1 teaspoon lemon zest

½ teaspoon ground cumin

¼ teaspoon ground coriander

Pinch sea salt

Pinch cayenne pepper

1 bunch parsley, minced

1 Add all ingredients, except for the parsley, to a high-speed food processor and process until it becomes the consistency of a dense, hummuslike paste. Remove from the food processor, scoop it onto a serving dish, and top it with minced parsley.

 JASON'S TIP

For extra fanciness, add sliced cucumber, baby cherry tomatoes, and olives.

ROASTED BRUSSELS SPROUTS
WITH COCONUT BACON

SERVES 2

BRUSSELS SPROUTS HAVE A NASTY REPUTATION, generally from some horrible childhood dish. When prepared correctly, however, they can take on a sweet undertone and roasted, nutty flavor. This recipe accentuates the natural flavor of the sprouts and complements it with sweet yacon syrup and the addictive crunch of coconut bacon. For potlucks or family gatherings, this delicious dish is always one of the first to get completely scarfed up. Brussels sprouts' vitamin content also keeps your skeleton strong. It contains vitamin C, a nutrient you need to make collagen abundant in bone tissue, as well as vitamin K that promotes bone mineralization.

2 pounds brussels sprouts, sliced in half

2 tablespoons organic virgin coconut oil

¼ cup yacon syrup

½ teaspoon garlic powder

1 teaspoon ground white pepper

2 teaspoons sea salt

One 3.5-ounce bag coconut bacon, crushed

1 Preheat the oven to 400 degrees Fahrenheit.

2 Add the brussels sprouts to a 3-quart glass baking dish and add all remaining ingredients, except the coconut bacon. Mix together thoroughly.

3 Bake for 35 minutes. Cut a sprout to check doneness; if the knife goes through the sprout cleanly and smoothly, your sprouts are done. If not, bake for another 5 to 10 minutes.

4 Add the coconut bacon and mix slightly so that the coconut bacon can absorb some of the flavors. Serve.

STUFFED
BELL PEPPERS
WITH MEXICAN "RICE"

SERVES 4

GROWING UP, I ENJOYED A WIDE variety of stuffed-vegetable dishes (you really can't avoid it in a Polish family!). These fully raw stuffed bell peppers are crammed with a crunchy, light salad featuring a radical rainbow of colors. I can't think of a better pairing than with cauliflower rice. With an array of Mexican spices, it's amazing how good it tastes. This is the kind of raw dish that you can enjoy for days on end and not grow tired of it. Plus, red bell peppers and cauliflower provide essential manganese and vitamin K, respectively, to build strong connective tissues and superhero bone strength.

MEXICAN "RICE":

1 large head cauliflower

2 teaspoons chili powder

½ teaspoon ground cumin

½ teaspoon cayenne pepper

1 tablespoon plus 1 teaspoon minced cilantro

1 lime, juiced

½ teaspoon sea salt

STUFFED BELL PEPPERS:

4 small beets, peeled

4 medium carrots, peeled

1 large head purple cabbage

1 large red onion, peeled

1 burdock or taro root, peeled (optional)

1 jalapeno pepper, seeded

1 cup green olives, pitted and diced

4 teaspoons oregano, minced

¼ cup cilantro, minced, plus more for garnish

½ cup apple cider vinegar

1 large orange, juiced

2 limes, juiced

4 limes, quartered

¼ teaspoon liquid stevia

4 yellow or orange bell peppers, seeded and cored, reserved for plating

1 **To make the Mexican "Rice":** add the cauliflower to a food processor and pulse just a few times until it becomes ricelike. Transfer to a paper towel–covered plate and press out any excess water. Add to a small mixing bowl and toss with the remaining rice ingredients. Mix well and set aside.

2 **To make the Stuffed Bell Peppers:** attach the shredder disc attachment to your food processor. Add beets, carrots, cabbage, onion, burdock, and jalapeno to the food processor and shred into small ribbons. Transfer the mixture to a bowl and add the olives, oregano, and cilantro. Mix to combine well. Add the apple cider vinegar, juiced orange, juice from 2 limes, and stevia directly to the bowl, then toss again until well incorporated.

3 Using a large spoon, fill the bell peppers with the mixture until slightly overflowing. Plate with a side of the Mexican "Rice" and garnish with the remaining limes and cilantro.

11

EAT FOR

GREAT SKIN

IF YOU WANT TO GET the glow and have youthful, radiant skin, it all starts with great nutrition and maximum hydration. Yes, eating mindfully and drinking a boatload of water will do wonders for your complexion. Beautiful skin truly starts from the inside out. I mean, c'mon, they don't call me Jason "Glowbell" for nothin', honey.

However, it wasn't always that way for me. I remember being in my teens and using really powerful pharmaceutical topical creams and medicines to combat my acne. Brainwashed by all the TV and magazine advertising, I thought that was the only way to win the war against pimples. My dermatologist mentioned that the cause of my acne could be the oily food and chocolate I was eating, but for some reason, I brushed it off. Little did I know, there was a correlation between my dietary choices and my skin issues (but the chocolate got a bad rap for years).

Before I learned how to take care of my skin by eating a clean, organic, plant-based diet, I was all too familiar with the challenges detailed below:

- Acne is the most common skin disorder in the U.S., affecting 40 to 50 million people
- Nearly 85 percent of all people have acne at some point in their lives
- In 2004, the total cost associated with the treatment of acne exceeded $2.2 billion

As it turns out, healthy foods work from the inside out to brighten your complexion and give you an attractive, radiant glow. Good nutrition plays a vital role in maintaining awesome, youthful, and supple skin. Blueberries, spinach, walnuts, kiwis, dark chocolate, and nondairy yogurts are just a few great choices that come to mind—and there are lots more!

NECESSARY NUTRIENTS FOR SEXY, SUPPLE SKIN

Omega fatty acids, antioxidants, and trace minerals are all essential nutrients that contribute to flawless skin throughout your lifetime. According to research from the University of Maryland Medical Center, increasing your intake of omega-3 fatty acids can reduce skin dryness and inflammation. Inflammation can cause your skin

to age faster, and the research shows that getting too few omega-3s may contribute to inflammatory disorders like eczema and psoriasis. Omega-3 fatty acids can also help keep the heart's arteries clear and thus improve circulation. Good circulation is absolutely crucial for skin health. Omega-3 fatty acids also help to keep the top outer layer of the skin strong and intact so that external toxins and pollutants are kept out.

One of the big-kahuna antioxidants, vitamin E, combats skin-aging free radicals, protecting your skin from sun damage caused by these UV-sunlight-generated culprits. Vitamin E also tends to help skin retain moisture, relieving dryness and making your skin look younger. Pairing vitamin E with selenium can enhance its powerful antioxidant abilities, so go ahead and munch on some raw almonds or Brazil nuts (both great sources of selenium) for a skin-revitalizing snack. Other antioxidants like lycopene (found in watermelon and tomatoes) and beta-carotene (found in carrots and peppers) are superfood skin saviors that can curb any potential damage from free radicals.

Vitamin C is a prime skin care ingredient in tons of beauty creams on the market. This vitamin aids in the body's production of collagen, a protein that forms the basic structure of your skin. Collagen breakdown, which starts speeding up significantly around the age of 35, can leave your skin looking saggy. Consuming extra vitamin C in foods like oranges, grapefruits, camu camu, acerola cherries (a single acerola has 100 percent of your vitamin C for the day), and tomatoes can help to tighten up your skin and prevent wrinkles. Vitamin C may also fight inflammation, and its high levels of antioxidants can neutralize the free radicals (highly reactive oxygen molecules) that damage your cells and prematurely age your face. In case you get tired of eating all that fruit, hot peppers, bell peppers, and organic sprouts also have good amounts of vitamin C.

Zinc, a trace mineral, can help your skin by fighting acne. Zinc is involved in metabolizing testosterone, which affects the production of an oily substance called sebum, one of the primary causes of acne. Zinc also assists in new cell production and the sloughing off of dead skin cells, which gives skin a nice, healthy glow and plump appearance.

FOODS THAT HELP YOU LOOK FOXY

Your skin is your body's largest organ. It makes sense, then, that what's healthy for your whole body is also great for your skin. As far as food choices, it doesn't get much better than fresh, organic vegetables. You'll especially want to look for brightly colored red-orange and green vegetables like carrots, sweet potatoes, peppers, and dark, leafy greens.

Orange- and red-colored vegetables are full of beta-carotene. Our bodies convert beta-carotene into vitamin A, which acts as an antioxidant, thereby preventing cell damage and premature aging.

Spinach and other dark, leafy greens also provide tons of vitamin A, which helps your skin produce more fresh new cells and get rid of the old ones, reducing dryness and keeping your face looking bright and young.

Mangoes are also a great source of vitamin A and taste amazing in smoothies or dessert recipes. Truthfully, it's best to get vitamin A from your food and not from supplements, as extremely high levels of vitamin A can cause health problems. The primary risks of too much vitamin A (either acute or chronic excess) are birth defects, liver abnormalities, central nervous system disorders, and lower bone mineral density that might increase osteoporosis risk.

Oatmeal is nature's balm for dry, itchy, irritated skin—just ask the ancient Romans and Egyptians! Colloidal oatmeal, which is made by pulverizing and boiling oats, is an ingredient you'll often see in skin care products. It fights itch, helps to retain moisture, and contributes to the barrier your skin maintains to protect you from harsh, outside elements.

In essence, a nutrient-dense, whole-food vegan diet offers a wide range of whole-body advantages, most notably great-looking skin. Whole foods are natural, unprocessed foods with high nutrient value—an example would be organic, sprouted whole-grain buckwheat instead of white bread. Whole-grain buckwheat is a great source of the antioxidant rutin, which helps to combat inflammation-related skin damage. Wheat germ provides the B vitamin biotin, which assists cells in processing fats. If you don't have enough biotin in your body, your skin can become dry and scaly.

In general, whole grains instead of processed carbohydrates can improve your complexion. Processed or highly refined flours can cause insulin spikes, which in turn can promote acne. Replacing your refined-flour cereal with buckwheat cereal is a great acne-reducing move. Incidentally, this would also help reduce your risk of developing adult-onset diabetes.

Not feeling the crunchy texture and nutty taste of buckwheat? It's all good, baby. Avocados and mushrooms can provide many of the same nutritive benefits. Remember: a healthy body usually means healthy skin. So just make time to feed your body good, healthy, unprocessed, whole plant foods, get your daily exercise, and keep your stress levels low—and your skin will see some seriously beautiful benefits.

WHAT ELSE CAN YOU DO?

The ideal way to get the nutrients you need for a lifelong radiant complexion is eating a healthy, balanced, plant-based diet. But it can also be a good idea to take a whole-food-derived daily multivitamin with lots of organically derived minerals and antioxidants to boost your overall nutrient intake if you're not consistently eating a balanced diet. Taking high-quality vitamins and supplements is important if you spend a lot of time outdoors in an urban environment or are exposed to high levels of air pollution and secondhand smoke.

Your skin also needs sleep, regular exercise, hydration, and protection. On days of really high-intensity sun exposure, apply a natural, mineral-rich sunblock with an SPF of at least 30. The label should say "broad-spectrum," meaning that it protects against the sun's UVA and UVB rays. If you're going to be outdoors during peak hours of intense sun, limit your exposure time, especially between the hours of 10 A.M.

and 2 P.M. on hot days. A good 15 minutes of direct exposure on your skin should be adequate to maintain healthy vitamin D levels. The important thing is finding the balance of just the right amount of sun exposure to be healthy and not increase your risk for skin cancer. If you have a genetic history of skin cancer in your family, it may be a better idea to obtain higher levels of vitamin D from your food sources and keep sun exposure to a minimum. Use your own best judgment and make smart choices with this one.

From a topical perspective on skin care, shea butter is usually the first recommendation to anyone looking for smoother skin. This soft substance from sub-Saharan Africa has been used for generations to treat ailments from stretch marks to arthritis to leprosy. Shea butter is composed mainly of triglycerides, such as palmitic, stearic, oleic, and linoleic fatty acids. These make it a fantastic emollient, and, combined with its thick texture and creaminess, it's a moisturizer that really sticks. But it's the other aspect of shea butter that researchers are more interested in: the unsaponifiables—the parts of oils and fats that don't form soaps. Shea butter is full to the brim with them, and they have antioxidant, anti-inflammatory, and antimicrobial properties. And, to make it even better, cinnamic acids in the unsaponifiables actually absorb UV radiation.

Gettin' your sweat on is a great way to detoxify your skin and open your pores. I recommend using a far-infrared sauna to penetrate deep into the layers of your epidermis and to release the maximum amount of toxins through your skin. Here's a personal story to highlight the effectiveness of far-infrared sauna therapy for skin detox: My cousin Steve spent the better part of a year in China working on a project. While in Shanghai, he was exposed to some of the most horrific, toxic air pollution in the world. The air quality there is so bad that many people wear masks on the street during their commutes to and from work or even while jogging! When he finally returned to the U.S. after the project wrapped, he started a hardcore detox protocol that integrated far-infrared sauna therapy. He told me that once the temperature got above 150 degrees Fahrenheit, he noticed that black soot started to ooze out of his pores. Can you imagine this happening to you? Needless to say, he was totally freaked out but very relieved to be getting those potentially damaging toxins out of his body.

THE PITHY MYTH OF DRINKING A TON OF WATER

There are many important reasons to drink copious amounts of water every day. It helps your brain function, maintains consistent energy levels, regulates your body temperature, supports efficient digestion, and ultimately keeps your body healthy. But human beings aren't necessarily like houseplants. Our skin doesn't become instantly nourished when we consume a lot of water. In fact, when you drink water, it doesn't go straight to your skin. It first travels through your intestines, gets absorbed into your bloodstream, and is filtered by your kidneys. Its final task is to hydrate your cells.

When it comes to deeply moisturizing your skin, water isn't really all that efficient at moisturizing your skin. Whether it's dry, oily, or a combination, your skin type is largely determined by your genetics. Your natural moisture level tends to fluctuate depending on what your skin's protective lipid barrier is exposed to. This lipid layer helps keep moisture in and germs and irritants out. If the irritants get past the layer, that's when dry skin can become red and itchy. Minimizing your exposure to harsh elements like low humidity, strong winds, dry heat, high altitude, prolonged and intense sun exposure, alcohol, moisture-stripping soaps, and hot baths can prevent the loss of your natural oils.

Going back to your diet again: choosing foods rich in the essential fatty acids found in walnuts, flaxseed, and olive oil can help your skin cells stay hydrated and well nourished. A study by the Institute of Experimental Dermatology in Germany revealed that women who took flaxseed or borage oil supplements for 12 weeks experienced a significant increase in skin moisture and a reduction in roughness. A healthy diet with three to five servings a week of omega fatty acids will do wonders for most everyone. But if you suffer from extremely dry skin or eczema, try flaxseed, evening primrose, or borage oil supplements. All three oils are awesome sources of alpha and/or gamma linolenic fatty acids.

Make no mistake, you want to stay hydrated—but the foods and supplements are the real game changers when it comes to your epidermis!

When it comes to first impressions, your skin tells other people a lot about you. As your largest organ, it's a direct reflection of your overall level of vitality and health. I think the REAL test of a person's skin health is when you see him or her with no camera makeup and no fancy Instagram filters or tricky lighting angles. Unfortunately, we live in a quick-fix culture that values illusion over real, authentic, natural beauty. But you want the real thing, right? So, baby, blow off the Botox, forget the face-lift, and let nature nurture your skin the old-school way like a classic Hollywood diva from the '20s. Armed with the awesome information and shine-worthy recipes in this chapter, we'll have your skin glowing like newborn-baby butt cheeks in no time!

MY TOP NUTRIENTS FOR HEALTHY SKIN

Biotin: A coenzyme and a member of the B-vitamin family that's partly responsible for healthy nails, hair, and (of course) skin.

Vitamin E: A fat-soluble antioxidant that is essential for the maintenance of healthy skin. Naturally occurring vitamin E is not a single compound; instead, vitamin E is a group of molecules with related structures, some of which may have unique properties in skin.

Essential fatty acids (EFAs): Essential fatty acids like omega-3s and omega-6s are the building blocks of healthy cell membranes. They are fats that also help produce the skin's natural oil barrier, critical in keeping skin hydrated, plumper, and fresh looking.

Polyphenols: These guys belong to a group of antioxidant compounds known as catechins that aid in detoxifying skin.

MY TOP FOODS FOR HEALTHY SKIN

- aloe vera
- arugula
- avocado
- bell peppers
- blueberries
- borage oil
- cacao
- calendula
- cannellini beans
- chamomile
- citrus fruits
- coconut
- coconut oil
- evening primrose oil
- flaxseed
- goji berries
- green tea
- hemp seeds
- hot peppers
- Irish moss
- kale
- non-GMO soy products (tofu, tempeh, miso, natto)
- olive oil
- olives
- pomegranate
- pumpkin
- spinach
- sunflower seeds
- tomatoes
- walnuts

RECIPES
FOR
GREAT SKIN

....

WATERMELON
AGUA FRESCA

AGUA FRESCA IS A TRADITIONAL MEXICAN beverage made with fresh fruit. With the inclusion of watermelon as the star, you have an ultra-hydrating drink that is perfect for maintaining deliciously dewy skin year-round. Research shows that watermelon cuts the risk of sun-related skin damage by 40 percent. That's because watermelon is nature's richest source of lycopene, an antioxidant that scavenges the UV-induced free radicals that cause sunburn and wrinkling. Lycopene may also help reduce the risks of cancer and other diseases. With a tangy undertone of flavor from fresh lime and camu camu, this fantastic fresca will be your go-to bevvy during the dog days of summer. (FYI—you'll look especially badass while sipping this drink poolside.)

4 cups fresh watermelon

1 lime, juiced

½ tablespoon coconut nectar

Pinch sea salt

¼ teaspoon camu camu powder

1 cup ice cubes

1 Blend all ingredients in a high-speed blender for 30 seconds until smooth. Serve.

SERVES 2 TO 4

MAKING YOUR OWN NONDAIRY MILK AT home can be a great way to save money, increase your nutrient intake, and add a fresh flavor to your smoothies, cereal, or oatmeal. This milk has a high amount of omega fatty acids and protein, while the fresh strawberries add a sweet, fruity touch to the flavor profile. This milk is so darn good, you can drink it straight up on its own. Plus, the macadamia nuts contain several antiaging compounds that not only prevent the signs of aging but also remove them, for a supple, youthful appearance. Mac nuts are the mack daddy for your skin health.

5 cups raw coconut water

¼ cup hemp seeds

½ cup macadamia nuts

½ teaspoon ground vanilla bean

1 teaspoon maca powder

3 pinches sea salt

¼ teaspoon liquid stevia

Handful fresh strawberries

¼ teaspoon ground cinnamon

1 Blend all ingredients in a high-speed blender for 30 seconds until smooth and frothy.

PINE NUT MARINARA
QUINOA BOWL

YOU CAN'T GO WRONG WITH THIS magical marinara sauce. The secret is using a combination of lycopene-rich fresh tomatoes and sun-dried tomatoes, which give it a nice depth and rich, smoky flavor. Lycopene helps eliminate skin-aging free radicals caused by ultraviolet rays—in other words, it protects against sun damage. Instead of pasta, which is so passé, serve this with fluffy, nutty quinoa and deliciously rich pine nuts. Those diminutive little pine nuts have vitamin E to protect your skin from cell damage and support healthy skin growth. There are so many skin-enhancing nutrients in this dish, I'm tempted to rename it "The Glow Bowl" and call it a day.

2 cups sun-dried tomatoes

¼ cup extra-virgin olive oil

2 tablespoons fresh lemon juice

1¼ tablespoons coconut nectar

2 large tomatoes, diced

½ yellow onion, chopped

3 to 4 cloves garlic, crushed

1 handful fresh basil leaves, plus more for garnish

2 teaspoons dried oregano

1 teaspoon sea salt

Pinch crushed red pepper flakes

4 cups cooked quinoa

¼ cup pine nuts, reserved for garnish

1. Soak the sun-dried tomatoes in water for 2 hours. Drain and reserve 1 cup of the water.

2. Blend the olive oil, lemon juice, coconut nectar, sun-dried tomatoes, diced fresh tomatoes, onions, garlic, basil, oregano, salt and red pepper flakes in a high-speed blender until smooth, 30 to 45 seconds. (Use a tamper if necessary to support the proper blending of the sauce.) Add the reserved tomato-soaking water to thin as needed. Serve as is or simmer at a low temperature in a medium saucepan for 25 to 30 minutes.

3. Spoon the marinara sauce over the cooked quinoa in a serving bowl and top with the pine nuts and reserved basil. Serve immediately.

Store the quinoa and marinara sauce separately. They will stay fresh for up to five days in sealed containers in the refrigerator.

SUPERFOOD
CAESAR SALAD

SERVES 4 TO 6

FOR YEARS, CAESAR SALAD WAS ONE of the holy grails of vegan cuisine. My friend Gary and I had a firm restaurant policy: anytime we saw a vegan Caesar on the menu, we HAD to order it. Eventually, the time came to see if I could top those tasty take-out salads and become the supreme salad master. My superfood version of a classic Caesar goes a few steps further by eliminating the oil and extra fat while retaining the creamy texture and zesty flavor you know and love. If you're on an anti-wrinkle diet, take note: aside from offering protection against certain diseases, the free-radical-disarming activities of the delectable cannellini beans may also offer beauty benefits by preventing premature aging of the skin triggered by excessive exposure to sunlight. In addition to fighting wrinkles by providing skin-protecting antioxidants, these beauty-preserving beans provide zinc, copper, and protein, which can also help fight premature wrinkling of the skin.

DRESSING:

1 cup cooked cannellini beans, rinsed

⅓ cup filtered water

2 tablespoons fresh lemon juice

1 tablespoon apple cider vinegar

1½ teaspoons salt-free herb blend seasoning

2 teaspoons vegan Worcestershire sauce

1½ teaspoons Dijon mustard

½ teaspoon ground black pepper

1 teaspoon ground chia seeds

3 to 4 cloves fresh garlic, crushed

4 tablespoons nutritional yeast flakes or vegan Parmesan cheese

SALAD:

4 to 6 heads of baby romaine lettuce

½ cup wild or organic capers

¼ cup hemp seeds

¼ cup vegan Parmesan cheese or nutritional yeast flakes

¼ cup dulse flakes or thinly shredded nori sheets

Dash ground black pepper

1 **To make the dressing:** blend all ingredients in a high-speed blender for 30 to 40 seconds until very smooth and creamy. Set aside at room temperature.

2 **To make the salad:** make a small, lengthwise base cut on the underside of each lettuce head so that they can lie flat on a plate without rolling or tipping over. Drizzle the dressing over the top of each romaine head and top with the capers, hemp seeds, vegan Parmesan cheese, dulse flakes, and ground black pepper. Serve immediately.

GRILLED SHISHITO PEPPERS
WITH CHILI MINT SALT SHAKE

GRILLING PEPPERS ON SKEWERS IS A primal, beautiful act of ancient culinary wizardry. I love taking these cute little shishito peppers and grilling them over an open flame. The Chili Mint Salt Shake is really the star of this recipe, though. It's a pleasant mix of spicy, salty, and sweet flavors with a refreshing finish of fresh mint. It pairs brilliantly with any type of roasted vegetables or potatoes. The peppers themselves are packed with vitamin C, vitamin A, and carotenoids. Carotenoids are one class of phytochemicals that offer great skin protection from the sun's rays. After you consume carotenoid-rich foods like peppers, carotenoids accumulate in your skin, where they oppose UV-induced oxidative stress. This is a beautifully unique recipe for barbeque season!

PEPPERS:

1 pound shishito peppers

2 teaspoons extra-virgin olive oil

2 limes, quartered

CHILI MINT SALT SHAKE:

1 teaspoon sea salt

1 teaspoon chili powder or ground chipotle pepper

1 teaspoon hemp seeds

1 to 1½ teaspoons fresh mint leaves, minced

1 teaspoon coconut sugar

1 **To make the peppers:** add the shishito peppers to a small bowl and drizzle with oil. Stir until the peppers have a light coating of oil. Dip some bamboo skewers in water to prevent burning over the flames. Skewer the peppers at an angle. Grill them over an open flame (either a stovetop or grill) until softened and charred slightly around the edges, with just a little bit of grill marks.

2 **To make the Chili Mint Salt Shake:** mix all ingredients in a small mixing bowl. Sprinkle on top of each pepper.

3 Squeeze lime juice over the top of the peppers.

CEVICHE

CEVICHE IS A REFRESHING LATIN APPETIZER traditionally made with fish. My version uses the closest substitute I've yet found: coconut meat. It's important to use only young Thai coconuts for this dish, as the meat has a soft, chewy, slightly firm texture that absolutely sings with the tang and spice of the other fresh vegetables. This ceviche is refreshing, healthy, and addictive. Plus, the coconut meat has antioxidant and anti-inflammatory properties that help prevent signs of aging.

2½ cups young Thai coconut meat

¼ cup fresh lime juice

¼ cup fresh orange juice

2 medium tomatoes, diced

5 scallions, minced

½ large cucumber, diced

½ green bell pepper, seeded and diced

½ cup fresh parsley, chopped

¼ cup fresh cilantro, chopped

½ jalapeno pepper, seeded and minced

1½ tablespoons extra-virgin olive oil

½ teaspoon sea salt, or to taste

Pinch cayenne pepper, to taste

1 large avocado, peeled, pitted, and diced

One 16-ounce bag tortilla chips or vegetable chips, for plating

1 Crack the coconuts open using a sturdy cleaver: make four identical cuts on the top, forming a square. Using the back of the blade for leverage, gently "pop" open the top of the coconut. Drain the coconut water and refrigerate in a covered glass storage jar. Crack the coconuts in half and scrape out the coconut meat with the backside of a large metal spoon. The coconut meat should be thick enough to remove it as one large piece. Rinse the coconut meat to remove any shell bits or debris. Using a paring knife, fillet any pieces of hard shell that won't easily wash off.

2 Chop the coconut meat into ½-inch square pieces. Add them to a medium mixing bowl and toss with the lime and orange juice. Marinate in the refrigerator for at least 2 hours.

3 Add the remaining ingredients, except the avocado and tortilla chips. Mix gently. Add the diced avocado last and mix well. Serve immediately or chill in the refrigerator for 30 minutes to 1 hour prior to serving. Serve with tortilla chips.

Purchase a total of 5 young Thai coconuts for this recipe, as the thickness and consistency of the coconut meat can vary greatly, depending on the age of the coconuts. Use coconut meat that is on the firm side so that it can marinate well with the lime juice and retain its "fishlike" mouthfeel. Stay away from coconuts that have brown spots and soft areas on the bottom or ones that have a slight pink hue to the exterior. They are much too young and the meat will be too gelatinous to work well in this ceviche.

SUPREME
KALE BLT SALAD

SERVES 4

KALE IS KING. AND WHAT BETTER way to really make it sing than to turn it into the base for a BLT salad? In this recipe, the "B" comes from tempeh bacon, which is a package of premarinated tempeh strips that you can find at most grocery stores. The "honey" mustard dressing provides a sweet, tangy, and tantalizing flavor that pairs perfectly with the smoky tempeh and fresh tomatoes. If I had to pick a favorite salad in my recipe arsenal, this would absolutely be number one. And, if I have a number-one skin food, it's probably kale, too. Kale boosts the health of your skin because of its vitamin C content, which helps you make the collagen needed for skin strength. Kale also comes packed with skin-friendly copper. This mineral boosts the synthesis of melanin, a pigment that protects your skin from the sun. Kale also boosts your vitamin A intake, which promotes the growth of healthy cells that make up the dermis and epidermis of your skin.

TEMPEH BACON:

1 tablespoon organic virgin coconut oil

One 6-ounce package tempeh bacon

"HONEY" MUSTARD DRESSING:

½ cup and 2 tablespoons coconut nectar

¼ cup and 1 tablespoon Dijon mustard

2 tablespoons coconut vinegar

⅛ teaspoon sea salt

Pinch ground black pepper

SALAD:

1 large bunch lacinato kale, chopped and destemmed

1 avocado, pitted and diced

½ cup red pepper, diced

½ cup cherry tomatoes, sliced

¼ cup shallot, finely minced

¼ cup sunflower sprouts

1. **To make the tempeh bacon:** heat the coconut oil in a large skillet over medium heat. Add the tempeh bacon strips and cook them on both sides for a couple of minutes, then set aside.

2. **To make the "Honey" Mustard Dressing:** blend the coconut nectar, Dijon mustard, coconut vinegar, salt, and black pepper in a high-speed blender for 30 seconds until creamy and set aside.

3. **To make the salad:** add the kale to a large mixing bowl and massage in the diced avocado. Add red bell pepper, cherry tomatoes, shallot, and the tempeh bacon. Drizzle the dressing over the top and toss. Top with the sunflower sprouts.

ROASTED GARLIC
BEAN DIP

SERVES 6 TO 8

INSTEAD OF RELYING ON A TON of olive oil for flavor and texture in this delectable dip, cannellini beans are the perfect stand-in. Their buttery taste and dense texture make them a great choice. Pairing them with roasted garlic and balsamic vinegar creates a classic flavor profile. Serve this recipe with multigrain crackers, vegetable crudités, or toasted pita bread, or use it as a sumptuous spread for sandwiches. Along with the cannellini beans, the ridiculously flavorful roasted garlic is the skin star of this recipe. Garlic's high sulfur content tones your skin and gives hair more luster. The sulfur reportedly works with B-complex vitamins to support body metabolism and keep youthful elasticity in your tissues. Garlic also is a source of the mineral selenium, which works with vitamin E to boost antioxidant power and slow the signs of aging. Selenium is critical for the production of glutathione peroxidase, the body's primary antioxidant found in every cell.

One 15-ounce can cannellini beans

2 bulbs garlic, roasted

1 teaspoon extra-virgin olive oil

1 teaspoon fresh rosemary, minced

Pinch sea salt

1 tablespoon balsamic vinegar

Pinch truffle salt

1 teaspoon pumpkin seed oil, optional

1 teaspoon pumpkin seeds

1 Preheat the oven to 400 degrees Fahrenheit.

2 Drain the cannellini beans and reserve ½ cup of the liquid from the can.

3 Slice off the top of each head of garlic to expose some of the cloves inside. Place the heads on a piece of foil. Drizzle with olive oil and wrap in the foil. Roast until the cloves are lightly browned and tender, about 30 to 35 minutes.

4 Process the garlic, rosemary, sea salt, and balsamic vinegar in a high-speed food processor. Gradually add the bean liquid as it processes. Process until you get a nice consistency, scraping the sides down with a spatula as necessary. Give it a taste and add additional salt if necessary.

5 Serve the dip in a bowl and top with the truffle salt, pumpkin seed oil, and pumpkin seeds.

PEAR & PECAN
SALAD

SERVES 2 TO 4

THERE ARE SO MANY ALKALIZING INGREDIENTS in this recipe, it's enough to make your head spin. Think of this dish as the great equalizer if you've been eating too much acidic food. This salad is sweet, savory, crunchy, and well balanced. It's a great side dish or main course if you're doing a cleanse. Pears are naturally high in vitamins C and K, as well as nutrients such as copper—all of which act as antioxidants to protect our cells from free-radical damage. Geeky nutrition fact alert: pears are also said to have more nutrients per calorie than calories per nutrient. Power to the pears, people!

1 large pear, diced

1½ cups carrot, diced

1 cup golden beets, diced

1 cup raw pecans, crushed

¼ cup cilantro, minced

4 scallions, minced

1 orange, juiced

2 tablespoons extra-virgin olive oil

2 tablespoons coconut aminos

¼ cup hemp seeds

Small handful sprouted pumpkin seeds

Dash cayenne pepper

1 Combine the pear, carrots, beets, and pecans in a large mixing bowl. Add the cilantro, scallions, orange juice, olive oil, coconut aminos, and hemp seeds. Mix well. Top with the pumpkin seeds and cayenne pepper.

PUMPKIN
GELATO

WHEN YOU TRY THIS UBER-CREAMY, DAIRY-FREE gelato, all the awesome autumn flavors unleash simultaneously in your mouth. The pumpkin and coconut base creates a sweet taste and thick, voluminous texture while the maple syrup and coconut sugar deliver a sweet, caramel flavor palette. The dynamic duo of pumpkin seeds and oil needs to be in your skin care regimen, stat. Boasting vitamin E and zinc, they aid in the formation of new skin cells as well as collagen, which is responsible for maintaining the elasticity of your skin. Moreover, they've got free-radical-killing carotenoids and essential fatty acids to bring out that healthy, youthful shine.

One 15-ounce can unsweetened pumpkin puree

2 cups coconut milk

½ cup young Thai coconut meat

½ cup coconut sugar

¼ cup plus 2 tablespoons organic virgin coconut oil

¼ cup maple syrup

1 tablespoon vanilla extract

4 teaspoons pumpkin pie spice

¼ teaspoon ground cinnamon

½ teaspoon sea salt, to taste

¼ cup pepitas (pumpkin seeds), crushed, reserved for topping

1 teaspoon toasted pumpkin seed oil, reserved for topping

½ cup organic candied ginger, diced, reserved for topping (optional)

1 Blend all ingredients, except pepitas, pumpkin seed oil, and candied ginger, in a high-speed blender about 60 seconds, until very smooth and creamy. Transfer to a 2-quart automatic ice cream maker and allow it to mix for 45 to 50 minutes until thick and creamy. Top with the crushed pepitas, pumpkin seed oil, and candied ginger pieces, if using. Store any remaining gelato in a covered glass storage container in the freezer.

JASON'S TIP

Make sure that the metal bowl of your ice cream maker is completely frozen and chilled prior to using, or you won't get the proper consistency during the churning process. You can also substitute fresh, roasted pumpkin in the recipe instead of canned pumpkin.

SHEPHERD'S PIE

PREPARING COMFORT FOODS IS A SERIOUS business. You are taking someone's emotional security into your hands and providing something deeply nourishing and soul soothing. This delicious Shepherd's Pie definitely accomplishes both tasks with ease and grace. The classic mix of vegetables is slathered in a soy-free chickpea miso gravy that has the perfect salty and savory flavor balance, while the purple potatoes offer a creamy topping that encases all this glorious goodness in cute ramekins. And those purple potatoes pack some serious skin-saving power! Purple potatoes have more than four times the free-radical-annihilating antioxidant potential of other potatoes. Those purple spuds score as high as brussels sprouts, kale, or spinach on the antioxidant power scale. They're also a good source of complex carbohydrates, potassium, vitamin C, folic acid, and iron.

VEGETABLE FILLING:

1½ tablespoons organic virgin coconut oil

½ yellow onion, diced

3 cloves garlic, minced

2 stalks celery, diced

1 carrot, chopped

1 leek, chopped

1 large Yukon Gold potato, chopped

½ cup green peas

1½ tablespoons minced parsley

2 teaspoons sage leaves, chiffonaded, plus more for garnish

1 teaspoon rosemary, minced

1 tablespoon thyme, minced

½ teaspoon sea salt

¼ teaspoon ground black pepper

¼ cup low-sodium vegetable broth

1 **To make the vegetable filling:** preheat the oven to 350 degrees Fahrenheit. Heat the coconut oil in a large skillet on medium-high heat. Add the onion and garlic and cook until translucent. Add the remaining ingredients and cook for another 6 to 10 minutes, then transfer to a large mixing bowl.

2 **To make the sauce:** blend all sauce ingredients in a high-speed blender until fully combined. Pour over the pie filling ingredients and mix well.

3 **To make the purple potato topping:** sauté the purple potatoes and vegetable broth in the same skillet that was used for the filling, for about 6 minutes. Transfer the mixture to a blender and add the remaining ingredients. Pulse until you get a smooth puree.

SAUCE:

⅛ cup dry white wine

1 tablespoon chickpea miso

1 cup low-sodium vegetable broth

½ cup filtered water

1 teaspoon arrowroot powder

⅛ cup sunflower seeds, soaked
    for 2 hours

⅛ teaspoon ground white pepper

⅛ teaspoon ground coriander

3 tablespoons unsweetened
    coconut milk

PURPLE POTATO TOPPING:

2 large purple potatoes, peeled,
    quartered, and thinly sliced

1 cup low-sodium vegetable broth

½ cup plus 2 tablespoons
    coconut milk

½ teaspoon sea salt

4 Liberally spoon the vegetable filling and sauce mixture into five 3½-inch porcelain ramekins. Top with the purple potato topping, using the back of a spoon to smooth out the top, starting in the center and spiraling out to the rim. Place the ramekins on a baking sheet to catch any spillage in the oven. Bake for 30 minutes. Remove and let cool for 10 minutes. Garnish with fresh sage and enjoy!

JASON'S TIP

For more protein, add 8 ounces of cubed tempeh to the vegetable filling mixture and sauté with the rest of the ingredients. For a 100 percent oil-free recipe, feel free to substitute filtered water or low-sodium vegetable broth for the coconut oil.

12

EAT FOR

STRONG EYESIGHT

WANT TO ENJOY PERFECT PORTIONS
to polish your peepers? Well, I've got some useful tips and recipes that will help give you holographic vision and laser-powered retinas! I'm kidding. But we'll get you pretty darn close! Now, if there's one thing that's critically important to maintain as you age, it's your eyesight. With the right foods and supplements combined with some eye-strengthening exercises, you'll be on track to keep your future looking bright . . . and clear!

I don't remember much of my life without lenses. I've worn glasses since I was five years old and contact lenses since age 14. To say the least, they've been interesting filters through which I view the world. I've sometimes felt a lot of anger and confusion as to why my eyesight declined at such a young age and why nobody seems to know the reason. I've yet to see any substantive, clinical research studies regarding the causes of macular degeneration or near-sightedness. Furthermore, modern science has yet to find a reversal or cure. On another note, it's also amusingly ironic how the script can get flipped in life: I went from being relentlessly teased in my teens for having "four eyes" to being publicly adored as a frame-wearing, culinary Casanova in my 30s. Go figure. Social commentary and style preferences aside, my vision has definitely changed as I've gotten older, and my prescription changes slightly about every ten years. As I age, I'm more mindful than ever about my dietary choices and making sure I'm setting myself up for a lifetime of good eyesight.

Can you relate? Do you experience issues with your vision, or do you currently wear corrective lenses of some kind? I wouldn't be surprised. It looks like eyesight issues are pretty common for a whole lot of folks in the U.S., with many people needing corrective aids later in life:

- Americans spend more than $400 million on reading glasses each year
- People typically start needing higher prescription lenses in their 40s

- By 55 or 60, many people find that they need reading glasses in two strengths

Besides getting a boost from glasses or contact lenses, there's an abundance of perfect foods and nutrients to keep your eyesight strong (or prevent it from getting worse). Essential antioxidants like carotenoids are fantastic for maintaining sharp eyesight. You can find them in brightly colored foods like carrots, squash, pumpkin, gourds, and other nutritious root vegetables. Nature gives you some pretty easy-to-follow clues regarding which foods contain carotenoids, as indicated by orange, yellow, or red pigmentation.

EYE LOVE THESE NUTRIENTS AND FOODS!

Thanks to Bugs Bunny, most of us think of carrots as the best food for helping our eyesight, with their abundance of beta-carotene and vitamin A. But there are other key nutrients and foods that are just as important for keeping your eyesight sharp as you age.

Vitamins C, A, and E, along with minerals such as copper and zinc, are essential to eyesight. Antioxidants, including lutein, zeaxanthin, and beta-carotene, as mentioned, protect the macula, a small area of the eye near the retina, from sun damage. You can get these awesome antioxidants from dark, leafy greens, yellow peppers, pumpkin, sweet potatoes, and carrots. Notice any more color patterns happenin' here? Current research shows that consuming yellow and green vegetables can help prevent age-related macular degeneration (AMD), a leading cause of blindness.

Foods rich in sulfur, cysteine, and lecithin help protect the lens of your eye from cataract formation, which is the clouding of your lenses. Excellent choices to prevent this include garlic, onions, shallots, and capers.

Anthocyanin-rich blueberries, blackberries, grapes, and goji berries have antioxidant and anti-inflammatory properties that can help improve your vision. And DHA, an essential fatty acid found in seaweed and ocean microalgae, provides structural support to the cell membranes, boosting eye health.

As always, it's best to get these nutrients from whole-food sources, as these foods may contain many other macronutrients and phytochemicals that haven't been discovered by research yet.

VISIONARY WAYS TO STRENGTHEN YOUR EYES

With the current pace of modern life and the technology that we have at our disposal, we're constantly staring at very large amounts of text and images on computers, televisions, and smartphones. Staring at these types of screens for long periods can lead to eye fatigue and an increase in age-related eye problems. But we're not going to stop using our smartphones anytime soon. So what are we supposed to do?

Diminished eyesight does not have to be an inevitable part of a long life. In addition to eating a nutrient-dense diet, there are exercises you can do to sharpen your vision so you can see your way to a future of joyful and healthy longevity.

These simple daily exercises will help you maintain optimal vision and may also keep eye floaters at bay. You can perform these exercises first thing in the morning, before bedtime, or anytime your eyes feel fatigued.

- Warm your eyes. Rub your palms together to create heat, and then place them against your eyes for five seconds. Repeat this 3 times.
- Roll your eyes. Start by looking up and then slowly circle 10 times clockwise and 10 times counterclockwise.
- Focus. Hold a pen at arm's length, focus your eyes on it, and slowly bring the pen closer until it's about six inches away from your nose. Then slowly move it back, keeping your eyes focused on the pen, 10 times in all.
- Massage your temples. Using your thumb knuckles, massage your temples in small circles, 20 times in one direction and 20 in the other. Repeat the same actions above the midpoint of the eyebrows at the forehead, then below the eyes on both sides of the bridge of the nose.
- Take a mini nap. Put your head back, close your eyes, and relax for ten minutes.

THE IMPORTANCE OF REST AND SLEEP

It goes without saying that we need to take a break from technology every once in a while. How you do this depends on your personal lifestyle, career, family, and other commitments—some of us need to be "on call" more than others. If your schedule allows it, give your eyes a ten-minute break once an hour during your workday. Whether it's a quick, five-minute break every half hour or a daylong electronic Sabbath, your eyes will thank you!

In addition to these much-needed breaks, getting enough sleep is essential for eye health. Sleep allows your eyes to fully rest, repair, and recover. Insufficient sleep may weaken your vision, so shoot for eight hours of sound sleep a night. You need to be a good sleeper for strong peepers!

STAVING OFF MACULAR DEGENERATION AND CATARACTS

Macular degeneration comes in two forms, wet and dry, and occurs when the central part of the retina is damaged due to deterioration of retinal cells (dry form) or to leaking blood vessels in or under the retina (wet form). This degeneration, as mentioned, may be slowed by diets high in antioxidants such as vitamin C and carotenoids. A study by the National Institutes of Health published in the *Journal of the American Medical Association* linked overall macular health with a high lutein content in the eye. Lutein and its related compound, zeaxanthin, are found in high concentrations in the center of the retina. These compounds contribute to the macular pigment, which helps protect the eye against harsh light. In a study at the University of Florida, Department of Ophthalmology, it was shown that taking 20 milligrams of lutein daily brings the amount of pigment to normal levels within 120 days, though taking a higher dosage does not significantly affect the levels in the eye.

The clouding of the lens, typical of cataracts, may be related to exposure to sunlight and the accompanying oxidation process. As with macular degeneration, this process appears to be slowed by a diet rich in antioxidants, especially vitamin C. The key vitamins for both conditions appear to be vitamin C, folic acid, selenium, and zinc. These are found in leafy, green vegetables, carrots, citrus fruits, and sweet melons. Spinach, kale, and collard greens, which provide lutein and zeaxanthin, seem to be particularly beneficial for the macula. Caution should be exercised regarding three antioxidants: vitamin A, beta-carotene, and vitamin E. Vitamin A in excess of 5,000 units has been linked with osteoporosis. Beta-carotene has been associated with lung cancer in smokers. And finally, vitamin E in excess of 400 units has been linked with excessive blood thinning. Patients who are on medications such as coumadin or aspirin should be particularly cautious about their vitamin E dosage.

KNOCKOUT NUTRIENTS FOR LONG-TERM EYE HEALTH

If you are at serious risk for age-related macular degeneration, there are special supplements that may help slow it or keep it from getting worse. They are called AREDS, named after the age-related eye disease studies that tested and fine-tuned the formula. These supplements combine high doses of nutrients in some of the foods that were mentioned earlier: vitamin C, vitamin E, beta-carotene, vitamin A, zinc, and copper. The newest version of these supplements, called AREDS 2, is especially good if you get very little lutein and zeaxanthin in food. It's also safe if you're a smoker or recently quit, because it doesn't have beta-carotene in it. You can buy AREDS 2 formula supplements over the counter, but talk to your eye doctor first. Some people shouldn't take high doses of antioxidants for various health reasons.

Experts say it's hard to get the same high levels of nutrients in the AREDS 2 supplements from food alone. Monica L. Monica, M.D., Ph.D., a clinical spokeswoman for the American Academy of Ophthalmology, says to avoid a do-it-yourself approach like taking extra vitamin C or E, because the specific AREDS combination has been known to work.

IMPORTANT LIFESTYLE CHANGES

While vitamins can be obtained by taking natural supplements, I believe that you should get as many of these nutrients as you can through food. A diet high in fresh, organic fruits and vegetables and low in saturated fat, trans fats, and refined sugar will not only support your eyesight but also your overall level of health and vitality. Although increasing your intake of antioxidants will probably not restore vision that's already lost, it may help to slow the progress of degeneration.

Remember: good nutrition and vitality are lifelong goals. Don't wait until you develop an eye problem or other health concern to make changes in your lifestyle. Being proactive and making well-informed nutritional choices goes a long way with maintaining your eyesight and your overall state of well-being!

MY TOP NUTRIENTS FOR STRONG EYESIGHT

Anthocyanins: This is the largest group of water-soluble pigments in the plant kingdom, known collectively as flavonoids. Similar to chlorophyll, they convert light into pigment and may have a similar effect on eye health, helping to reduce retina fatigue.

Beta-carotene: This is the compound we are all familiar with that gives carrots, pumpkins, and sweet potatoes their bright orange color. Many studies have proven its effectiveness against cataracts and other eye degenerative diseases.

DHA: A major structural fat in the retina of the eye, DHA plays an important role in both infant visual development and visual function throughout life.

Lutein: A specific carotenoid that may block blue light from reaching the underlying structures in the retina, thereby reducing the risk of light-induced oxidative damage that could lead to macular degeneration. There are more than 600 known carotenoids and lutein is one of only two found in the retina.

Zeaxanthin: With protective properties very similar to lutein, this is the other retinal carotenoid with antioxidant effects on the eye.

MY TOP FOODS FOR STRONG EYESIGHT

- arugula
- bell peppers
- bentonite clay
- bilberries
- blueberries
- Brazil nuts
- broccoli
- brown rice
- brussels sprouts
- butternut squash
- carrots
- cherries
- chrysanthemum
- cicada chantui
- citrus fruits
- collard greens
- daikon radish
- fennel
- figs
- flaxseed
- ginkgo biloba
- goji berries
- green tea
- kale
- legumes
- milk thistle
- nectarines
- parsley
- pumpkin
- pumpkin seeds
- red wine
- saffron
- soy products
- spinach
- squash
- strawberries
- sweet potatoes
- turnip greens

RECIPES FOR BETTER EYESIGHT

·····················

PINEAPPLE MANGO
SALSA

I LOVE MY FOOD EXTRA SPICY, especially Latin cuisine like Mexican, Cuban, and Puerto Rican. What I love even more is having a nice amount of sweet with my spicy. This low-fat, low-calorie salsa is infused with sweet pineapple and mango while bringing the detox duo of cilantro and cayenne pepper to the party. Tomato—this ain't your party, pal. It's time to let the tropical fruit take the dance floor. Pineapple contains beta-carotene and vitamin A that are good for eyesight. Eating pineapple helps to prevent macular degeneration and reduces the risk of vision loss as you age. The presence of antioxidants helps to solve eye-related problems and maintains good overall eye health. That right there is cause for a fiesta!

2 cups diced fresh pineapple

2 cups diced fresh mango

1 cup diced red bell pepper

¼ cup fresh cilantro leaves, chopped

¼ cup fresh lime juice

Pinch cayenne pepper

Pinch ground cumin

Pinch sea salt

1 jalapeno, seeded and diced

One 16-ounce bag organic tortilla chips, for dipping

1 Add all of the ingredients, except tortilla chips, to a mixing bowl and gently stir to combine well. Serve with the organic tortilla chips.

SPAGHETTI SQUASH
PRIMAVERA

SERVES 4 TO 6

WHEN YOU NEED A PASTA FIX but you're sick of the same old noodles, this is the recipe to reach for. Spaghetti squash, aka nature's noodles, is one of my favorite ingredients. Whether it's used in mac n' cheese, fettucine alfredo, or this delightful primavera recipe, it holds up well with dense sauces and retains its slightly sweet flavor and crunchy texture. Apart from being a rich source of vitamins and minerals, spaghetti squash has high levels of beta-carotene, which along with lutein can reduce the risk of eye problems like macular degeneration and cataracts.

1 spaghetti squash, halved

3 tablespoons extra-virgin olive oil, divided

3 to 4 cloves garlic, minced

2½ cups broccoli, chopped into small florets

1 cup oyster mushroom, sliced

2½ teaspoons fresh rosemary, chopped

1 teaspoon fresh thyme, chopped

Pinch crushed red pepper flakes

1 cup cherry tomatoes, halved

¼ cup green olives, pitted and chopped

Ground black pepper, to taste

Truffle salt or sea salt, to taste

¼ cup pine nuts, lightly toasted, reserved for garnish

1 Preheat the oven to 350 degrees Fahrenheit.

2 Place both spaghetti squash halves, cut side down, in a shallow glass baking dish and lightly drizzle with 1 tablespoon of olive oil and the truffle salt. Bake for 35 to 40 minutes until a fork glides through the squash easily and with little effort. Remove from the heat and use a fork to shred the "noodles" inside the squash. Place the spaghetti squash "noodles" in a medium mixing bowl and set aside.

3 Heat 1 tablespoon of olive oil in a large skillet over medium heat and sauté the minced garlic for about 5 minutes, until lightly browned. Add the broccoli florets and cook for another 8 minutes or until tender. Add the oyster mushrooms, rosemary, thyme, and red pepper flakes, cooking for 3 minutes. Add the cherry tomatoes and green olives, cooking for another 2 minutes. Remove from the heat and add to the mixing bowl with the spaghetti squash. Season to taste with salt and pepper. Add the remaining 1 tablespoon of olive oil and mix well. Top with the toasted pine nuts. Serve immediately.

CARROT ALMOND
ICE CREAM FLOAT

INSPIRED BY MY TIME WORKING WITH a Middle Eastern gypsy café in Venice Beach, California, this smoothie highlights the addictive flavor combination of sweet carrot and creamy, nondairy vanilla ice cream. At first, I thought this combo was pure insanity until my taste buds convinced me otherwise. The texture is somewhere between that of a smoothie and a juice. Hence, the term "smuice" was invented to best describe its unique culinary glory. Carrots, as we all know, have good amounts of beta-carotene, which your body uses to make vitamin A. Vitamin A helps the eye convert light into a signal that can be transmitted to the brain, allowing you to see under conditions of low light. This float won't give you X-ray vision, but it may help you see a bit better as you get on in age.

6 medium carrots, peeled and juiced

1 cup raw coconut water

¾ cup coconut nectar

1 tablespoon almond extract

¼ cup young Thai coconut meat

½ cup cashews, soaked for 2 hours

1 cup macadamia nuts

½ cup organic virgin coconut oil

1½ teaspoons maca powder

2 teaspoons vanilla extract

Pinch sea salt

Pinch ground cinnamon

¼ cup mulberries, reserved for garnish

¼ cup almonds, crushed, reserved for garnish

1 Place the peeled carrots in a juicer and process into carrot juice. Set aside.

2 Blend the remaining ingredients, except the mulberries and almonds, in a high-speed blender for 40 seconds until smooth and creamy. Transfer to an automatic ice cream maker and process for 30 to 45 minutes, until a smooth, dense, creamy consistency is achieved. After your ice cream is ready, place a few scoops into a big glass and pour the fresh carrot juice over it. Top with the mulberries and almonds.

PUMPKIN SPICE
PARFAIT

SERVES 6

I'LL ADMIT—THIS RECIPE IS LYING TO you. It says "pumpkin" in the title, but there's actually no pumpkin here. The pumpkin flavor comes from the butternut squash's signature fall spices. I know, you're sad. But trust me, you'll get over it when you try the light, fluffy, creamy texture and sweet flavors of this parfait, baby. Plus, the awesome antioxidants beta-carotene, lutein, and zeaxanthin in butternut squash help you squash out potential eyestrain, dry eyes, the inability to make out fine details, and deteriorating vision as you age.

1 ounce Irish moss (by weight)

1 cup coconut milk

3 cups butternut squash, finely chopped

½ cup maple syrup

2 tablespoons vanilla extract

2 tablespoons fresh lemon juice

1 teaspoon ground cinnamon

½ teaspoon pumpkin pie spice

¼ teaspoon ground nutmeg

⅛ teaspoon ground cloves

¼ teaspoon sea salt

2 tablespoons sunflower lecithin

½ cup organic virgin coconut oil

1 cup pecans, crushed, reserved for garnish

1 Remove any stones, pebbles, or dark pieces from the Irish moss. Soak the Irish moss in hot water for 30 minutes. Rinse with cold water and finely mince. Blend the minced Irish moss and coconut milk in a high-speed blender until the Irish moss is completely broken down. Scrape the top and sides of the blender, making sure that all small chunks are blended well with the liquid. You'll notice the mixture start to firm up and become more jellylike.

2 Add the remaining ingredients, except the sunflower lecithin, coconut oil, and pecans. Blend until smooth and creamy.

3 Add the sunflower lecithin and coconut oil and blend until fully incorporated. Pour the mixture into parfait glasses or another type of serving glass. Set in the fridge for 30 to 45 minutes until solid. Garnish with the crushed pecans.

BUTTERNUT SQUASH MAC N' CHEESE
WITH CRISPY SAGE

SERVES 4 TO 6

WHEN ATTEMPTING A VEGAN MAC N' cheese, there are a lot of ways to tackle a recipe. My version features a mighty tag team of butternut squash and sage. These two ingredients add a sweet, buttery flavor and savory, wintertime feel to the dish, while the cheesy flavor comes full force thanks to the nutritional yeast, coconut milk, and lemon. This is healthy comfort food at its absolute finest. In addition to boasting a bodacious amount of beta-carotene, butternut squash is also a great source of two other powerful antioxidants, zeaxanthin and lutein. Your body concentrates these two carotenoids in the macular region of your eyes, where they protect your vision from damaging UV and blue-light radiation.

- 1 small to medium butternut squash, about 2 pounds
- 3 tablespoons organic virgin coconut oil, divided
- One 16-ounce package gluten-free elbow noodles, shells, or rigatoni
- 4 cloves garlic, minced
- 1 teaspoon dried oregano
- 3 cups heavy coconut milk, divided
- 2 tablespoons arrowroot powder
- 1½ cups nutritional yeast
- 2 tablespoons Dijon mustard
- 2 tablespoons fresh lemon juice
- 2 teaspoons truffle salt, divided
- 1 teaspoon fresh ground black pepper
- 1½ cups collard greens, chopped
- Pinch smoked paprika, to taste
- ½ cup toasted pecans, crushed
- 1 handful fresh sage leaves

JASON'S TIP

If you can't find gluten-free pasta, feel free to use whatever natural, whole-grain pasta you can find and cook according to the directions on the box. For topping the mac n' cheese, you can use toasted, crushed pecans; pepitas; almonds; or bread crumbs.

1. Preheat the oven to 425 degrees Fahrenheit.

2. Peel and dice the butternut squash. Toss the diced butternut squash with 1 tablespoon of coconut oil in a 13 x 9-inch metal baking pan until evenly coated. Roast for 30 to 35 minutes.

3. Cook the pasta according to the package instructions. Drain and set aside.

4. Heat 1 tablespoon of coconut oil in a medium saucepan over medium heat for 1 minute. Add the garlic and dried oregano and cook for a few minutes or until the garlic is soft and slightly golden brown. Reduce the heat to medium low and then whisk in 1½ cups of coconut milk and the arrowroot powder, making sure there are no lumps. Add the nutritional yeast and whisk vigorously until the sauce thickens. Stir in the mustard, lemon juice, 1 teaspoon of the truffle salt, and the pepper, and cook for another 3 to 5 minutes. Remove the saucepan from the heat and set aside.

5. Remove the squash from the oven and allow to cool for a few minutes. Reduce the oven temperature to 350 degrees Fahrenheit.

6. Blend the butternut squash and remaining coconut milk in a high-speed blender until very smooth, about 30 to 45 seconds. Transfer to the saucepan and whisk together until well combined.

7. Transfer the cooked pasta and butternut squash sauce to a large glass baking dish. Add the chopped collard greens and smoked paprika and mix well. Top with the crushed pecans. Bake for 20 minutes.

8. Heat the remaining 1 tablespoon of coconut oil in a medium skillet over medium-low heat. Add 6 to 7 individual sage leaves at a time, flipping once, until crispy, about 1 minute total. Watch the sage leaves carefully to ensure they do not burn; you want them slightly browned. Let them drain on a paper towel and lightly season with the remaining 1 teaspoon of truffle salt. Remove the mac n' cheese from the oven and serve with the crispy sage leaves on top.

NECTARINE SALAD

SERVES 4

I FEEL SOMETIMES LIKE NECTARINES DON'T get the same amount of love that peaches do. 'Tis a shame, really, because this sweet stone fruit really shines when paired with a great dressing and the right vegetable companions. In this salad, the nectarines play off fresh field greens, pine nuts, and vegan cheese. The tangy, spicy balsamic Dijon dressing brings all the fantastic flavors together in what may be the ultimate summer salad. Nectarines contain lutein and beta-carotene, which encourage eye health and help reduce the risk of age-related eye diseases. Plus, they taste like pure sunshine!

DRESSING:

3 tablespoons extra-virgin olive oil

2 tablespoons balsamic vinegar

1 teaspoon Dijon mustard

2 teaspoons coconut sugar

⅛ teaspoon sea salt

Pinch ground black pepper

SALAD:

4 cups field greens, arugula, or baby lettuce, torn by hand

¼ cup cultured vegan cheese

2 large nectarines, pitted and sliced

¼ cup raw pine nuts

1 **To make the dressing:** add the olive oil, balsamic vinegar, and Dijon mustard to a small mixing bowl. Add the coconut sugar, salt, and black pepper, and whisk together.

2 **To make the salad:** toss together the field greens and dressing. Top with vegan cheese, sliced nectarines, and pine nuts.

ROASTED VEGETABLE
PASTA

SERVES 4

FILE THIS RECIPE UNDER THE HEADING, "I really want a filling, comforting meal, but I don't wanna work that hard!" Sometimes, you just want to throw some pasta on boil, roast some veggies, and call it a night. If that's your fancy, make this roasted-veggie pasta, and you'll be chillin' like a Rasta. The butternut squash has some of the highest eye-protecting levels of beta-carotene and lutein in the cucurbitaceae family. Hey—just use that word the next time you want a seriously freakin' high word score in *Scrabble!*

1 cup butternut squash,
 chopped

1 cup potatoes, chopped

1 cup red onion, sliced into
 ½-inch-thick circles

2 tablespoons extra-virgin olive
 oil, divided

Pinch sea salt, plus more for
 garnish

Pinch ground black pepper, plus
 more for garnish

One 16-ounce package gluten-free
 pasta, cooked

2 tablespoons garlic, minced

1 cup cherry tomatoes, halved

½ cup basil, chiffonaded

2 tablespoons balsamic vinegar

1 Preheat the oven to 425 degrees Fahrenheit.

2 Mix together the butternut squash, potatoes, and red onion in a large bowl. Add 1 tablespoon of olive oil and toss to combine. Add the salt and pepper and spread the vegetables out over two baking sheets to ensure that the vegetables aren't touching. Roast the veggies for 25 to 35 minutes. Halfway through their roasting time, flip the vegetables to make sure both sides are cooking evenly. Once the vegetables are crisp at the edges, remove from the oven and set aside.

3 Cook the pasta according to the package instructions. Drain and set aside.

4 Heat a large skillet over medium heat and add the remaining 1 tablespoon of olive oil and the garlic. Let the garlic cook for about 2 minutes, and then add the cherry tomatoes. Allow the tomatoes to cook for about 3 to 4 minutes, until soft.

5 Add the roasted vegetables to the skillet, stirring to combine well. Add the pasta to the skillet. Cook for 1 to 2 minutes to meld the flavors. Remove from the heat and plate the pasta. Garnish with the fresh basil, a drizzle of balsamic vinegar, and salt and pepper to taste.

MIXED BERRY
PARFAIT

THIS RECIPE IS A MODIFIED VERSION of a classic dessert recipe I learned from my wedding cake mentor, Tiziana. Normally, you might use this recipe as a pie or layer cake filling, as the Irish moss helps the mixture set with a creamy, fluffy texture, but it works great on its own as a parfait. I love the bright flavor of the mixed berries with the sweet coconut nectar. These berries are bursting with vitamin C, which helps protect your eyes from age-related vision loss. This light, deliciously satisfying dessert won't make you feel like you need a nap after you're done enjoying it.

1 ounce Irish moss (by weight)

1 cup coconut milk

3 cups fresh mixed berries, chopped

½ cup coconut nectar

2 tablespoons vanilla extract

2 tablespoons fresh lemon juice

¼ teaspoon sea salt

2 tablespoons sunflower lecithin

½ cup organic virgin coconut oil

¼ cup fresh blueberries, reserved for garnish

¼ cup fine coconut shreds, reserved for garnish

1 Soak the Irish moss in very warm water for 20 minutes. Rinse the Irish moss and finely dice. Blend the diced Irish moss and coconut milk until the Irish moss is completely broken down. Scrape the top and sides of the blender, making sure that all small chunks blend with the liquid. You'll notice the mixture start to firm up and become more jellylike.

2 Add the remaining ingredients, except for the sunflower lecithin, coconut oil, fresh blueberries, and coconut shreds. Blend for an additional 30 seconds or so until creamy. Add the sunflower lecithin and coconut oil and blend for another 30 seconds.

3 Pour the mixture into parfait glasses or another type of serving glass. Set in the fridge for 2 hours or until solid. Garnish with the fresh blueberries and coconut shreds.

NO-GLUTEN NEWTONS

SERVES 6 TO 8

A HEALTHY TAKE ON THE CLASSIC childhood cookies, these gluten-free fig cookies are as sweet, soft, chewy, and delicious as the originals. The hazelnuts and flaxseed are a dynamite combination, rich in omega fatty acids and folate. What's more, hazelnuts are great for those hazel eyes! They're chock-full of nearly one-third of your RDA of vitamin E, which helps to prevent macular degeneration. This recipe is straight-up comfort food and is so ooey, gooey, moist, and delicious, a fight might break out over who gets the last one.

3 cups dried black mission figs, rehydrated

¾ cup golden flaxseed, ground

1½ cup raw hazelnuts

¾ cup gluten-free oats

1 teaspoon vanilla extract

Pinch sea salt

½ teaspoon ground cinnamon

⅓ cup coconut nectar

1 Soak the figs in room-temperature water for 20 minutes. Drain and reserve ¼ cup of the soak water.

2 Transfer the figs to a food processor and pulse, adding water slowly and as needed until a thick paste is formed. Set aside.

3 Blend flaxseed, hazelnuts, and gluten-free oats in a high-speed blender and pulse until a fluffy powder forms. Add the remaining ingredients and pulse a few more seconds. At this point, you may need to use a spatula or mix by hand until you get a nice doughy consistency.

4 Transfer the dough to a counter lined with parchment paper. Roll the dough out to a ¼-inch thickness. Slice the dough into 2 equal squares, side by side. Spread the fig paste on top of 1 square, then use the parchment paper to fold the other square onto it as the top crust. Press lightly. Freeze for 15 to 20 minutes to set, then cut into bite-size squares and enjoy.

PERSIMMON
GELATO

HOW DO YOU DO THE VOODOO that you do, Fuyu? That's my persimmon rap, yo. My stone-fruit game is real tight. And your lips will be tight around the spoon that carries a scoop of this gelato, which is so sweet you'll be singin' with vibrato! When persimmons are in season, I get a big bag full of them, halve them, and freeze them just so I can have this glorious gelato year-round, Jackie Brown. Plus, word on the street is that persimmons are a nutritional powerhouse, with 55 percent of your RDA of vitamin A and 21 percent of your vitamin C. Low in calories and fats, this little fruit contains all kinds of phytonutrients, flavonoids, and antioxidants such as beta-carotene, lycopene, lutein, and cryptoxanthin. Among other wondrous feats, they absorb into your eyes and help you filter light more efficiently. Neat trick, huh?

5 large persimmons, peeled, halved, and frozen

2 tablespoons baobab powder

¼ teaspoon ground cardamom

½ teaspoon ground cinnamon

¾ cup coconut milk

¼ cup fresh blueberries, plus more for garnish

1 Blend all ingredients in a high-speed blender for 30 to 45 seconds. Dish into parfait cups and garnish with blueberries.

STUFFED SQUASH BLOSSOMS
WITH RED PEPPER HARISSA

SERVES 4 TO 6

NEARLY EVERY CHEF UNDER THE SUN insists on frying stuffed squash blossoms to death. And, you know, I just felt like there was a more unusual and simple way to preserve their delicate floralness and crunchy texture . . . by keeping them raw. In this recipe, the Pine Nut Ricotta cheese is so good, you could eat it on its own, while the Red Pepper Harissa sauce adds zing and spice by the mile. For the few short weeks in summer when squash blossoms are widely available, use that time wisely to enjoy this sensual dish. Thanks to their rich stores of lutein, zeaxanthin, and vitamin C, the red bell peppers in the harissa sauce can stave off age-related macular degeneration and cataracts. Plus, the cute squash blossoms add some awesome vitamin A to the beach party. Those sweet summer sunsets are going to look better than ever now.

RED PEPPER HARISSA:

2 large red bell peppers, seeded and diced

2 garlic cloves, minced

1 tablespoon fresh lemon juice

2 teaspoons extra-virgin olive oil

1 teaspoon coconut nectar

1 teaspoon fresh oregano, minced

2 teaspoons dry harissa spice

¼ teaspoon sea salt

PINE NUT RICOTTA:

2 cups raw pine nuts, soaked for 1 to 2 hours

2 tablespoons extra-virgin olive oil

2 tablespoons fresh lemon juice

2 tablespoons nutritional yeast flakes

2 teaspoons shallot, minced

1 teaspoon lemon zest

1 teaspoon dried tarragon

¼ to ½ teaspoon sea salt

Pinch garlic granules

Pinch ground black pepper

SQUASH BLOSSOMS:

15 to 20 zucchini squash blossoms

¼ cup diced black olives or capers

3 tablespoons hemp seeds

3 cups arugula or watercress leaves, reserved for plating

1 **To make the Red Pepper Harissa:** blend the red bell peppers and garlic in a high-speed blender until smooth. Add the remaining ingredients and process until very smooth. Set aside.

2 **To make the Pine Nut Ricotta:** blend all ingredients in a high-speed blender for about 30 seconds until very smooth, thick, and creamy. Set aside.

3 **To make the squash blossoms:** gently cut a 1-inch lengthwise slit in each zucchini squash blossom. Transfer the Pine Nut Ricotta to a gallon-size, zip-top plastic bag. Cut the corner off the bag of ricotta and use it to pipe about 1 tablespoon of ricotta into each zucchini squash blossom. Pinch each blossom closed at the opening and then top each blossom with 1 to 2 teaspoons of the Red Pepper Harissa. Sprinkle the blossoms with the chopped black olives and hemp seeds. Transfer the blossoms to a bed of fresh arugula on a plate. Serve immediately.

JASON'S TIP

Traditionally, stuffed squash blossoms are sautéed or deep-fried. To cook the squash blossoms, combine ⅓ cup organic all-purpose flour with a pinch of dried oregano and thyme and ½ teaspoon baking powder in a medium mixing bowl. Whisk together vigorously. Once the squash blossoms are filled with the Pine Nut Ricotta, dunk each stuffed squash blossom gently into the flour mixture to coat evenly. Heat a few heaping tablespoons of coconut oil in a medium skillet on medium-low heat. Fry the stuffed squash blossoms in the skillet for a few minutes. Be mindful to not overcook the stuffed blossoms, as they can get burnt very quickly.

13

EAT FOR A
HEALTHY
HEART

YOU WANT A ROCK-SOLID RECIPE for a healthy heart? All right, here you go, baby. Don't say I never did nothin' for ya. Learning from my good friend and world-renowned cardiologist, Dr. Joel Kahn—aka "America's Holistic Heart Doc"—the equation for lifelong heart health looks a little something like this: stress reduction techniques + daily exercise + reducing your cholesterol + eating heart-healthy, plant-based foods + adding more joy and gratitude to your life = one top-notch ticker! The recipes and recommendations in this chapter are fun, flavorful, and absolutely fantastic for your long-term heart health.

Before I started writing this book, I knew that heart disease was a big issue. I've had acquaintances whose parents underwent bypass surgery, and I'd occasionally see social media posts from people trying to heal after open-heart surgery. But when I saw the entire scope of the issue and the sheer number of people dying from this disease, it really hit home: people are not taking good care of their most vital organ. The good thing is that we are seeing more and more practical solutions to healing the heart, from dietary choices to lifestyle modifications and mindfulness practices. The nuggets of wisdom you get from this chapter are more useful than ever, simply due to the number of people who suffer from heart disease:

- One-third of all people in the world are currently at risk of developing heart disease
- About 600,000 people die of heart disease in the U.S. every year—that's one in every four deaths
- Coronary heart disease alone costs the U.S. $108.9 billion each year

Looking at this from a sheer numbers perspective—from the number of people dying to the hundreds of billions of dollars in health care costs—it's clear that, as a society, we need to turn this equation around and start taking more responsibility for our health.

Along with poor nutrition, stress and anxiety can be extremely detrimental to your heart health. Studies have shown that high levels of cortisol (the stress hormone) are correlated to higher rates of heart disease. Reducing your levels of stress and anxiety through daily walks, regular exercise, meditation, deep breathing, lovemaking, or regular massage can lower your cortisol levels and, in turn, help to preserve your heart.

IS OIL-FREE THE ONLY WAY TO GO?

The oil-free, vegan diet craze has been all the rage for the past few years, and it's easy to see why. When you reduce the total amount of saturated fat and cholesterol in your diet, you can significantly reduce your overall risk of heart disease. However, making a blanket statement that ALL oils and fats are dangerous for your heart is a bit extreme, in my opinion. Not all oils and fats are created equal. And I strongly believe that the *quality* of the oil you consume is just as relevant as the overall *quantity*. Partially hydrogenated, trans-fatty-acid-laden, genetically modified cooking oils have a drastically different effect on your body and heart health than raw, cold-pressed, organic, extra-virgin oils made from nuts or seeds. In moderate amounts, healthy, plant-based fats are absolutely essential for nourishing your brain (which, as we learned, is mostly composed of fat) and producing healthy amounts of testosterone.

I don't recommend a completely oil-free or fat-free diet except for truly high-risk individuals who need to drastically cut their intake to stave off the acceleration of major diseases. For those of us in great overall health with no current heart issues or history of heart disease, a mild, monitored intake of high-quality, unprocessed, organic, raw, plant-based oils and fats can be a fantastic way to supplement your healthy lifestyle and add essential nutrients such as omega fatty acids into your diet.

Now, if you want to quit cooking with oil completely, I suggest you use low-sodium, organic vegetable stock or filtered water as a substitute when sautéing. For salad dressings, you can use organic apple cider vinegar, citrus juices and spices, or even cannellini beans to add extra creaminess and a rich texture without the additional oil.

PROTECTING YOUR HEART WITH PLANT-BASED DIETS

When you eat heart-healthy, plant-based, organic, whole foods, you nourish health-promoting bacteria in your digestive tract that emit by-products that lower inflammation, neutralize toxins, and nourish your cells and tissues. Conversely, when you consume heart-harming foods laden with chemicals, toxins, pesticides, sugars, processed salts, and animal protein, your bacteria emit poisons and toxins. One of these is called endotoxin, and the immune system treats it as a poison. When this toxin gets into your bloodstream, your level of inflammation goes up.

Pistachio Ice Cream
(see recipe page 321)

Certain foods are highly medicinal for your blood vessels. Healthy blood vessels are flexible and widen to accommodate increased blood flow. Organic, whole fruits and vegetables, such as pomegranates; grapes; green, leafy vegetables; beets; cacao; omega-rich oils; teas; and non-GMO, organic soy products all help your arteries to relax, driving down your blood pressure and making it easier for your heart to pump more blood. By consuming more of the right foods—raw, unprocessed, organic, plant-based foods—and minimizing or eliminating your consumption of highly processed, chemical-laden, high-fat animal products or artificial foods, you can protect your heart and greatly minimize your chance of coronary disease.

The Harvard Nurses' Health Study and Health Professionals Follow-Up Study found that people who eat more fresh fruits and vegetables have a lower risk of developing heart disease. People who ate eight or more servings a day were 30 percent less likely to have a heart attack or stroke than people who consumed one and a half servings or fewer. What's more, the symptoms of heart disease can even be *reversed* with a plant-based diet and holistic lifestyle. As we learned in a previous chapter, Dr. Dean Ornish is a pioneer in the medical industry who successfully reversed atherosclerosis, coronary artery disease (CAD), and other chronic diseases in his patients. His approach features a plant-based diet, quitting smoking, moderate exercise, and stress-management techniques.

In short, the absolute best approach to creating and maintaining long-term heart

health is through active and conscientious prevention. Through your dietary choices, you are creating a healthy internal bioterrain in which your heart can efficiently do its job by getting blood to vital organs, cells, and tissues. Combine this with healthy lifestyle practices, and you've got a powerful prescription for lifelong heart health!

MEDITATION IS MAGICAL FOR HEART HEALTH

Taking a few minutes to relax each day could help you exponentially lower your risk of heart disease. Daily meditation is a practice that often uses deep breathing, quiet contemplation, or sustained focus on something benign such as a color, phrase, or repetitive sound (known as a mantra) that helps you let go of stress, free yourself of anxiety, feel peaceful, and maintain a relaxed, clear state of mind. Think of it as a daily vacation from the stress in your life.

Stress is your body's natural alarm system. It releases a powerful hormone called adrenaline that causes your breathing and heart rate to quicken and your blood pressure to rise. However, this primal "fight or flight" response and heavy adrenaline cascade flowing through your veins can take a massive toll on your body if it's consistently repeated over time, as if there's always a threat waiting around the next corner to annihilate you.

Instead of dealing with real predators like our ancestors did, the only monsters that cause us stress now are the ones created in our minds. What I'm saying is a bit esoteric, but follow me on this: there are no stressful events—it's only our thoughts, fears, and judgments about those events that create acute stress responses in our bodies. To feel stressed-out about something is a choice based on our interpretation, judgment, and reaction to it. The proverbial saber-toothed tiger chasing us down in the wild has been replaced by money worries, family dramas, work stresses, and a multitude of other modern psychological maladies. The problem is that your body can't tell the difference between a real physical threat and an image in your mind, so it continues to release the same stress hormones in response.

For people with cardiovascular disease, meditation provides a pathway to reduce their stress and focus on things they can do to be healthier. Meditation is a way to bring balance into your life. It can also help you to sleep better, which is a very important restorative part of physical health and heart vitality.

Recent studies have offered promising results regarding the impact of meditation in reducing blood pressure. A 2012 study showed African-American adults with heart disease who practiced Transcendental Meditation regularly were 48 percent less likely to have a heart attack or stroke or to die compared with African-Americans who attended a health education class more than five years earlier.

There are countless types of meditation, so it's important to find an approach that you feel comfortable with. Try local yoga classes with gentle movements. Yoga not your thing? Check out a meditation workshop, pick up a few books about mindfulness, or download a meditation online (there are tons of free apps and videos online). I also recommend asking a family member or friend to do it with you so you can share the learning experience with someone.

Not all meditation is done sitting down with your legs crossed like many people believe. In addition to yoga, there's tai chi, also called "moving meditation," which incorporates gentle movements that require deep concentration and balance.

While meditation can offer a technique for lowering stress and your risk for heart disease, it's not a replacement for other important lifestyle changes like eating a clean diet, lowering your sodium and sugar intake, or getting daily physical exercise.

THE HEALING POWER OF FORGIVENESS

In terms of a spiritual approach, the practice of forgiveness and "letting go" is a very powerful and effective way to let go of toxic, negative emotions that can cause stress and put extra strain on your heart. Practicing forgiveness toward yourself and others allows you to let go and release painful emotions such as anger, regret, shame, resentment, and grief—which in turn will allow you to accept things as they are and let more love into your life. This practice of radical forgiveness and emotional healing is a critical component in the pursuit of longevity. When you take full responsibility for your emotional state of well-being and choose to heal your heart, you gain a deep sense of self-worth, empowerment, and a feeling of lasting acceptance that "all is well." Basically, you learn to stop sweating the small stuff, let the negativity go, and start to forgive. It's a very powerful practice and a perfect complement to a heart-healthy diet.

WHEREVER YOU GO, GO WITH ALL YOUR HEART

Relatively simple in function, your heart's primary purpose is to pump . . . 24 hours a day, 70 to 80 times a minute. With each beat, your heart pumps blood that delivers life-sustaining oxygen and nutrients to more than 300 trillion cells in your body. Your heart is the lil' engine that keeps chugging along, keeping you alive every day. With that much work to do, it's worth noting that ALL whole, plant-based foods are intrinsically cholesterol free, which gives you a great indication of the perfect sources of fuel for your ticker.

Beyond your diet, though, I think your lifestyle plays a huge role in your overall heart health. Of course, please eat a ton of nutrient-rich fruits and veggies—but also cultivate more deep love in your life, let go of lingering resentments, explore meditation or prayer, and remember to have more fun and let loose! Your heart is a very intuitive, receptive organ and will respond to all of the goodness you can cultivate in life. Come to think of it, I think the basic formula is even easier than the one I shared with you in the first paragraph of this chapter. Here's the new, simplified formula for a healthy heart:

Happy Life = Healthy Heart.

MY TOP NUTRIENTS FOR A HEALTHY HEART

Alpha-carotene: A precursor to vitamin A that acts as an antioxidant. Studies are showing that this phytonutrient may help to prevent oxidative damage to the heart.

B vitamins: These support a key process called methylation, which regulates homocysteine levels and plays a role in DNA regulation.

Capsaicin: A powerful compound in hot peppers that has been scientifically proven to improve heart health.

Catechins: Types of natural phenols and antioxidants that are known to greatly improve cardiovascular health.

Coenzyme Q10: CoQ10 acts as a powerful antioxidant to fight the damage caused by free radicals and helps mitochondria produce more energy.

Magnesium: Most Americans are deficient in this critical nutrient, which helps to lower blood pressure, normalize irregular heartbeats, ease anxiety, support sleep, reduce headaches, resolve constipation, and improve energy levels.

Phytoestrogens: Studies suggest that phytoestrogens may lower the risk of blood clots, stroke, and cardiac arrhythmias. They may also help lower total and "bad" low-density lipoprotein (LDL) cholesterol and triglycerides, and even blood pressure.

Resveratrol: The key ingredient in red wine that helps prevent damage to blood vessels, reduces LDL cholesterol, and prevents blood clots.

Vitamin D: Adequate vitamin D levels are necessary for the prevention of heart failure and cancer. It's also critical for maintaining low levels of blood pressure and blood sugar as well as the health of your brain and bones. Mild to moderate sun exposure on your bare skin for up to 30 minutes per day is ideal; however, depending on your climate and exposure, supplementation is usually necessary.

MY TOP HEART-HEALTHY FOODS

- acorn squash
- almonds
- artichokes
- asparagus
- beets
- bell peppers
- black beans
- blackberries
- blueberries
- bok choy
- broccoli
- brown rice
- butternut squash
- cacao
- carrots
- cantaloupe
- flaxseed
- garlic
- hazelnuts
- kidney beans
- leeks
- non-GMO soy products (tofu, tempeh, miso, natto)
- oatmeal
- onion
- oranges
- papaya
- pistachios
- pumpkin seeds
- red bell peppers
- spinach
- sunflower seeds
- sweet potatoes
- tomatoes
- walnuts

RECIPES FOR A HEALTHY HEART

....

PISTACHIO
ICE CREAM

SERVES 4

PISTACHIOS ARE, SHELLS DOWN, MY FAVORITE nuts of all time. There's something hauntingly addictive about them, from the cracking of their tough cases to their rich, buttery flavor. I thought, why not make a vegan ice cream with 'em? So I did! Here, the pistachio plays off the sweetness of ripe banana and coconut water, finding its true, creamy potential with avocado in the mix. High in fiber, vitamins, minerals, and phytochemicals, pistachios are the only nuts besides peanuts that offer resveratrol, a compound also found in the skin of red grapes. Resveratrol has been shown to decrease risk of heart disease and some cancers. Thanks to this recipe, the phrase "healthy ice cream" is no longer an oxymoron.

2 frozen bananas

1 cup raw coconut water

¼ cup coconut nectar or maple syrup

1 tablespoon ground vanilla bean

1 whole avocado, pitted

2 cups ice cubes

¼ teaspoon almond extract

½ cup raw pistachios, shelled and crushed, plus more for topping

4 teaspoons hemp seeds

1 Blend the bananas, coconut water, coconut nectar, vanilla bean, avocado, and ice cubes for 20 seconds in a high-speed blender until smooth, dense, and creamy. Add the almond extract and pistachios and pulse a few times until the pistachios are broken up a bit.

2 Dish the ice cream into serving bowls and top with the crushed pistachios and hemp seeds. Any remaining ice cream can be stored in a covered glass container in the freezer.

BLOOD ORANGE
BRUSCHETTA

SERVES 4

BRUSCHETTA, AS AN APPETIZER, IS JUST okay. On many menus, it's a bit played out, frankly. So, I combined fava beans and fresh blood oranges to take it into another realm of flavor. This gives the dish a Middle Eastern–inspired twist while surprising your palate with smoky, hummuslike flavor and the tart infusion of orange. I love serving this dish with fresh arugula, as the spicy overtone of flavor adds more depth and complexity. Blood oranges' distinctive maroon color is due to the antioxidant anthocyanin. Antioxidants help prevent cancer and heart disease, while anthocyanins help lower LDL cholesterol (that's the bad kind) to keep your blood vessels flexible and strong.

½ small baguette, gluten-free if possible, sliced into rounds

1¾ cups cooked fava beans

1 clove garlic, minced

2 tablespoons fresh lemon juice

6 tablespoons extra-virgin olive oil, divided

2 tablespoons fresh blood orange juice

2 teaspoons orange pulp

1 tablespoon coconut vinegar

Pinch salt

Pinch ground black pepper

1 to 2 cups spicy greens

2 blood oranges, peeled and sliced

1 Toast the bread slices and set aside.

2 Blend 1½ cups of the fava beans, garlic, lemon juice, and 3 tablespoons of the olive oil in a high-speed blender or food processor for about 30 seconds, until about hummus consistency, adding water if needed. Set aside.

3 Combine the blood orange juice, grated orange pulp, remaining 3 tablespoons of olive oil, coconut vinegar, salt, and black pepper in a small bowl. Whisk away for a few seconds to create dressing, and set aside.

4 Mix spicy greens, the remaining ¼ cup of fava beans, blood orange slices, and dressing. Toss well to combine.

5 Spread fava bean puree on toasted bread slices. Top with greens mixture.

Any bread will work with this recipe—rye, ciabatta, or even pita bread (or gluten-free versions thereof) will serve the spread in superhero style.

THAI CUCUMBER PEANUT SALAD

SERVES 2

PEANUTS ARE ONE OF THE TRADEMARK ingredients in Thai cuisine. They taste truly amazing on everything from rice noodles to spring rolls. In this salad, these legumes bring a nutty flavor and crunchy depth to the fresh vegetables. It's a refreshing appetizer and incredibly easy to make. In addition, peanuts pack a potent punch to protect your heart. Peanuts contain resveratrol, a powerful phenolic compound, which is also found in red wine. Resveratrol helps to prevent blood platelet aggregation, which is a risk factor for heart attacks and strokes, and may regenerate vitamin E, which further strengthens antioxidant effects.

4 small cucumbers, diced

½ small red onion, diced

1 cup cilantro, minced

¼ cup peanuts, crushed

2 tablespoons extra-virgin olive oil

½ tablespoon coconut aminos

½ tablespoon vegan Worcestershire sauce

¼ cup fresh lime juice

2 cloves garlic, minced

2 small Thai bird chilies, minced, or 1 teaspoon crushed red pepper flakes

Pinch sea salt

1 tablespoon coconut sugar

1 Mix the cucumbers, red onion, cilantro, and crushed peanuts in a large bowl. Set aside.

2 Combine the remaining ingredients in a medium bowl. Whisk for 20 to 30 seconds to create the dressing.

3 Drizzle the dressing all over your salad. Toss everything together and serve.

GARLIC AIOLI WITH
STEAMED ARTICHOKES

SERVES 2

ARTICHOKES AND AIOLI. A FAMOUS DUO almost as fly as Jay-Z and Beyoncé. And much like that power couple, this dish is a double dose of healthy, yo. For the aioli, I love using a Greek-style coconut yogurt to allow the garlic, dill, and lemon to shine through and brighten the flavor. The artichoke puts a choke hold on potential heart issues with its high quantities of potassium to help you maintain normal heart rhythm. Research studies have shown a strong link between high-potassium diets and reduced risk of stroke. Potassium also tones down the effect of sodium on blood pressure, helping to maintain the healthy levels that promote a good heart. Enjoy!

3 large artichokes

1 cup plain Greek-style coconut yogurt

2 teaspoons fresh lemon juice

1 clove garlic

¾ teaspoon dried dill

Pinch salt

Pinch ground black pepper

1 Fill a large stockpot with lightly salted water and bring to a boil. Add the artichokes and reduce heat to low. Simmer, covered, for about 20 to 30 minutes or until you can easily pull out a leaf from the center of an artichoke.

2 Blend the remaining ingredients in a high-speed blender for 30 seconds to create garlic aioli. Transfer to a small bowl.

3 Serve artichokes with garlic aioli for dipping.

ROCKIN' RED
SMOOTHIE

SERVES 2 TO 4

IN RESPONSE TO THE AVALANCHE OF green smoothie recipes that have infiltrated the pages of cookbooks 'round the world, I created this ultra-red smoothie recipe. I think it might literally explode with all of the amazing antioxidants from the acai, raspberries, and beets. Speaking of those badass beets, think of them as red spinach—nutritionally speaking! Just like Popeye's power food, this crimson vegetable is one of your best sources of both folate and betaine. These two nutrients work together to lower your blood levels of homocysteine, an inflammatory compound that can damage your arteries and increase your risk of heart disease. Plus, the natural pigments in beets called betacyanins have been proved to be potent cancer fighters!

1 small beet, peeled and chopped

1 bunch of beet greens (from 1 beet)

One 3.5-ounce pack frozen acai berry

1 apple, peeled, cored, and chopped

⅓ cup raspberries

½ fresh lime, juiced

1 tablespoon superfood red blend powder or beet juice powder

½ teaspoon ground cinnamon

Pinch ground cardamom

1 cup filtered water

10 ice cubes

1-inch piece of ginger root, peeled and chopped

Pinch sea salt

1 Blend all ingredients for 30 seconds in a high-speed blender until smooth and creamy.

SPICY COCONUT ALMOND NOODLES

THIS IS ONE OF MY FAVORITE old-school original raw food recipes. It requires a large chunk of time to prepare the fresh young Thai coconut noodles, but the results are well worth it. Contrary to popular belief, coconut is actually a heart-friendly food. Most of the saturated fat in coconut is a medium-chain fatty acid, which is broken down much faster than long-chain fatty acids, so it does not contribute to high cholesterol. The almond butter dressing with ginger and habanero gives this dish a rich, nutty texture and spicy kick to your taste buds. It's incredibly filling, and you'll only need a small portion to feel really satisfied.

4 young Thai coconuts

2 cups raw pistachios

¼ cup coconut aminos

¼ cup ginger root, peeled and minced

¼ to ½ habanero pepper, seeded

3 tablespoons coconut nectar

½ cup fresh lime juice

¾ cup raw almond butter

1 cup julienned jicama root

1 cup julienned green papaya or mango

1 cup julienned bok choy

1 cup julienned radishes

2 scallions, sliced thin on a bias

1 large handful cilantro

1 small handful basil

1 tablespoon finely minced habanero, seeded

½ teaspoon sea salt

½ cup crushed pistachios

2 tablespoons extra-virgin olive oil

2 tablespoons coconut aminos

2 limes, halved

1. Open 1 young Thai coconut and drain 1½ cups of coconut water into a blender. Scrape out the meat, clean it, and reserve ⅓ cup of it.

2. Blend the coconut water, pistachios, coconut aminos, ginger, habanero pepper, coconut nectar, and lime juice until thick and creamy. Add almond butter and blend once more. Set aside.

3. Open the other 3 young Thai coconuts, drain the coconut water, and scoop out the meat in large, uniform pieces. Clean the meat and julienne the coconut into long, thin noodle strips. Transfer the coconut noodles to a large mixing bowl. Add the jicama, papaya, and the almond butter sauce. Combine to coat evenly. Add the bok choy, radishes, scallions, cilantro, half the basil, ½ tablespoon of habanero, and the salt, and gently toss.

4. Divide among 4 serving plates and sprinkle with the crushed pistachios and the remaining basil and habanero. Drizzle the olive oil and coconut aminos around the noodles and garnish with lime halves.

JASON'S TIP For a sweeter sauce, add more coconut nectar or yacon syrup. For more tropical noodles, add more mango and papaya and fewer coconut noodles.

FIG & FENNEL
CHOCOLATES

SOME OF THE BEST IDEAS FOR new recipes are totally unexpected. The inspiration for these chocolates came from an artisan cacao bar that was so good, I just had to re-create it at home. The chewy, soft sweetness of the dried figs plays so well with the fennel pollen and complements the dark, smoky cacao. Bonus: raw cacao beans help to protect your cardiovascular system due to their high concentration of plant nutrients called flavonoids. Flavonoids have other potential benefits, such as lowering blood pressure, improving blood flow to the brain and heart, and making blood platelets less sticky and able to clot. There is a delicate balance of earthy, floral, and spicy flavors in these chocolates that will mesmerize and hypnotize your palate!

1¾ cups raw cacao butter, shredded

1 teaspoon ground vanilla bean

10½ ounces raw cacao powder (by weight)

½ cup plus 2 tablespoons coconut sugar

1 scoop chocolate-flavored vegan protein powder (optional)

Dash cayenne pepper

½ teaspoon ground cinnamon

2 teaspoons fennel pollen

½ teaspoon sea salt

⅔ cup coconut nectar

¼ cup dried figs, finely diced

1 Melt the cacao butter in a double boiler. Whisk in the vanilla bean and stir to combine well. Transfer the cacao butter and vanilla mixture to a food processor. Add 5¼ ounces of the raw cacao powder and process the mixture. Gradually add in the remaining raw cacao powder and all of the other ingredients, except for the figs. When the chocolate is well combined, fold in the diced figs. Use a spoon to press the chocolate mixture into chocolate molds. Use a butter knife or offset spatula to level off the tops. Place in the freezer, uncovered, for 60 minutes to set the chocolates.

SUNFLOWER BUTTER
COOKIES

MAKES 10 SMALL COOKIES

IF THERE'S ONE INGREDIENT THAT'S SLIGHTLY overplayed in healthy baking, it's almond butter. Not only does it get awfully boring when you see it so often, but using it eliminates people with nut allergies from enjoying these recipes. With these glorious, gluten-free cookies, I chose to use sunflower seed butter to make your eyes flutter. Sunflower seeds are an excellent source of vitamin E, the body's primary fat-soluble antioxidant, which plays an important role in the prevention of cardiovascular disease. They're also packed with phytosterols, which are known to reduce blood levels of cholesterol, enhance your immune response, and decrease your risk of certain cancers. The rich, delicious nutty taste of the sunflower seeds plays nicely with the dense, gluten-free oats and sweet maple syrup. These cookies are great as an on-the-go snack or delightfully healthy dessert.

1 cup gluten-free oats

½ cup sunflower seed butter

⅓ cup maple syrup

⅓ cup organic virgin coconut oil

½ teaspoon ground vanilla bean

½ teaspoon sea salt

2 tablespoons vegan vanilla protein powder (optional)

1 Add the oats to a food processor and grind into a nice, coarse, slightly mealy texture—not a fine powder—about 10 seconds or so. Add the sunflower seed butter, maple syrup, coconut oil, ground vanilla, salt, and protein powder, if using, to the food processor. Process about 20 seconds, until the dough easily balls together in your hands.

2 Form cookies of your preferred size and shape and refrigerate overnight. Or, if you can't wait that long, freeze them for an hour and then enjoy.

DARK CHOCOLATE
PANCAKES

HOW DO YOU TAKE SOFT, FLUFFY pancakes on the fast track to fantasy land? Put some raw chocolate in there! These deliciously decadent, dark chocolate pancakes are surprisingly healthy, satisfying, and gluten free. Made with nondairy milk, sunflower seed butter, and coconut oil, they're going to fool your taste buds into thinking they're bad for you. But in reality, the antioxidants, magnesium, medium-chain triglycerides, vitamin E, and selenium in these pancakes will have you shining like the sun, hon! What's more, the fiber and polyphenols in raw cacao work together to help control your blood pressure and blood glucose levels. At least part of the beneficial effect of cacao on your blood sugar level may be due to the slowing of starch-digestive enzymes by polyphenol procyanidins in your small intestine. A crazy technical benefit, yes, but really awesome, too!

⅔ cup gluten-free pancake mix

1½ tablespoons raw cacao powder

½ teaspoon baking powder

Pinch sea salt

¾ cup hemp milk

1 tablespoon maple syrup

¼ teaspoon vanilla extract

1 tablespoon sunflower seed butter

1 tablespoon organic virgin coconut oil

1 Mix the gluten-free pancake mix, raw cacao powder, baking powder, and salt in a large bowl.

2 Mix the hemp milk, maple syrup, vanilla extract, and sunflower seed butter in a separate bowl.

3 Add the dry ingredients to the wet ingredients and whisk together. Once mixed, refrigerate for 10 minutes to set the pancake batter.

4 Add the coconut oil to a heated pan over medium heat. Add ¼ cup of the batter to the heated pan. Cook for about 90 seconds. Flip when the edges are brown and bubbles come through the batter. Transfer each cooked pancake to a plate. Repeat until the batter is used up. Serve.

JASON'S TIP

Top pancakes with cacao nibs, extra-fine shredded coconut, fresh berries, and maple syrup. So yummy!

SQUASH
CROSTINI

SOMETIMES, I GET REALLY INSPIRED IDEAS and turn them into recipes. It's kind of like being the host of *Ingredient Matchmaker*. The sweet, roasted flavor of butternut squash melds so well with the mild onion taste of the shallot and the rich nuttiness of the almond butter. In terms of heart health, butternut squash is an excellent source of potassium, which is important for maintaining healthy blood pressure. Plus, the bodacious beta-carotene in butternut squash is a powerful antioxidant that may prevent the free-radical damage that can lead to heart disease. Why don't you give your baguette a break from bruschetta and crash the dinner party with these killer squash crostini?

1 butternut squash, halved

2½ tablespoons extra-virgin olive oil, divided

1½ cups shallot, minced

¾ teaspoon sea salt

1 large baguette, sliced diagonally into rounds

3 tablespoons raw almond butter

1. Preheat the oven to 350 degrees Fahrenheit. Bake the squash on a baking sheet for 45 minutes or until tender. Allow to cool.

2. Heat ½ tablespoon of the olive oil in a skillet over medium heat and sauté the shallots with the salt until tender and golden.

3. Brush the bread slices with the remaining 2 tablespoons of olive oil and toast in the oven.

4. Scoop out 2½ cups of the squash. Process the squash with the shallots and almond butter in a food processor until it's at your desired consistency. Spread it over the toasted bread and serve.

HEART BEETS
SALAD

NOT ONLY DOES THIS SALAD blow away your taste buds with blood-building beets, it's chock-full of heart-healthy superfoods exploding with high levels of beneficial zinc, magnesium, and antioxidant all-stars such as vitamin C. Even better, beets can lower your systolic blood pressure by an average of four to five points. This dish packs in a lot of variety with a nice, crunchy texture and is light enough to enjoy any time of day. Plus, it's a surefire potluck pleaser—even if one of your guests is a grump like Ebenezer! (Scrooge, get it? Man . . . tough crowd in here.)

4 beets, peeled and shredded

1½ cups pomegranate seeds

¾ cup cilantro, chopped

¼ cup extra-virgin olive oil

¼ teaspoon crushed red pepper
flakes

¼ cup hemp seeds

⅓ cup cacao nibs

¼ cup pumpkin seeds

¼ teaspoon camu camu powder

⅛ teaspoon stevia powder

1 lemon, squeezed

Pinch sea salt

1 Add all ingredients to a large mixing bowl and stir gently until well combined.

14

EAT FOR

LESS STRESS

STRESS IS LIKE A KILLER COCKTAIL

made from the Grim Reaper's personal liquor cabinet: it's powerful, insidious, highly addicting, and can strike anyone, anywhere, at any time. Try to name a single person you know who's consistently stress free other than freakin' Bobby McFerrin. Don't worry, be happy? Yeah, easy for him to say. It was the freewheeling '80s back then.

Stress may be an even bigger killer than poor diet, genetics, or environmental toxicity. As a culture, we are extremely stressed-out to the point of an epidemic, with 20 percent of Americans reporting their stress levels at an eight, nine, or ten (on a one-to-ten scale). That's a ferocious national health issue if I've ever seen one. And the crazy part is, many people accept these high levels of stress as, y'know, just another normal part of their day.

Be honest: How often do you get really stressed-out? Daily? Every other day? Maybe even a few times a day? Check in with yourself and really be honest about your emotional balance and ability to handle stress in your life. It may be that you've become so used to (or even chemically addicted to) stress that it's just an everyday norm for you. Unfortunately, that's when stress can do the most damage and balance must be restored. If you feel like a stress case on a consistent basis, so do a

lot of people in modern society. Indeed, the startling statistics about stress tell a potentially grim tale:

- One in five Americans experiences "extreme" stress, resulting in body shakes, heart palpitations, and depression
- 40 percent of people with high stress levels overeat or consistently eat unhealthy foods, while 44 percent lose sleep every night
- Stress increases your risk of heart attack by 25 percent, your risk of heart disease by 40 percent, and your risk of stroke by more than 50 percent

I'll be the first to admit that I can let stress steer my ship a little too often. It's usually when I take on too much in my life—too many projects, too many friends, too many dates . . . and end up overcommitting myself. And, as a result, I just can't do it all. I'm sure you know the feeling: we are trying so hard to please the people in our lives, succeed in our careers, make enough money to be secure and comfortable . . . and play the role of superhero for our co-workers, family, and friends. Holy crap, that sounds impossible, doesn't it? I mean, really, it's enough to make Spiderman climb the walls with anxiety. So, how can you maintain your responsibilities in life without allowing stress to break you down and throw off your balance? It's all about finding daily equilibrium in your life through stress-management techniques and eating the right foods to keep your nervous system happily humming along.

STRESS: IT CAN MAKE YOU A HOT MESS

So, how does stress affect you on a biological level? And what are the long-term effects of prolonged stress? Well, at the risk of freaking you out, there's a number of ways that chronic stress can ruin your life. Prolonged stress can shrink your brain, add fat to your belly, and even unravel your chromosomes. The brain cells of stressed individuals are dramatically smaller, especially in the area of their hippocampus, which is the seat of learning and memory. Stress disrupts your neuroendocrine and immune systems and appears to trigger a degenerative process in your brain that can result in Alzheimer's disease. Stress can also accelerate aging by shortening your telomeres, the protective genetic structures that regulate how your cells age. And we'll go into more detail about cortisol and belly fat later on, but let's just say it ain't pretty.

The stress response is a natural bodily reaction that was designed to help us run from predators or take down prey. As touched upon in the "Eat for a Healthy Heart" chapter, these days, we are turning on the same "life-saving" stress response to cope with $4-per-gallon gasoline prices, fear of public speaking, asshole bosses, and traffic jams during rush hour. The problem is that most people don't know how to proactively avoid this stress reaction. Constantly being in a stress response can have you needlessly marinating in corrosive stress hormones around the clock.

There's a quote I love by Dr. Lissa Rankin, author of *Mind Over Medicine*: "Our bodies know how to fix broken proteins, kill cancer cells, retard aging, and fight infection. They even know how to heal ulcers, make skin lesions disappear and knit together broken bones! But here's the kicker—*those natural self-repair mechanisms don't work if you're stressed!*"

I know this all sounds a bit scary, but it's good to recognize what our bodies are capable of. We need to support our bodies so that they can do what they were originally intended to do: keep us alive and well!

"BAD" AND "GOOD" STRESS

Understanding how stress works can help you figure out ways to combat it and reduce its negative impacts. First, we need to acknowledge that we have essentially become addicted to stress in modern society. There is "bad" stress and "good" stress: you experience certain stressful experiences as unpleasant and seek to avoid them, but you may actually seek out other

stress-inducing experiences because you think they're fun. For example, skydiving, roller coasters, and horror movies are experiences that may turn on your adrenaline and give you a "rush." However, your body responds to the stress in the exact same way as if the creepy serial killer from the movie was ACTUALLY chasing you down the street. Wait a second, creepy villains don't really run . . . they kind of . . . fast walk with a grim stride. Anyway, you get the picture here!

Your muscles tense, your heart pounds, your respirations increase, and your body stops all of its nonessential processes. This can be pleasantly exhilarating and feel freakin' amazing—and, for some people, rather addictive. You might have a friend or family member whom you could describe as an "adrenaline junkie." A thrill is simply the relinquishing of a bit of control in a setting that feels safe. But when you're in that heightened state of arousal and adrenaline rush all the time, the accumulated stress takes its toll on your body, whether you perceive the stress as "good" or "bad." That's why it's important to find balance and ways to de-stress.

CORTISOL: THE BELLY OF THE BEAST

Science has established that stress can lead to cardiovascular disease, but did you know that it also leads to weight gain? You've probably heard about the link between cortisol and belly fat—but what *is* cortisol, and how does it work? Cortisol is a critical stress hormone that performs many actions in the body, both good and bad. Normally, cortisol is secreted by the adrenal glands in a pattern called a diurnal variation, meaning that levels of cortisol in the bloodstream vary depending upon the time of day (normally, cortisol levels are highest in the early morning and lowest around midnight). Cortisol is important for the maintenance of blood pressure as well as regulating energy levels. Cortisol stimulates fat and carbohydrate metabolism for fast energy and stimulates insulin release and maintenance of blood sugar levels. The end result of these actions can be a marked increase in appetite.

Cortisol has been dubbed the "stress hormone" because excess cortisol is secreted during times of major physical or psychological stress, and the normal pattern of cortisol secretion can be drastically altered. A disruption of cortisol secretion may not only promote weight gain, but it can also affect where you put on the weight. Studies have shown that stress and elevated cortisol tend to cause fat deposition in the abdominal area. This belly fat has been referred to as toxic fat because it is strongly correlated with the development of cardiovascular disease, including heart attacks and strokes.

But stress is not the only reason for weight gain. Weight gain or loss is dependent on a number of factors including resting metabolic rate, food intake, amount of exercise, and even the types of food consumed and the times of day when you eat. Genetic factors also likely influence our metabolism and may explain some people's tendency to gain or lose weight more rapidly than others.

Whether or not your stress levels result in high cortisol levels and weight gain is not really a predictable thing. The amount of cortisol secreted in response to high stress can vary among individuals, with some people being innately more reactive and less able to cope with stressful events. Published in the *Journal of the American Dietetic Association*, a recent study by the Psychology Research Laboratory at San Guiseppe Hospital in Italy showed that women who reacted to stress with high levels of cortisol secretion also tended to eat more while stressed than women who secreted less cortisol. Another study by the Healthy Psychology Program at the University of California, San Francisco, demonstrated that women who stored excess fat in their abdominal area had higher cortisol levels and reported more lifestyle stress than women who stored fat primarily in the hips.

HOW TO HAVE FUN MANAGING STRESS

Stress is not an inevitable, unchangeable experience. As they say, you may not be able to control everything that happens to you, but you can control how you respond.

You have the power to change your mind, and this alters your body's reaction.

Make it your practice to handle stressful situations differently by responding with a conscious intention to maintain a positive state of being. As you practice this positive response, your body will learn how to effectively decrease your stress, your cortisol levels will stabilize, your blood pressure will drop, and your health will dramatically improve in a multitude of ways.

It's also important to adopt a consistent practice. Stress management isn't something you just take care of on the weekends. You need to handle it on a daily basis, because that's how often debilitating stress rears its monstrous head. There are many different stress-reduction techniques, and what works best for you may not have the same results for someone else. You might really enjoy meditating, but someone else may feel calmer just by cleaning house. Stress management is a highly selective and individual thing. The last thing you want to do is to nullify any potential benefit by getting stressed-out with your chosen stress-busting activity. You'll have to find what kind of daily activity works best for you.

As you'll guess, making smart food choices will support your overall health and increase your body's resiliency. Be sure to get adequate sleep, too, as sleep deprivation dramatically impairs your body's ability to handle stress. And make your chosen stress-relief activities an adventure—experiment with different things and see what brings you joy. Some popular stress relievers include:

- Exercise (e.g., yoga, weight training, hiking)
- Meditation or breathing practices
- Having fun with family and friends
- Enjoying time alone in nature (or wherever your "happy place" is)
- Music (both listening to it and making it)
- Sex (duh!)

Be sure to deal with stress in healthy ways. When people use alcohol, tobacco, or drugs to try to deal with their stress, sadly, instead of providing the body with relief, they tend to keep it in a stressed state and cause even more problems, including addiction.

LAUGHTER TRULY IS THE BEST MEDICINE!

Whether you're guffawing at some inane YouTube video or giggling at an episode of *Saturday Night Live*, laughing does your body a whole lot of good. Laughter is a great form of stress relief, and that's no joke. A strong funny bone can't cure all of your ailments, but research data is steadily mounting about all of the positive things that laughter can do for you.

A good laugh has great short-term effects. Laughter doesn't just lighten your mental stress load; it also induces physical changes in your body. Laughter has more than a few tricks up its sleeve. It can stimulate many organs by enhancing your intake of oxygen-rich air. This stimulates your heart, lungs, and muscles and increases the endorphins released by your brain. Laughter also activates and relieves your

stress response. A rollicking laugh fires up and then cools down your stress response and increases your heart rate and blood pressure, which results in a good, relaxed feeling. Laughter can soothe tension by stimulating circulation and aiding in muscle relaxation, both of which help reduce some of the physical symptoms associated with stress.

Laughter isn't just a quick "wham, bam, thank you, ma'am." It's also good for you over the long haul. Consistent daily laughter can improve your immune system. Negative thoughts manifest into

chemical reactions that affect your body by bringing more stress into your system and decreasing your immunity. In contrast, positive thoughts actually release neuropeptides that help fight stress and potentially more serious illnesses. Laughter may also ease physical pain by causing the body to produce its own natural painkillers. It may also break the pain-spasm cycle common to some muscle disorders. Laughter can increase your feelings of personal satisfaction and make it easier to cope with difficult situations. It also helps you connect with other people. And, without a doubt, laughter can greatly improve your mood. Many people experience depression, sometimes due to chronic illnesses. Laughter can help lessen your depression and anxiety and make you feel happier.

C'mon now. Just stop resisting the idea of cracking up and give it a try. Turn the corners of your mouth up into a smile, think about something hilariously ridiculous, and then let out a hearty chortle, even if it feels a bit forced. Once you've had your guffaw, pay attention to how you feel. Pretty happy and relaxed, I'd venture to guess. That's the power of laughter to instantly take away stress.

THE TRUTH ABOUT COMPLEX CARBS

All carbohydrates prompt the brain to make more serotonin. For a steady supply of this feel-good chemical, it's best to eat complex carbs from whole-food sources, which take longer to digest and assimilate. Good choices include whole-grain or gluten-free breads, pastas, and breakfast cereals, including good, old-fashioned oatmeal. Fresh, organic fruits are a fantastic source of sustainable carbohydrates and provide essential hydration to your cells. Complex carbs can also help you feel balanced by stabilizing your blood sugar levels.

Those that can tolerate gluten may benefit from foods with whole grains, like whole-grain pasta and bread. If you're intolerant to gluten or have celiac disease, there are a plethora of delicious and healthy gluten-free breads, cereals, pastas, and wraps available. Studies have shown that true whole grains have multiple benefits for those with anxiety. Whole grains are rich in magnesium—and magnesium deficiency may lead to anxiety. They also contain tryptophan, which becomes serotonin (a calming neurotransmitter). They create healthy energy while reducing hunger, both important for reducing anxiety. Whole-grain foods contain nutrients that have been stripped out of processed and artificial foods and are a great building block for a stress-reducing diet.

It's important to eat foods that will calm your nerves amid the chaos of your most stressful days. It's all too easy to forget to eat or skip nutrient-dense meals amid a busy, hectic schedule. (I'm still working on improving this one myself!) I think a lot of people become overwhelmed and tend to overthink what it takes to achieve a healthier lifestyle—including the right foods to put in their kitchens. Trust me—it doesn't have to be a stressful science project. Adding nutritious new foods into your current lifestyle can be really easy, fun, and highly educational.

ADAPTA-WHAT?

Adaptogens are a unique and powerful group of herbal ingredients you can use to improve the health of your adrenal system—the system that manages your body's hormonal response to stress. Adaptogens enhance your body's ability to cope with stress and fight fatigue. They're called adaptogens because they can adapt their functionality according to your body's current needs. Though their effects may initially be subtle and take time to be felt, they are lasting and undeniable. Unlike addictive pharmaceutical drugs, adaptogens aren't synthesized in a laboratory. In fact, they've been used in Chinese and Ayurvedic medicine for centuries to boost energy and resilience in the face of heavy stress. Research studies have shown evidence that adaptogens offer positive benefits and are safe for long-term use.

Adaptogens work a bit like a thermostat. When a thermostat senses that the room temperature is too high, it brings it down—and vice versa. Adaptogens can calm you down and boost your energy at the same time without overstimulating your nerves. They can normalize body imbalances. By supporting adrenal function, they counteract the adverse effects of stress. They enable the body's cells to access more energy, help cells eliminate toxic by-products of the metabolic process, and help the body to utilize oxygen more efficiently.

From a culinary perspective, I like to use adaptogenic herbs in my tonic drink recipes, ice creams, desserts, soups, salad dressings, and smoothies to increase my body's stress-management powers and my immune system's resiliency. Depending on my state of being, I use powerful adaptogenic herbs to combat stress, including: ginseng, eleuthero, rhodiola, holy basil, shatavari, ashwagandha, and reishi mushroom. You'll find these herbs either whole or in capsule form.

Before you start experimenting with any new adaptogens or herbal medicine, please notify your doctor. With the majority of these potent herbs available on store shelves or available to order online, it can be all too easy for you to screw up your dosage amounts and potentially cause greater imbalances if you don't know what you're doing. Consult with a licensed Ayurvedic herbalist or a doctor specializing in Traditional Chinese Medicine (TCM) for expert evaluation and guidance.

FROM STRESSED TO BLESSED

Unless you're burning to become a Benedictine monk or cramming to find a killer real estate deal on a cave in the Mojave, you're just going to have to handle the stress of modern life—one way or another. Rather than "let the bastards wear you down," be proactive and positive with your stress management! Breathe deeply, let go of stuff that doesn't matter, eat "feel-good," healthy, plant-based foods, and make sure you're getting the right nutrients to help your body effectively deal with stress.

And remember: Feeling stress is a choice. You're not a victim of stress—you either allow it to affect you or let it pass on by like one of those scary floats in the Thanksgiving Day parade. When we learn to allow and dissolve stressful thoughts before they can lodge themselves in our minds, our bodies will likely never feel the effects of the potential stress. Key word: POTENTIAL. So practice being the loving, watchful guardian of your daily thoughts, count your blessings with gratitude, and make conscious, supportive food choices. You'll likely notice that nasty ol' stress will have a much tougher time scaling the castle walls of your consciousness!

MY TOP STRESS-REDUCING NUTRIENTS

Folate: Our bodies cannot synthesize folate, so we must consume it through diet. Folate is crucial for regulating many bodily functions, including DNA repair, which in turn, eases stress in our brains and our bodies.

Glutathione: Another essential nutrient that aids in cellular repair and fights against free-radical damage, glutathione helps to relieve anxiety and stress.

Polyphenols: Another micronutrient responsible for aiding against free-radical damage.

Potassium: Potassium ion diffusion is a key mechanism in nerve transmission, and potassium depletion results in various dysfunctions relating to the nervous system and—you guessed it—stress!

Probiotics: Probiotics, or living cultures, are believed to be beneficial for many areas of our health and wellness as well as curing stress and depression.

Sulforaphane: A powerful antioxidant said to have neuroprotective effects on the brain, thus preventing tension and anxiety.

MY TOP STRESS-REDUCING FOODS

- almonds
- apricots
- ashwagandha
- asparagus
- avocado
- banana
- black tea
- blue-green algae
- blueberries
- broccoli
- cacao
- camu camu
- carrot
- cashews
- celery
- chia seeds
- collard greens
- dark green, leafy vegetables
- dates
- eleuthero
- flaxseed
- ginseng
- green tea
- hemp seeds
- holy basil
- kale
- lemons
- limes
- mushrooms
- nondairy nut or seed yogurts (fortified with vitamin D)
- non-GMO soy products (tofu, tempeh, miso, natto)
- oatmeal
- oranges
- peanuts
- pecans
- pistachios
- pumpkin seeds
- raspberries
- reishi mushroom
- rhodiola
- sesame seeds
- shatavari
- spinach
- spirulina
- St. John's wort
- sunflower seeds
- sweet potatoes
- Swiss chard
- valerian root
- walnuts
- whole grains

RECIPES TO REDUCE STRESS

· · · · · · · · · · · · · · · ·

PEANUT BUTTER
ICE CREAM

AS MUCH AS I WISH I had a soft-serve ice cream machine, I must face reality and realize I just don't have the room; neither do I want to carry it up my staircase! Instead, I make instant ice cream in the blender. The coconut milk ice cubes are the secret in this creamy delight, which you can use for the base in any instant blended ice cream recipe. If you're not down with OPP (other people's peanuts), you can substitute almond or pecan butter in this recipe, G. And if life's got you pulling out your hair, take solace in the fact that peanuts contain magnesium, a mineral that helps regulate the stress hormone cortisol our bodies produce. So eat some of this PBIC and chill the fudge out, baby.

28 coconut milk ice cubes

1 cup full fat coconut milk, reserved for blending

⅔ cup peanut butter, plus more for topping

1 teaspoon vanilla extract

½ cup coconut sugar

2 tablespoons cacao nibs, plus more for topping

1 Start by filling two standard-size ice cube trays with coconut milk and freezing them. When the cubes are frozen solid, blend the coconut milk ice cubes and all remaining ingredients in a high-speed blender for about 40 to 50 seconds at maximum speed. After blending, you'll have a thick and creamy soft-serve ice cream consistency. Fill some fancy parfait glasses with the ice cream and top with cacao nibs and an additional dollop of peanut butter.

JASON'S TIP

I don't recommend you attempt this recipe with a standard, low-speed blender. High-speed blenders such as Blendtec and VitaMix will allow you to execute this ice cream recipe to perfection.

LEMON CASHEW CREAM
TARTLETS

THESE LITTLE CUTIE PATOOTIES ARE ADORABLE dessert options that will make your smile widen, but not your waistline. Lemon is a fantastic stress reliever and lends the perfect tart flavor to the cashew cream. Cashews have a high concentration of tryptophan, magnesium, and healthy monounsaturated fats, which directly ward off mild depression and anxiety naturally. This recipe is super easy and is a great dish to make for anyone who's never tried raw vegan desserts before. These beautiful baby tarts are sure to steal their hearts!

LEMON CASHEW CREAM FILLING:

1 cup soaked cashews

1 to 2 tablespoons filtered water, as needed

¼ cup coconut nectar

Pinch sea salt

1 tablespoon organic virgin coconut oil

1 teaspoon vanilla extract

1 large lemon, juiced and zested

CRUST:

1 cup raw walnuts

5 medjool dates, pitted and chopped

½ teaspoon vanilla extract

Pinch sea salt

TOPPING:

½ cup fresh blueberries

2 tablespoons mint leaves

1 **To make the Lemon Cashew Cream filling:** blend all ingredients 30 seconds or until the filling becomes frothy and smooth. Transfer to an airtight container and place in the refrigerator.

2 **To make the crust:** place the walnuts in a food processor and process for 10 to 15 seconds, until the "dough" achieves a coarse, mealy consistency. Add the dates and process for another 15 seconds. Check the texture to see that the mixture has a malleable, doughlike consistency. Add the remaining ingredients and gently pulse for another 10 seconds.

3 Divide the crust dough into 3 even balls and place them into 5-inch ramekins lined with cupcake paper. Form the crust with your hands, pressing the ball of your hand into the center of the ramekin and using thumbs to work it out into the sides, forming a miniature pie crust shape. Continue with the other two until complete.

4 Spoon the Lemon Cashew Cream filling into each ramekin evenly and top with fresh blueberries and mint leaves. Transfer to the refrigerator and chill for 2 hours to set.

CREAM OF BROCCOLI
SOUP

SERVES 2

OH, CREAM OF BROCCOLI, HOW YOU'VE always made me knock-kneed. I've been in love with the C.O.B. since 1983. Seriously, I've adored this soup practically since I came out of the womb. In crafting a vegan version here, I also made it raw. It tastes dense, creamy, and hearty. If you want to deepen the flavor profile and have a cooked soup, steam the broccoli first and then simmer the soup for 15 minutes after blending. Either way, this soup will make you wanna shoop-a-doop like Salt-N-Pepa. And, as if you didn't have enough reasons to dance with delight, broccoli boasts impressive levels of folic acid (also known as vitamin B9), which can help boost serotonin levels and improve your overall mood, dude.

3 cups filtered water

½ cup hemp seeds

1 teaspoon coconut nectar

2 cups broccoli florets

1 tablespoon extra-virgin olive oil

1 tablespoon minced red onion

3 cloves garlic, crushed

1 tablespoon nutritional yeast

1 teaspoon ground cumin

¼ teaspoon ground black pepper

1 teaspoon sea salt

1 avocado, pitted

1 Blend all ingredients in a high-speed blender for 40 seconds until smooth and super creamy.

RED PEPPER
GAZPACHO

EATING A GREAT GAZPACHO IS LIKE getting hit in the face by Hector "Macho" Camacho. Just like the famous Puerto Rican boxer, this soup is quick, light, and will knock you out with a big mouthful of flavor! Truthfully, there's a bit of a fine line between salsa and this gazpacho, and I'm inclined to tell you to dunk some tortilla chips in this mix and get yourself a spicy lil' fix. Red bell peppers are an excellent source of vitamin B6, an essential nutrient for normal brain development and function. It helps your body make the hormones serotonin and norepinephrine, which influence melatonin production and your stress levels.

½ cup filtered water

1 red bell pepper, seeded and chopped

1 large roma tomato, chopped

¼ cup red onion, chopped

1 clove garlic, minced

½ cup cilantro, chopped, plus more for garnish

½ jalapeno pepper, seeded and chopped

1 lime, juiced

¼ teaspoon ground cumin

1 teaspoon sea salt

Dash ground black pepper

1 teaspoon extra-virgin olive oil

1 Blend all ingredients in a high-speed blender until the desired consistency is met. Garnish with additional cilantro.

SPICY
JACKFRUIT TACOS

I FIRST TRIED JACKFRUIT TACOS BACK in 2009 at an L.A. restaurant called Mooi. I was never a fan of pulled pork when I used to eat meat, but the idea of vegan "pulled pork" tacos was intriguing nonetheless. With my version of the recipe, I faithfully tried to re-create the same awesome, dynamic flavor from that first experience at Mooi with these spicy and delicious jackfruit tacos. Jackfruit contains a plethora of B vitamins, including pyridoxine, niacin, riboflavin, and folic acid, which are great for mood enhancement and boosting your immune system. To get this recipe right, make sure you only use young, green shredded jackfruit and not the thick, fruity, sweet mature fruit.

JACKFRUIT FILLING:

2 tablespoons extra-virgin olive oil

½ cup yellow onion, diced

1 tablespoon minced garlic

One 14-ounce can young jackfruit

4 limes, juiced

2 tablespoons maple syrup

1 teaspoon ground cumin

½ teaspoon ground coriander

1 teaspoon chili powder

½ teaspoon ground cinnamon

1 teaspoon apple cider vinegar

12 ounces gluten-free ale

1 teaspoon sea salt

Dash ground black pepper

TACOS:

6 organic tortillas

1 cup salsa or pico de gallo

½ cup guacamole

¼ cup cilantro, minced (optional)

1 lime, quartered

1 **To make the jackfruit filling:** add the olive oil to a large skillet and bring to a medium heat. Sauté the onion for 3 to 4 minutes, until translucent, and then add the garlic. After about a minute, add the remaining ingredients and cook for 15 to 20 minutes on medium-low heat or until the liquid is mostly absorbed.

2 Fill each taco shell with a generous amount of the jackfruit filling and top with salsa, guacamole, and fresh cilantro, if using. Garnish with a squeeze of fresh lime.

Edward & Sons brand organic young jackfruit is the perfect ingredient to execute this recipe.

SALTED CARAMEL
WAFFLES

THE PRIMAL REACTION MOST PEOPLE HAVE to these waffles looks something like an out-of-body experience: heads back, mouth curled into a blissful grin, and lots of deep, guttural "mmmmmm" noises. The crispy, chewy, fluffy texture of these waffles is pure Heaven, while the salted caramel sauce takes it over the top in terms of sweetness. The macadamia nuts in the caramel sauce are one of nature's most masterful mood boosters. These little heart-healthy Hawaiian treasures are rich in thiamine as well as folate, making them a great mood-boosting and stress-reducing food. Serve this at your next brunch, and your friends will love you forever. Seriously, you'll need restraining orders.

CARAMEL SAUCE:

1 cup macadamia nuts, soaked 2 hours

¼ cup coconut milk

½ cup coconut nectar

2 teaspoons yacon syrup or maple syrup

¼ teaspoon vanilla extract

2 teaspoons mesquite powder

½ teaspoon sea salt

⅛ teaspoon ground cardamom

WAFFLES:

1 cup gluten-free waffle/pancake mix

1 tablespoon golden flaxseed, ground

1 teaspoon ground cinnamon

1 tablespoon vegan vanilla protein powder (optional)

1 cup coconut milk

1 tablespoon organic virgin coconut oil

TOPPINGS:

¼ cup fine coconut shreds

½ cup vegan chocolate chips, preferably stevia sweetened

½ cup sliced banana

½ cup sliced strawberries

1   Preheat a two-sided waffle iron.

2   **To make the caramel sauce:** blend all ingredients in a high-speed blender for 40 seconds until ultra smooth, dense, and creamy.

3   **To make the waffles:** combine all dry ingredients in a medium mixing bowl and whisk well. Add the coconut milk and combine with a large mixing spoon until you get a smooth, yet slightly lumpy batter. Let sit for 5 minutes.

4   Lightly coat the hot waffle iron with coconut oil and pour the waffle batter into the grooves. When the grooves are fully covered, close the waffle iron and cook for about 5 minutes. Before removing, check to see that your waffle is a nice golden-brown color and cook a little longer if needed to achieve perfect crispiness. Continue the steps until all the remaining batter has been used.

5   Layer each waffle with toppings and drizzle with salted caramel sauce. Serve.

KOHLRABI FRITTERS

SERVES 2 TO 4

KOHLRABI, WHY DON'T PEOPLE LOVE YOU the way you deserve? I just don't understand why this vegetable is so underutilized in recipes. Its light, crisp texture and nutty, radish-like flavor will make your eyes glitter for these fritters. With the cooling yogurt sauce, I find myself eating an entire batch of these in one sitting—no joke! I'm also not joking about the awesome, mood-boosting benefits of sweet potato. Sweet potatoes are a good source of magnesium, which is the relaxation and antistress mineral.

FRITTERS:

2 bulbs kohlrabi, peeled

1 medium sweet potato, peeled

2½ tablespoons of ground flax "egg" (see instructions, right)

3 tablespoons coconut flour

½ teaspoon sea salt

⅛ teaspoon ground black pepper

¼ teaspoon cayenne pepper

2 tablespoons organic virgin coconut oil

3 tablespoons minced chives, reserved for plating

YOGURT SAUCE:

½ large avocado, pitted

1 cup unsweetened coconut yogurt

½ lemon, juiced

¼ teaspoon sea salt

1 To make the flax "egg": combine 1 tablespoon of ground flaxseed (measure after grinding) with 3 tablespoons of filtered water. Stir well and place in the fridge to set for 15 minutes. After 15 minutes, the result should be a thick, sticky, egglike substitute. Set aside at room temperature.

2 To make the fritters: shred the kohlrabi and sweet potato in a food processor, or by hand using a grater. Squeeze the shredded vegetables in cheesecloth, a nut milk bag, or with several paper towels to remove excess moisture, then transfer to a medium bowl. Add the flax egg, coconut flour, sea salt, black pepper, and cayenne pepper. Mix well to combine. Shape the mixture into 3½-inch round patties with your hands, no more than ¾ inch thick.

3 Place a dollop of coconut oil in a large skillet. Heat the oil over medium-high heat, then place small patties of the fritter mixture into the oil. Fry on one side until browned, then fry on the other side. Remove and place on a plate lined with a paper towel to drain excess oil.

4 To make the yogurt sauce: blend the avocado, coconut yogurt, lemon juice, and sea salt in a high-speed blender until thoroughly combined.

5 Serve the fritters with the yogurt sauce and top with the minced chives.

DRAGON FRUIT
SODA

SERVES 2 TO 4

FORGET MOLLY RINGWALD. THIS DRINK IS *truly* pretty in pink! Subtle is not in its repertoire. Not only does it look totally cool in a martini glass, it tastes out-of-this-world. The dragon fruit seeds stay crunchy after you blend it, which lends a surprisingly curious mouthfeel to this drink. Go on. Make some of this soda and say yes to Duckie Dale's invitation to the prom. To ensure you can dance the night away, dragon fruit is booming with bountiful B-complex vitamins to support the formation and maintenance of nerve cells, keep you mentally alert, and reduce your overall stress.

1 cup coconut kefir

½ cup fresh dragon fruit, peeled and chopped

½ teaspoon ginger root, peeled and chopped

2 teaspoons fresh lime juice

⅛ teaspoon liquid stevia

1 handful of ice cubes

1 Blend all ingredients for 30 seconds in a high-speed blender and serve immediately.

CREAMY
FENNEL SOUP

FENNEL IS FANTASTIC FOR NOT ONLY fresh breath, but also fancy nails, hair, and skin. It's an awesome source of silica and gives this soup a savory undertone of licorice-like flavor. I love this recipe as an "in-between" soup—it's not as light as, say, a miso soup, but it's not as hearty and dense as chowder. It just works its magic in the in-between. Fennel bulbs and seeds have high levels of potassium, which acts as a vasodilator to help lower your blood pressure (which can get sky high when you're stressed-out!). A cup of fresh fennel in your daily diet will pump you full of powerful potassium to help keep you balanced.

One 32-ounce carton low-sodium vegetable broth

¼ cup organic virgin coconut oil

½ yellow onion, diced

5 small fennel bulbs, destalked and chopped

½ teaspoon garlic granules

½ teaspoon sea salt

Pinch ground black pepper, to taste

1 teaspoon fresh tarragon, minced

¼ teaspoon ground coriander

3 tablespoons fennel fronds, reserved for garnish

1 teaspoon dry fennel seeds, reserved for garnish

1 Bring the vegetable broth to a boil in a medium stockpot; reduce the heat to low and then cover. Melt the coconut oil in a large skillet on medium-high heat and sauté onion for about 5 minutes, until it becomes translucent. Add the fennel pieces and sauté for an additional 10 minutes or until they're lightly golden brown. Transfer the vegetables to the veggie broth in the stockpot. Add the garlic granules, sea salt, pepper, tarragon, and coriander, and simmer on low heat for 15 to 20 minutes.

2 Garnish with the fennel fronds and fennel seeds and serve.

PUMPKIN
ALFREDO PASTA

SERVES 2

FOR A MOSTLY RAW NOODLE RECIPE, this Pumpkin Alfredo rocks the roof like Rocky Balboa in the ring! This sauce is rich, creamy, and subtly sweet, and it complements the crunch of the raw butternut squash noodles so perfectly that you may never crave another pasta dish again. Low in fat, yet rich in phytonutrients and antioxidants, butternut squash provides significant amounts of vitamin B6, essential for the proper functioning of your nervous system, which in turn helps your body deal more effectively with stress. This recipe is a great overall stress reducer, not only because of its powerful nutrition, but the movement in your jaw from eating crunchy foods helps to relieve tension as well.

PUMPKIN ALFREDO SAUCE:

½ cup filtered water

1 cup unsweetened pumpkin puree

1 cup raw cashews, soaked for 1 hour

1 teaspoon extra-virgin olive oil

½ teaspoon ground coriander

½ teaspoon ground cumin

½ teaspoon ground white pepper

2 teaspoons sea salt

1 teaspoon garlic powder

Dash ground nutmeg

1 teaspoon fresh sage, chiffonaded

NOODLES:

1 small butternut squash, seeded and spiralized

TOPPINGS:

2 tablespoons pumpkin seed oil

2 tablespoons pumpkin seeds

4 sage leaves, reserved for garnish

1 **To make the Pumpkin Alfredo Sauce:** blend all ingredients in a high-speed blender for 40 seconds or until smooth and creamy. Stop and scrape the sides down with a rubber spatula if needed to be sure all the cashews are well blended.

2 **To assemble:** combine the sauce with the butternut squash noodles in a large bowl. Mix well with your hands or tongs. Drizzle pumpkin seed oil and garnish with pumpkin seeds and fresh sage and serve.

FANCY GRILLED CHEESE
WITH GOLDEN FIG JAM

SERVES 2

THIS IS THE KIND OF GRILLED cheese sandwich that creates REALLY long lines at a food truck. The smoky flavor and crispy texture of the tempeh bacon pairs phenomenally well with the fresh sliced pear and golden fig jam. Figs are full of antioxidants and are fantastic as general stress reducers. And after the vegan cheese melts and combines with the figs' subtle sweetness . . . boy, the hand gets dealt. And then it's coming up all aces with this slammin', jammin' sammie. You'll be asking for seconds before you even know it.

- 3 tablespoons organic virgin coconut oil, divided
- One 6-ounce package tempeh bacon
- 4 slices gluten-free sandwich bread
- 1 large pear, cored and sliced
- 1 cup vegan cheddar cheese shreds
- ¼ cup golden fig jam

1 In a small skillet on medium high, melt 2 tablespoons of the coconut oil and add the tempeh. Cook for about 5 minutes on each side or until golden brown.

2 While the tempeh is cooking, fire up your panini press and coat your bread slices with the remaining coconut oil. Once the press is hot enough, heat your bread for about 1 minute, then transfer the bread to a plate.

3 Layer the bread with the cooked tempeh bacon, pear slices, vegan cheddar cheese, and golden fig jam. Return the sandwich to the panini press and grill for an additional 5 to 7 minutes or until the bread is crispy around the edges, golden brown in color, and the cheese is fully melted. Serve immediately.

EPILOGUE

Writing this book was probably the closest thing I'll experience to giving birth. Unless, of course, they perfect the advanced fertility technology from that classic Arnold Schwarzenegger movie *Junior* . . . then I *might* consider volunteering as the first man in history to bear a child. But for now, this book is my baby. As such, I've been very mindful of its evolution and development so that it may inspire you to live a more conscious, joyful, energized, purposeful, and (hopefully) longer life. My true aim here is not to encourage you to achieve some magical, lofty number of legendary longevity (which, for me, would be 120 years old, by the way). Seriously, though, in pursuit of longevity, the intention is not to restrict your life choices or make yourself feel stressed about being the perfect eater or the perfect person. It's about living with maximum vitality, joy, love, and inspiration while you're here . . . however long that may be.

The truth is, the future isn't promised to any of us, the past is merely a footprint, and certainty is an illusion. The only thing we truly have is the present moment. All the goodness of life is happening RIGHT NOW. As scary and liberating as this is, it's the absolute nature of our reality here. So, whether you've got three weeks or 30 years left, I encourage you to cultivate authentic and loving relationships in your life: with yourself, your family, your career, your food choices, and all of the sentient beings you share this planet with. You've been given this beautiful and precious gift

called life and have been entrusted with the innate wisdom and compassion to care for it. I encourage you to strip away the layers of conditioning, self-imposed limitations, judgments, and the illusion of separation from your fellow earthlings—so you can finally get a taste of your true essence as a human being.

And, you know, there's no point in being the healthiest eater on Earth if you're feeling miserable about your life. I hate to break it to you, but there are no gold medals being given out on this planet for being the longest-lived human being or the most vegan or being able to drink the most amount of green juice in five minutes (although that *would* be a fun video!). Lighten up and don't take life so damn seriously. It makes you a drag to be around, and it'll shorten your lifespan from all the stress. Trust me. I used to be that guy . . . Mr. Freakin' Serious-About-EVERYTHING. I often annoyed myself and everyone else around me.

Life is a beautiful, mysterious, delightful, and often confusing paradox: scary, fun, heartbreaking, joyful, magical, amazing, and confusing—sometimes all in the same ten minutes! I believe we are all doing our best to figure out the puzzle pieces of our lives, every day. So I hope that the tools, health tips, recipes, and humorous philosophies in this book have touched your life and uplifted you in a positive and lasting way. Remember to experiment, take risks, be yourself, and stop caring so much about

what other people think of you. It's WAY more important what you think of yourself. Thanks to the constant bombardment of social media, most people have attention spans of about 6.2 seconds these days. They'll likely forget what you said or did tomorrow anyway. So have a blast, let it rip, be courageous, and let your own personal truth guide your way.

Thank you so much for sharing this journey with me, for taking the time to read this book, and for letting the information seep into your pores like a fresh avocado face mask. For now, I'll leave you with one of my all-time favorite quotes. I hope that it serves as a reminder to live your life with big love and reckless abandon!

COOKING IS LIKE LOVE.
IT SHOULD BE ENTERED INTO WITH
ABANDON OR NOT AT ALL.

—**Harriet Van Horne**

JASON'S PERFECT PANTRY LIST

Here are my favorite healthy ingredients that I have on hand in my pantry and refrigerator. Stock your kitchen with these splendid, super powerful staples so you can easily make any of the recipes in this book or liberally experiment with your own delectable culinary creations whenever the mood strikes.

Almond butter

Almonds

Amaranth

Apple cider vinegar

Baking soda

Balsamic vinegar

Black beans

Black olives

Black pepper

Brown rice

Buckwheat groats

Cacao butter

Cacao nibs

Cacao powder

Cannellini beans

Capers

Cardamom

Cashews

Cayenne pepper

Chaga mushroom powder

Chia seeds

Chickpea miso

Chickpeas

Chlorella powder

Cinnamon

Cistanche extract powder

Coconut aminos

Coconut milk

Coconut nectar

Coconut oil

Coconut sugar

Coconut vinegar

Coriander

Crushed red pepper flakes

Cumin

Curry powder

Dates

Dijon mustard

Extra-virgin olive oil

Figs

Finely shredded coconut

Frozen fruit (acai, mixed berries)

Garlic powder or granules

Ginger root

Gluten-free all-purpose baking flour

Gluten-free noodles

Goji berries

Golden flaxseed

Goldenberries

Grapeseed oil

Ground vanilla bean

Hemp milk

Hemp oil

Hemp seeds

Kelp noodles

Liquid stevia (plain and English toffee flavor)

Maca powder

Maple syrup

Millet

Nutritional yeast

Pecans

Pine nuts

Pistachios

Pumpkin puree

Pumpkin seed oil

Pumpkin seeds

Quinoa

Raw vegan protein powder (Sunwarrior is my favorite)

Reishi mushroom powder

Sea salt

Sea vegetables

Sesame seeds

Spirulina powder

Stevia powder

Sunflower seeds

Sunflower seed butter

Tahini

Teff

Tempeh

Tempeh bacon

Turmeric

Ume plum vinegar

Vanilla extract

Vegan probiotic powder

Walnuts

ESSENTIAL KITCHEN EQUIPMENT

Having high-quality kitchen equipment makes healthy food preparation easier and a lot more fun. Being prepared to rock your recipes with these professional tools will save you immeasurable amounts of time and energy so you can focus on what really matters: the divine pleasure of eating!

Baking pans

Bash and chop (aka cutting board scraper)

Can opener

Ceramic chef's knife (preferably 6- to 8-inch; my favorite is Kyocera)

Citrus reamer

Cookie sheets

Eco-friendly cooking pans and skillets (my favorites are Silit and Cuisinart)

Fine mesh strainer

Food processor (my favorite is Breville)

French press

Garlic press

Glass or ceramic casserole dish

Glass storage containers with locking lids (my favorite is Pyrex)

High-speed blender (my favorite is Blendtec)

Kitchen shears

Knife sharpener or whetstone (my favorite is Global)

Liquid measuring cup

Mandoline food slicer (my favorite is OXO)

Measuring cups

Measuring spoons

Metal ring molds

Metal tongs

Metric wonder cup

Microplane zester and grater

Mixing bowls

Nut milk bag or cheesecloth

Offset spatula

Oven mitts

Panini press (my favorite is Cuisinart)

Rubber spatula

Saucepans (multiple sizes from 1.5-quart to 6-quart or larger)

Silicon oil brush

Slow juicer (my favorites are Omega and Norwalk)

Snack bag clips

Soup ladle

Soup spoons

Stainless-steel chef's knife (preferably 6- to 8-inch; my favorites are Wüsthof and Shun)

Toaster (my favorite is Breville)

Vegetable dehydrator (my favorite is Excalibur)

Vegetable peeler

Vegetable spiralizer

Whisks, small and large

Wooden bamboo skewers

Wooden or bamboo cutting boards

Wooden spoons and spatulas

JASON'S FAVORITE PRODUCTS AND RESOURCES

SUPERFOODS

ULTIMATE SUPERFOODS

UltimateSuperfoods.com

Superfood powders, proteins, berries, nuts, oils, and seeds.

EARTH SHIFT PRODUCTS

EarthShiftProducts.com

Superfoods, supplements, and healthy lifestyle accessories at near-wholesale prices.

NAVITAS NATURALS

NavitasNaturals.com

Raw cacao, nuts, seeds, berries, and superfood powders.

ESSENTIAL LIVING FOODS

EssentialLivingFoods.com

Raw oils, nut butters, superfood berries, nuts, and seeds.

NUTIVA

Nutiva.com

Raw coconut butters, hemp oil, hemp seeds, and chia seeds.

BIG TREE FARMS

BigTreeFarms.com

Coconut sugar, nectar, water, and raw cacao products.

BOKU SUPERFOOD

BokuSuperfood.com

Berries, nuts, protein powders, superfood protein bars, and herbs.

SOLAY SUPERFOOD

SolaySuperfood.com

Organic, gluten-free, superfood meal-replacement shakes and raw cacao elixirs.

EARTH CIRCLE ORGANICS

EarthCircleOrganics.com

Bulk superfoods like nuts, seeds, berries, olives, oils, and natural sweeteners.

AMAZON PLANET

WonderFruitAcai.com

Frozen organic acai berry puree and sorbet.

JING HERBS

JingHerbs.com

Traditional Chinese herbs and herbal extracts.

DRAGON HERBS

DragonHerbs.com

Traditional Chinese herbs, teas, tonics, elixirs, extracts, nuts, and berries.

DAVID WOLFE FOODS/ LONGEVITY WAREHOUSE

LongevityWarehouse.com

Wide variety of superfood products, including beverages, drink mixes, herbs, berries, tonics, protein powders, and healthy lifestyle items.

NONDAIRY MILKS

SO DELICIOUS

SoDeliciousDairyFree.com

Coconut, almond, and cashew milk products.

OMEGA MILK

OmegaCreamery.com

Flax, hemp, and rice milk blends.

DREAM NONDAIRY MILKS

TasteTheDream.com

Dairy-free milk products, including rice, almond, soy, and cashew milks.

TEMPT HEMP MILK

LivingHarvest.com

Hemp seed milks.

PACIFIC NATURAL FOODS

PacificFoods.com

Variety of nondairy milks.

PLANT–BASED PROTEINS AND MEAT SUBSTITUTES

TOFURKEY

Tofurkey.com

Non-GMO, organic tempeh and vegan meat substitutes.

LIGHTLIFE

Lightlife.com

Tempeh, tempeh bacon, and plant-protein foods.

LIVING HARVEST

LivingHarvest.com

Nonsoy hemp tofu.

HILARY'S EAT WELL

HilarysEatWell.com

Gluten-free veggie burgers, veggie bites, and dressings.

SWEET EARTH NATURAL FOODS

SweetEarthFoods.com

Handmade traditional seitan products, burritos, and veggie burgers.

CARLA LEE'S NUT BURGERS

NutBurgers.com

Gluten-free and soy-free high-protein veggie burgers and tacos.

NATURAL SWEETENERS

OMICA ORGANICS

OmicaOrganics.com

Flavored liquid stevia, shilajit powder, and MSM products.

SWEET LEAF

SweetLeaf.com

Wide variety of flavored, liquid stevia products.

LAKANTO

Lakanto.com

Sugar-free, zero-calorie natural sweetener made from monk fruit and erythritol.

BEE FREE HONEE

BeeFreeHonee.com

Honeylike vegan syrups made from apples.

LILY'S SWEETS

LilysSweets.com

Gluten-free, stevia-sweetened vegan chocolate chips and bars.

ORGANIC TEAS

ORGANIC INDIA

OrganicIndia.com

Organic, medicinal teas and tea blends.

YOGI TEA

YogiProducts.com

Organic, specialty herbal teas and tea blends.

HEALTHY LIVING SUPPLEMENTS

NATURAL VITALITY

NaturalVitality.com

All-natural sleep aids and magnesium supplements.

GARDEN OF LIFE

GardenOfLife.com

Raw, plant-based vitamins, multi-vitamins, and plant proteins.

QUANTUM NUTRITION LABS

QNLabs.com

High-quality natural supplements, vitamins, minerals, detox products, and lifestyle tools.

MINERALIFE

MineralifeOnline.com

High-potency natural liquid mineral supplements.

COCONUT PRODUCTS

COCONUT SECRET

CoconutSecret.com

Coconut nectar, aminos, and vinegar.

HARMLESS HARVEST

HarmlessHarvest.com

Raw, organic coconut water.

EXOTIC SUPERFOODS

ExoticSuperfoods.com

Raw coconut meat and water.

NUTS AND NUT BUTTERS

ARTISANA FOODS

ArtisanaFoods.com

Organic, raw nut and seed butters.

LIVING TREE COMMUNITY FOODS

LivingTreeCommunity.com

Organic, raw nut and seed butters.

NUTS.COM

Nuts.com

Organic nuts, seeds, superfoods, and dried fruit.

STAPLE GROCERY ITEMS

THRIVE MARKET

ThriveMarket.com

Organic, vegan, raw, non-GMO, gluten-free, and nontoxic items from top-selling brands at wholesale prices.

EDWARD AND SONS

EdwardandSons.com

Canned young jackfruit, vegan Worcestershire sauce, and a wide variety of plant-based ingredients.

EDEN FOODS

EdenFoods.com

Organic beans, seaweeds, mirin, Japanese foods, cereals, and snacks.

BRAGG

Bragg.com

Apple cider vinegar, liquid aminos, nutritional yeast, beverages, and salad dressings.

ALTER ECO FOODS

AlterEcoFoods.com

Fair-trade organic quinoa, rice, natural sugars, and chocolates.

NATURAL SALT

SELINA NATURALLY

SelinaNaturally.com

Highly mineralized Celtic sea salt and salt blends.

REAL SALT

RealSalt.com

Mineral-rich natural sea salt.

FLOURS AND BAKING MIXES

BOB'S RED MILL NATURAL FOODS

BobsRedMill.com

Organic, gluten-free flours, baking mixes, ancient grains, cereals, and seeds.

ARROWHEAD MILLS

ArrowheadMills.com

Organic, gluten-free flours, cereals, and baking mixes.

MISO PRODUCTS

MISO MASTER ORGANIC

Great-Eastern-Sun.com

Chickpea- and soy-based miso paste, sea vegetables, and Asian-inspired sauces.

SOUTH RIVER MISO

SouthRiverMiso.com

Fine, traditional artisan organic miso paste.

GLUTEN-FREE PASTA AND GRAINS

TRUROOTS

TruRoots.com

Ancient grain and gluten-free pasta.

LOTUS FOODS

LotusFoods.com

Organic rice varietals and ramen-style rice noodles.

LUNDBERG

Lundberg.com

Organic brown rice and rice-based products.

SEA TANGLE

KelpNoodles.com
Raw kelp noodles.

ANCIENT HARVEST

AncientHarvest.com

Quinoa and ancient grain pasta.

HEALTHY OILS

RALLIS OLIVE OIL

IcePressed.com

Ice-pressed, extra-virgin olive oil.

OJIO

MyOjio.com

Plant-based oils and butters.

FLORA

FloraHealth.com

Flaxseed oils and plant-based oil blends.

NUTIVA

Nutiva.com

Plant-based oils and butters.

BULLETPROOF

UpgradedSelf.com

Fat-burning and brain-boosting medium-chain-triglyceride-rich coconut oils.

ORGANIC SPICES

FRONTIER

FrontierCoop.com

Organic spices and spice blends.

ENGAGE ORGANICS

EngageOrganics.com

Salt-free, organic spices and spice blends.

SPICE STATION

SpiceStationSilverlake.com

Premium spices and spice blends.

KITCHEN EQUIPMENT

BLENDTEC

Blendtec.com

High-speed blenders and accessories.

BREVILLE

Breville.com

Food processors, juicers, and kitchen accessories.

CUISINART

Cuisinart.com

Eco-friendly cookware, ice cream makers, food processors, and accessories.

OMEGA JUICERS

OmegaJuicers.com

Low-speed, masticating, and centrifugal juicers.

NORWALK JUICERS

NorwalkJuicers.com

Hydraulic, cold-press juicers.

EXCALIBUR DEHYDRATORS

ExcaliburDehydrator.com

Food dehydrators and accessories.

WÜSTHOF KNIVES

Wusthof.com

Fine German cutlery, chef's knives, and knife sharpeners.

SHUN KNIVES

Shun.Kaiusaltd.com/knives

Professional Japanese cutlery and chef's knives.

ROBERT WELCH

RobertWelch.com

Fine British chef's knives, kitchen gear, and home furnishings.

STRAWESOME

Strawesome.com

Eco-friendly, reusable glass drinking straws.

PROBIOTICS

BIO-K

BioKPlus.com

Powders and supplements.

INNER ECO

Inner-Eco.com

Liquid shots and bulk concentrates.

BODY ECOLOGY

BodyEcology.com

Fermented foods, culture starters, and drinks.

FARMHOUSE CULTURE

FarmhouseCulture.com

Cultured vegetables, sauerkraut, and kimchi.

HEALING MOVEMENT

HealingMovement.net

Coconut water kefir and cultured vegetables.

KEVITA

Kevita.com

Flavored, coconut-based probiotic beverages.

CUSTOM PROBIOTICS, INC.

CustomProbiotics.com

High-potency probiotic supplements.

COCONUT GROVE YOGURT

CoconutGroveYogurt.com

Coconut-based yogurts.

GOODBELLY

GoodBelly.com

Probiotic coconut waters.

NONDAIRY CHEESE

MIYOKO'S KITCHEN

MiyokosKitchen.com

Artisanal, gourmet, nut-based cheese products.

PUNK RAWK LABS

PunkRawkLabs.net

Cashew and macadamia cheese.

HEIDI HO

HeidiHo.com

Hazelnut-based, soy- and gluten-free, plant-based cheese, sauces, and spreads.

CHICAGO VEGAN FOODS

ChicagoVeganFoods.com

Vegan nacho cheese.

NARYDAIRY

NaryDairy.com

Cashew-based cheese and spreads.

PARMELA CREAMERY

ParmelaCreamery.com

Artisanal cashew and almond cheese.

PARMA

EatintheRaw.com

Nondairy Parmesan cheese.

DR. COW TREE NUT CHEESES

Dr-Cow.com

Nut-based cheeses and spreads.

TREELINE CHEESE

TreelineCheese.com

Cashew cheese and spreads.

KITE HILL

Kite-Hill.com

Almond-based gourmet cheese.

DAIYA FOODS

US.DaiyaFoods.com

Meltable, tapioca-based shredded cheese.

FIELD ROAST

FieldRoast.com

Meltable coconut- and soy-based cheese.

SEA VEGETABLES

MAINE COAST SEA VEGETABLES

SeaVeg.com

Seaweed snacks and supplements.

EDEN FOODS

EdenFoods.com

Wide variety of sea vegetables.

PROTEIN POWDERS AND WORKOUT SUPPLEMENTS

SUNWARRIOR

Sunwarrior.com

Raw, vegan protein blends, supergreens, fulvic acid, superfood vitamins, and protein bars.

CLEAN MACHINE

CleanMachineOnline.com

All-natural, vegan branch-chain amino acids and testosterone boosters.

VITAFORCE

Vitaforce.com

Multivitamin superfood plant-based greens powder.

HEALTHFORCE NUTRITIONALS

Healthforce.com

Multivitamin, superfood, green, and mineral powders and supplements.

LIVON LABS

LivonLabs.com

Super high-potency vitamin C, GSH, R-ALA, and B-complex supplements.

LONGEVITY POWER

LongevityPower.com

Longevity-promoting supplements, Chinese herbal formulations, and tonic herbs.

BRAIN AND ENERGY BOOSTERS

MUSHROOM MATRIX

MushroomMatrix.com

Medicinal mushroom-based energy drinks and sports recovery mixes.

BULLETPROOF

UpgradedSelf.com

Colloidal PQQ, MCT oils, and alkaline coffee products.

MEGAHYDRATE

PhiSciences.com

Oxygen-boosting supplements.

DETOXIFICATION AND CLEANSING

CLEARLIGHT FAR-INFRARED SAUNAS

HealWithHeat.com

Eco-friendly home sauna sales and installation.

OMICA ORGANICS

OmicaOrganics.com

Fulvic acids and other detoxification products.

BLESSED HERBS

BlessedHerbs.com

Ready-made home cleansing kits and products.

KITCHENWARE AND PORTABLE CONTAINERS

TO-GO WARE

To-GoWare.com

Bamboo utensils, stainless-steel and silicon travel containers.

KLEAN KANTEEN

KleanKanteen.com

Stainless-steel travel containers.

HYDRO FLASK

HydroFlask.com

Insulated stainless-steel travel thermoses.

NATURAL CLEANING SUPPLIES

EARTH FRIENDLY PRODUCTS

Ecos.com

Plant-based, eco-friendly cleaning products.

BIOKLEEN

BiokleenHome.com

Enzyme and essential-oil cleaning products.

VEGGIE WASH

Veggiewash.BeaumontProducts.com

Natural, plant-based fruit and vegetable wash.

FOOD PRESERVATION

BERRY BREEZE

BerryBreeze.com

Portable, battery-powered ozonator for your refrigerator.

DEBBIE MEYER GREEN BAGS

DebbieMeyer.com

Produce bags that mitigate ethylene gases and keep food fresh.

SPRING WATER AND ALKALINE FILTRATION SYSTEMS

CASTLE ROCK WATER

CastleRockWaterCompany.com

Mineral-rich spring water from Mt. Shasta in glass bottles.

MOUNTAIN VALLEY SPRING WATER

MountainValleySpring.com

Highly mineralized spring water from Arkansas in glass bottles.

OXYGEN OZONE

OxygenOzone.com

Alkaline water filtration systems based in Los Angeles.

TENSUI WATER PERFECTION SYSTEMS

TensuiWater.com

Alkaline water filtration systems.

KANGEN ALKALINE WATER SYSTEMS

Enagic.com

Alkaline water filtration systems.

ALKALUX ALKALINE WATER SYSTEMS

Alkalux.com

Alkaline water filtration systems.

NATURAL BODY CARE

LIVING LIBATIONS

LivingLibations.com

All-natural, handmade, and superfood body, hair, and skin care products.

SEVI ECO VEGAN HAIR & BODYCARE

EcoSevi.com

All-natural, botanical, vegan, plant-based skin, hair, and body care products.

WELL SCENT

Well-Scent.com

All-natural, handmade dental, skin care, essential oil, and aromatherapy products.

DR. BRONNER'S

DrBronner.com

All-natural, fair-trade soaps, lotions, shaving creams, and toothpaste.

AUBREY ORGANICS

Aubrey-Organics.com

Skin, hair, dental, body, and bath products.

ALAFFIA

Alaffia.com

Sustainable skin care products based on shea butter from Togo. Includes creams, lotions, soaps, hair care, and gift sets.

ACURE ORGANICS

AcureOrganics.com

Organic, plant-based body care, hair care, skin care, and facial care products.

SUNTEGRITY

SuntegritySkincare.com

Natural sun protection products.

KEYS SOAP

Keys-Soap.com

Natural and holistic skin care products.

BRUSH WITH BAMBOO

BrushWithBamboo.com

Eco-friendly bamboo toothbrushes, tongue cleaners, and natural dental products.

INDEX

ACKNOWLEDGMENTS

AS CLICHÉ AS IT MAY SOUND, this book was a massive labor of love. Many years of recipe testing and development, dozens of live cooking demos, hundreds of YouTube videos, and a lot of patience are infused into these pages. As the saying goes, you are only as good as the people who surround you. Well, if there's any truth to that phrase, then I'm doing spectacularly well. The culmination of my lifelong dream to publish a book was made possible through the support of my friends, family, business associates, mentors, and colleagues. It's the least I can do to thank you all—as you've inspired this work and much more to come. Here goes . . . something!

Kevin Motley of TGMD Talent, Marc Perman of Perman Management, and Sharon Bowers of Bowers Griffin and Associates—the talented business visionaries who have guided my career in various capacities for the past several years: your wisdom, guidance, patience, and unyielding belief in my talent helped to birth this book (uh, relatively painlessly)!

My culinary and creative assistant Michelle Marquis, aka The Alchemist Chef, whose diligent research skills, genius recipe contributions, world-class food styling, and hundreds of hours of hard work helped to focus the content, sharpen the recipes, and bring this book home to roost in the 11th hour: it's been such a delight to watch your culinary mastery unfold before my eyes.

My photography team: Jackie Sobon and Jeff Skeirik for your amazing attention to detail, incredible creativity, and eye for amazing, artful composition. Thank you for putting up with an anal, perfectionist vegan chef breathing down your neck the whole way. I say bravo to your collective badassery and

inimitable creative vision. You are both rock star artists of the highest caliber, and I'm grateful for your friendship and inspiration.

Recipe archivists Jessica Rene Hilzey, Jenelle York, Tina Tacorian, and G. Scott Hayes, for watching hundreds of hours of YouTube videos, online demos, and conference footage, and painstakingly annotating my recipes into legible, written form. Oh, and thanks for boosting my view count online, y'all.

Tess Masters, aka The Blender Girl, for introducing me to my first literary agent and showing me that the sky wasn't the limit in the publishing world . . . there IS no limit! Thank you for always being real, for thinking bigger than big, and for seeing the unlimited potential inside of me.

Whitney Lauritsen, aka Eco-Vegan Gal, for being my rock through all the doubts, fears, and "less than" thoughts that almost thwarted this book. Thank you for being such a gift to this world and for always holding me in my highest light. You're a shining example of a powerhouse leader and businesswoman—you continue to be a massive inspiration for me to be a better person, a better leader, and a better man.

Ele Keats, for being such a beacon of truth and abundance in my life. You continue to embody true grace and elegance. Thank you for your ever-present friendship and support . . . and for putting up with (and matching) my unique brand of crazy. And for reminding me to laugh, let go of my doubts, and stop giving a shit . . . also known as being free!

Lynx, Clawdia, and Figaro—you three were more than just fuzzy foot warmers during my writing process. You served as heart warmers, too . . . assuaging any sadness, fear, or pain I was feeling in my darkest moments. God bless your sweet little souls for clawing your way into my life.

Chad Sarno, the Michael Jordan of vegan cooking, for the awesome introduction to Hay House and your valuable guidance during the initial stages of the publishing process. Your culinary creativity is an absolute revelation and I'm humbled by your food mastery, my friend. And thank you for giving me the opportunity to generate some seriously awesome financial abundance during the writing of this book. You helped keep the boat afloat, brother!

To Jara Fairchild, for seeing my limitless potential so early. For being my very first PR rep and opening those huge doors with me. Thank you for being my cheerleader for all these years and one of my true soul sisters. You're an angel. Don't even try to hide that halo under those curly golden locks!

All of my dear friends and family who were present for the book photoshoots: Vince Lia, Kelly Serrano, Damon Valley, Kitten Kuroi, Aaron Ritter, Kevin Connelly, Abigail Cooper, and Theron Cook.

My culinary mentors and the healthy visionaries who've inspired my creativity and given me faith that plant-based cuisine is ready for the worldwide stage: Cherie Soria, Elaina Love, Alicia Ojeda, Cosmo Meens, David Wolfe, Matthew Kenney, Dr. Gabriel Cousens, Dr. Neal Barnard, Dr. Joel Kahn, Gary Yourofsky, Tiziana Alipo Tamborra, Matthew Rogers, Kris Carr, Tal Ronnen, and Isa Chandra Moskowitz.

Speaking of mentors, without the infinite compassion, love, and wisdom of Michael Park, I might be releasing this book posthumously. You are my soul brother, my mentor, and the father figure that I prayed for. Thank you for showing me how to walk the path with heart and reminding me "what's real here"!

My generous sponsors who've provided the platforms and venues for me to share my unique gifts, including Sunwarrior, Blendtec, Ultimate Superfoods, Ojio, Sweet Earth Natural Foods, Hilary's Eat Well, and Brush with Bamboo.

To the entire Crazy Legs Productions team—Alana, Tom, Alison, Wendy, Scott, Vanessa, and all of you crazy kids in the ATL on the production team for *How to Live to 100.* Y'all believed that the world was ripe for a national, prime time, mainstream vegan cooking series on TV, and we freakin' did it. We made television history, and you helped remind me that there's no dream too big or too crazy to come to fruition. Thanks for reminding me to keep thinkin' like a boss and swingin' for the fences!

My team at Hay House for instantly "getting it" and letting my freak flag fly with this book. To Stacey Smith, Marlene Robinson, Caroline DiNofia, Shay Lawry, Diane Thomas, and Noah Maldonado for your rock-star creative support and love-filled e-mails. To Christy Salinas and Laura Palese for designing an eye-popping, mouthwatering brazen beauty of a book. To my all-star editor Sally Mason, for massaging my prose like a master baker massages fresh challah bread (even after Laura delivered her own little bun from the oven). To Reid Tracy, for seeing the massive potential to contribute my unique vision here. To Patty Gift for being the first to recognize that vision and offering me my first major publishing deal. Your collective passion, joyfulness, dedication, and enthusiasm made it crystal clear that I wanted to be a part of the Hay House family. I am deeply grateful for you all—and this is just the beginning!

My childhood heroes, authors, and muses who inspired a stargazing little boy from Detroit with a serious case of wanderlust to take a chance on life and follow his dreams: Jim Carrey, Robin Williams, George Carlin, Gary Oldman, Jeff Buckley, Freddie Mercury, Stevie Wonder, David Bowie, Iggy Pop, Amos Lee, Marvin Gaye, Chris Cornell, Aretha Franklin, Tina Turner, Khalil Gibran, Joseph Campbell, Osho, Gurdjieff, Anthony Robbins, Byron Katie, Eckhart Tolle, George Lucas, and so many more that would require 100 books to mention them all.

To my family, I thank you for instilling a rock-solid work ethic and deep sense of self-worth in me. For helping me truly embody the classic Wrobel family motto: "We'll make it fit!" For believing in me and supporting my journey to chase my dreams so far away from home. Sending extra props and huge love to Aunt Mary Lou, Steve, Jenny, Sierra, Benjamin, and Uncle Bill for eating healthier and taking control of your lives with more empowered and aware food choices. You're living proof that if you can be healthy in Detroit, you can do it anywhere.

Finally, to my amazing mother and my "rock," Susan Wrobel, who is my original inspiration to create magic in the Universe. Your infinite support, patience, guidance, generosity, and unconditional love continue to move and inspire me to even bigger dreams and greater achievements. I can't think of a bigger blessing in my life than having such a supportive, conscious, loving, and generous parent. Thank you for showering me with unbounded goodness and for always reminding me that the only boundaries are the ones we create for ourselves. You raised a real rebel of a Wrobel—and just look where we are now. Top of the world, Ma!

ABOUT THE AUTHOR

Detroit-born chef Jason Wrobel (aka J-Wro) is a graduate of the Living Light Culinary Institute with national certification as a Professional Raw Food Chef and Instructor. An ethical vegan for nearly two decades, he has inspired hundreds of thousands of people worldwide to prepare deliciously easy and satisfying plant-based cuisine. The healing properties and outrageous tastes of his dishes have rendered his recipes hands-down favorites among celebrity clients and ravenous fans alike. His popular YouTube channel, *The J-Wro Show*, features hundreds of vegan recipe videos and vibrant living vlogs. As the first-ever celebrity vegan chef on Cooking Channel, his TV series *How to Live to 100* merged healthy, vegan comfort food recipes with a humorous blend of sitcom skits and innovative animation. He lives in Los Angeles with his rescued feline companions, Lynx, Clawdia, and Figaro. *Eaternity* is his first book with Hay House.

We hope you enjoyed this Hay House book. If you'd like to receive our online catalog featuring additional information on Hay House books and products, or if you'd like to find out more about the Hay Foundation, please contact:

Hay House, Inc., P.O. Box 5100, Carlsbad, CA 92018-5100
(760) 431-7695 or (800) 654-5126
(760) 431-6948 (fax) or (800) 650-5115 (fax)
www.hayhouse.com® • www.hayfoundation.org

Published and distributed in Australia by: Hay House Australia Pty. Ltd.,
18/36 Ralph St., Alexandria NSW 2015 • Phone: 612-9669-4299 •
Fax: 612-9669-4144 • www.hayhouse.com.au

Published and distributed in the United Kingdom by: Hay House UK, Ltd.,
Astley House, 33 Notting Hill Gate, London W11 3JQ • Phone: 44-20-3675-2450 •
Fax: 44-20-3675-2451 • www.hayhouse.co.uk

Published and distributed in the Republic of South Africa by: Hay House SA (Pty),
Ltd., P.O. Box 990, Witkoppen 2068 • info@hayhouse.co.za • www.hayhouse.co.za

Published in India by: Hay House Publishers India, Muskaan Complex,
Plot No. 3, B-2, Vasant Kunj, New Delhi 110 070 • Phone: 91-11-4176-1620 •
Fax: 91-11-4176-1630 • www.hayhouse.co.in

Distributed in Canada by: Raincoast Books, 2440 Viking Way, Richmond, B.C. V6V
1N2 • Phone: 1-800-663-5714 • Fax: 1-800-565-3770 • www.raincoast.com

TAKE YOUR SOUL ON A VACATION

Visit www.HealYourLife.com® to regroup, recharge, and reconnect
with your own magnificence. Featuring blogs, mind-body-spirit news, and
life-changing wisdom from Louise Hay and friends.

Visit www.HealYourLife.com today!